HTML5: Up and Running

HTML5: Up and Running

Mark Pilgrim

O'REILLY®

Beijing · Cambridge · Farnham · Köln · Sebastopol · Taipei · Tokyo

HTML5: Up and Running
by Mark Pilgrim

Published by O'Reilly Media, Inc., 1005 Gravenstein Highway North, Sebastopol, CA 95472.

O'Reilly books may be purchased for educational, business, or sales promotional use. Online editions are also available for most titles (*http://my.safaribooksonline.com*). For more information, contact our corporate/institutional sales department: (800) 998-9938 or *corporate@oreilly.com*.

Editor: Mike Loukides

Production Editor: Adam Zaremba

Copyeditor: Rachel Head

Proofreader: Emily Quill

Indexer: Fred Brown

Cover Designer: Karen Montgomery

Interior Designer: David Futato

Illustrator: Robert Romano

Printing History:

    August 2010:   First Edition.

RepKover™.

This book uses RepKover™, a durable and flexible lay-flat binding.

ISBN: 978-0-596-80602-6

[M]

[1/11]

1292866130

Table of Contents

Preface ix

1. **How Did We Get Here?** 1
   Diving In   1
   MIME Types   1
   A Long Digression into How Standards Are Made   2
   An Unbroken Line   7
   A Timeline of HTML Development from 1997 to 2004   9
   Everything You Know About XHTML Is Wrong   10
   A Competing Vision   11
   What Working Group?   12
   Back to the W3C   13
   Postscript   14
   Further Reading   14

2. **Detecting HTML5 Features** 15
   Diving In   15
   Detection Techniques   15
   Modernizr: An HTML5 Detection Library   16
   Canvas   16
   Canvas Text   17
   Video   18
   Video Formats   19
   Local Storage   21
   Web Workers   23
   Offline Web Applications   23
   Geolocation   24
   Input Types   25
   Placeholder Text   27
   Form Autofocus   27
   Microdata   28

Further Reading   29

3. **What Does It All Mean?** **31**
   Diving In   31
   The Doctype   31
   The Root Element   33
   The <head> Element   34
       Character Encoding   35
       Friends and (Link) Relations   36
   New Semantic Elements in HTML5   41
   A Long Digression into How Browsers Handle Unknown Elements   42
   Headers   45
   Articles   47
   Dates and Times   49
   Navigation   51
   Footers   52
   Further Reading   55

4. **Let's Call It a Draw(ing Surface)** **57**
   Diving In   57
   Simple Shapes   58
   Canvas Coordinates   60
   Paths   61
   Text   63
   Gradients   67
   Images   70
   What About IE?   73
   A Complete Example   75
   Further Reading   79

5. **Video on the Web** **81**
   Diving In   81
   Video Containers   81
   Video Codecs   83
       H.264   84
       Theora   84
       VP8   85
   Audio Codecs   85
       MPEG-1 Audio Layer 3   86
       Advanced Audio Coding   87
       Vorbis   87
   What Works on the Web   88
   Licensing Issues with H.264 Video   90

Encoding Ogg Video with Firefogg 91
Batch Encoding Ogg Video with ffmpeg2theora 98
Encoding H.264 Video with HandBrake 100
Batch Encoding H.264 Video with HandBrake 107
Encoding WebM Video with ffmpeg 108
At Last, the Markup 110
MIME Types Rear Their Ugly Head 113
What About IE? 114
A Complete Example 114
Further Reading 115

6. You Are Here (And So Is Everybody Else) 117
Diving In 117
The Geolocation API 117
Show Me the Code 118
Handling Errors 120
Choices! I Demand Choices! 121
What About IE? 123
geo.js to the Rescue 123
A Complete Example 125
Further Reading 126

7. The Past, Present, and Future of Local Storage for Web Applications 127
Diving In 127
A Brief History of Local Storage Hacks Before HTML5 128
Introducing HTML5 Storage 129
Using HTML5 Storage 130
Tracking Changes to the HTML5 Storage Area 131
Limitations in Current Browsers 132
HTML5 Storage in Action 132
Beyond Named Key/Value Pairs: Competing Visions 134
Further Reading 135

8. Let's Take This Offline 137
Diving In 137
The Cache Manifest 138
Network Sections 139
Fallback Sections 140
The Flow of Events 141
The Fine Art of Debugging, a.k.a. "Kill Me! Kill Me Now!" 142
Let's Build One! 145
Further Reading 146

9. **A Form of Madness** 147
    Diving In   147
    Placeholder Text   147
    Autofocus Fields   148
    Email Addresses   150
    Web Addresses   151
    Numbers As Spinboxes   153
    Numbers As Sliders   155
    Date Pickers   156
    Search Boxes   158
    Color Pickers   160
    And One More Thing...   160
    Further Reading   161

10. **"Distributed," "Extensibility," and Other Fancy Words** 163
    Diving In   163
    What Is Microdata?   164
    The Microdata Data Model   165
    Marking Up People   168
      Introducing Google Rich Snippets   174
    Marking Up Organizations   176
    Marking Up Events   180
      The Return of Google Rich Snippets   184
    Marking Up Reviews   186
    Further Reading   190

Appendix: The All-in-One Almost-Alphabetical Guide to Detecting Everything 191

Index 201

Preface

Diving In

What is HTML5? HTML5 is the next generation of HTML, superseding HTML 4.01, XHTML 1.0, and XHTML 1.1. HTML5 provides new features that are necessary for modern web applications. It also standardizes many features of the web platform that web developers have been using for years, but that have never been vetted or documented by a standards committee. (Would it surprise you to learn that the `Window` object has never been formally documented? In addition to the new features, HTML5 is the first attempt to formally document many of the "de facto" standards that web browsers have supported for years.)

Like its predecessors, HTML5 is designed to be cross-platform. You don't need to be running Windows or Mac OS X or Linux or Multics or any particular operating system in order to take advantage of HTML5. The only thing you *do* need is a modern web browser. There are modern web browsers available for free for all major operating systems. You may already have a web browser that supports certain HTML5 features. The latest versions of Apple Safari, Google Chrome, Mozilla Firefox, and Opera all support many HTML5 features. (You'll find more detailed browser compatibility tables throughout this book.) The mobile web browsers that come preinstalled on iPhones, iPads, and Android phones all have excellent support for HTML5. Even Microsoft has announced that the upcoming Version 9 of Internet Explorer will support some HTML5 functionality.

This book will focus on eight topics:

- New semantic elements like `<header>`, `<footer>`, and `<section>` (Chapter 3)
- Canvas, a two-dimensional drawing surface that you can program with JavaScript (Chapter 4)
- Video that you can embed on your web pages without resorting to third-party plug-ins (Chapter 5)
- Geolocation, whereby visitors can choose to share their physical locations with your web application (Chapter 6)
- Persistent local storage without resorting to third-party plug-ins (Chapter 7)

- Offline web applications that work even after network access is interrupted (Chapter 8)
- Improvements to HTML web forms (Chapter 9)
- Microdata that lets you create your own vocabularies beyond HTML5 and extend your web pages with custom semantics (Chapter 10)

HTML5 is designed, as much as possible, to be backward compatible with existing web browsers. New features build on existing features and allow you to provide fallback content for older browsers. If you need even greater control, you can detect support for individual HTML5 features (Chapter 2) using a few lines of JavaScript. Don't rely on fragile browser sniffing to decide which browsers support HTML5! Instead, test for the features you need using HTML5 itself.

Conventions Used in This Book

The following typographical conventions are used in this book:

Italic

Indicates new terms, URLs, email addresses, filenames, and file extensions.

`Constant width`

Used for program listings, as well as within paragraphs to refer to program elements such as variable or function names, databases, data types, environment variables, statements, and keywords.

`Constant width bold`

Shows commands or other text that should be typed literally by the user.

`Constant width italic`

Shows text that should be replaced with user-supplied values or by values determined by context.

> This icon signifies a tip, suggestion, or general note.

> This icon indicates a warning or caution.

Using Code Examples

This book is here to help you get your job done. In general, you may use the code in this book in your programs and documentation. You do not need to contact us for permission unless you're reproducing a significant portion of the code. For example, writing a program that uses several chunks of code from this book does not require permission. Selling or distributing a CD-ROM of examples from O'Reilly books does require permission. Answering a question by citing this book and quoting example code does not require permission. Incorporating a significant amount of example code from this book into your product's documentation does require permission.

We appreciate, but do not require, attribution. An attribution usually includes the title, author, publisher, and ISBN. For example: "*HTML5: Up and Running* by Mark Pilgrim. Copyright 2010 O'Reilly Media, Inc., 978-0-596-80602-6."

If you feel your use of code examples falls outside fair use or the permission given above, feel free to contact us at *permissions@oreilly.com*.

A Note on the Editions of This Book

•in fo

This book is derived from its HTML5 source, found at *http://diveintohtml5.org/* and maintained by the author. The ebook (*http://oreilly.com/catalog/9780596806033/*) and Safari Books Online (*http://my.safaribooksonline.com/9781449392154*) editions include all the original hyperlinking, while the print edition includes only a subset of the hyperlinks, set as URLs in parentheses. If you are reading the print edition, please refer to one of the other editions—or the original source—for a richer linking experience. Because the author maintains *http://diveintohtml5.org/* in HTML5, the site includes live examples of the code described in this book, many of which had to be modified for publication. Please visit *http://diveintohtml5.org/* to see these examples, but be aware that their rendering may vary across browsers.

Safari® Books Online

Safari Books Online is an on-demand digital library that lets you easily search over 7,500 technology and creative reference books and videos to find the answers you need quickly.

With a subscription, you can read any page and watch any video from our library online. Read books on your cell phone and mobile devices. Access new titles before they are available for print, and get exclusive access to manuscripts in development and post feedback for the authors. Copy and paste code samples, organize your favorites, download chapters, bookmark key sections, create notes, print out pages, and benefit from tons of other time-saving features.

O'Reilly Media has uploaded this book to the Safari Books Online service. To have full digital access to this book and others on similar topics from O'Reilly and other publishers, sign up for free at *http://my.safaribooksonline.com*.

How to Contact Us

Please address comments and questions concerning this book to the publisher:

O'Reilly Media, Inc.
1005 Gravenstein Highway North
Sebastopol, CA 95472
800-998-9938 (in the United States or Canada)
707-829-0515 (international or local)
707-829-0104 (fax)

We have a web page for this book, where we list errata, examples, and any additional information. You can access this page at:

http://oreilly.com/catalog/9780596806026/

To comment or ask technical questions about this book, send email to:

bookquestions@oreilly.com

For more information about our books, conferences, Resource Centers, and the O'Reilly Network, see our website at:

http://www.oreilly.com

## CHAPTER 1

How Did We Get Here?

Diving In

Recently, I stumbled across a quote from a Mozilla developer about the tension inherent in creating standards (*http://lists.w3.org/Archives/Public/public-html/2010Jan/0107 .html*):

> Implementations and specifications have to do a delicate dance together. You don't want implementations to happen before the specification is finished, because people start depending on the details of implementations and that constrains the specification. However, you also don't want the specification to be finished before there are implementations and author experience with those implementations, because you need the feedback. There is unavoidable tension here, but we just have to muddle on through.

Keep this quote in the back of your mind, and let me explain how HTML5 came to be.

MIME Types

This book is about HTML5, not previous versions of HTML, and not any version of XHTML. But to understand the history of HTML5 and the motivations behind it, you need to understand a few technical details first. Specifically, MIME types.

Every time your web browser requests a page, the web server sends a number of headers before it sends the actual page markup. These headers are normally invisible, although there are a number of web development tools that will make them visible if you're interested. The headers are important, because they tell your browser how to interpret the page markup that follows. The most important header is called `Content-Type`, and it looks like this:

```
Content-Type: text/html
```

`text/html` is called the "content type" or "MIME type" of the page. This header is the *only* thing that determines what a particular resource truly is, and therefore how it should be rendered. Images have their own MIME types (`image/jpeg` for JPEG images, `image/png` for PNG images, and so on). JavaScript files have their own MIME type. CSS stylesheets have their own MIME type. Everything has its own MIME type. The Web runs on MIME types.

Of course, reality is more complicated than that. Very early web servers (I'm talking web servers from 1993) didn't send the `Content-Type` header, because it didn't exist yet. (It wasn't invented until 1994.) For compatibility reasons that date all the way back to 1993, some popular web browsers will ignore the `Content-Type` header under certain circumstances. (This is called "content sniffing.") But as a general rule of thumb, everything you've ever looked at on the Web—HTML pages, images, scripts, videos, PDFs, anything with a URL—has been served to you with a specific MIME type in the `Content-Type` header.

Tuck that under your hat. We'll come back to it.

A Long Digression into How Standards Are Made

Why do we have an `<img>` element? I don't suppose that's a question you ask yourself very often. Obviously *someone* must have created it. These things don't just appear out of nowhere. Every element, every attribute, every feature of HTML that you've ever used—someone created them, decided how they should work, and wrote it all down. These people are not gods, nor are they flawless. They're just people. Smart people, to be sure. But just people.

One of the great things about standards that are developed "out in the open" is that you can go back in time and answer these kinds of questions. Discussions occur on mailing lists, which are usually archived and publicly searchable. So, I decided to do a bit of "email archaeology" to try to answer the `<img>` element question. I had to go back to before there was an organization called the World Wide Web Consortium (W3C). I went back to the earliest days of the Web, when you could count the number of web servers on the fingers of both hands, and maybe a couple of toes.

On February 25, 1993, Marc Andreessen wrote:[*]

> I'd like to propose a new, optional HTML tag:
>
> IMG
>
> Required argument is `SRC="url"`.
>
> This names a bitmap or pixmap file for the browser to attempt to pull over the network and interpret as an image, to be embedded in the text at the point of the tag's occurrence.
>
> An example is:
>
> `<IMG SRC="file://foobar.com/foo/bar/blargh.xbm">`
>
> (There is no closing tag; this is just a standalone tag.)

---

[*] *http://1997.webhistory.org/www.lists/www-talk.1993q1/0182.html*. The thread described over the next several pages can be followed by clicking the "Next message" and "Previous message" links.

This tag can be embedded in an anchor like anything else; when that happens, it becomes an icon that's sensitive to activation just like a regular text anchor.

Browsers should be afforded flexibility as to which image formats they support. Xbm and Xpm are good ones to support, for example. If a browser cannot interpret a given format, it can do whatever it wants instead (X Mosaic will pop up a default bitmap as a placeholder).

This is required functionality for X Mosaic; we have this working, and we'll at least be using it internally. I'm certainly open to suggestions as to how this should be handled within HTML; if you have a better idea than what I'm presenting now, please let me know. I know this is hazy with regard to image format, but I don't see an alternative than to just say "let the browser do what it can" and wait for the perfect solution to come along (MIME, someday, maybe).

This quote requires some explanation. Xbm and Xpm were popular graphics formats on Unix systems.

"Mosaic" was one of the earliest web browsers. ("X Mosaic" was the version that ran on Unix systems.) When he wrote this message in early 1993, Marc had not yet founded the company that made him famous, Mosaic Communications Corporation, nor had he started work on that company's flagship product, "Mosaic Netscape." (You may know them better by their later names, "Netscape Corporation" and "Netscape Navigator.")

"MIME, someday, maybe" is a reference to content negotiation, a feature of HTTP where a client (like a web browser) tells the server (like a web server) what types of resources it supports (like `image/jpeg`) so the server can return something in the client's preferred format. "The Original HTTP as defined in 1991" (the only version that was implemented in February 1993) did not have a way for clients to tell servers what kinds of images they supported, thus the design dilemma that Marc faced.

A few hours later, Tony Johnson replied:

I have something very similar in Midas 2.0 (in use here at SLAC, and due for public release any week now), except that all the names are different, and it has an extra argument `NAME="name"`. It has almost exactly the same functionality as your proposed `IMG` tag. e.g.,

```
<ICON name="NoEntry" href="http://note/foo/bar/NoEntry.xbm">
```

The idea of the name parameter was to allow the browser to have a set of "built in" images. If the name matches a "built in" image it would use that instead of having to go out and fetch the image. The name could also act as a hint for "line mode" browsers as to what kind of a symbol to put in place of the image.

I don't much care about the parameter or tag names, but it would be sensible if we used the same things. I don't much care for abbreviations, i.e., why not `IMAGE=` and `SOURCE=`. I somewhat prefer `ICON` since it implies that the `IMAGE` should be smallish, but maybe `ICON` is an overloaded word?

Midas was another early web browser, a contemporary of X Mosaic. It was cross-platform; it ran on both Unix and VMS. "SLAC" refers to the Stanford Linear Accelerator Center, now the SLAC National Accelerator Laboratory, which hosted the first web server in the United States (in fact, the first web server outside Europe). When Tony wrote this message, SLAC was an old-timer on the WWW, having hosted five pages on its web server for a whopping 441 days.

Tony continued:

> While we are on the subject of new tags, I have another, somewhat similar tag, which I would like to support in Midas 2.0. In principle it is:
>
> ```
> <INCLUDE HREF="...">
> ```
>
> The intention here would be that the second document is to be included into the first document at the place where the tag occurred. In principle the referenced document could be anything, but the main purpose was to allow images (in this case arbitrary sized) to be embedded into documents. Again the intention would be that when HTTP2 comes along the format of the included document would be up for separate negotiation.

"HTTP2" is a reference to Basic HTTP as defined in 1992. At this point, in early 1993, it was still largely unimplemented. The draft known as "HTTP2" evolved and was eventually standardized as "HTTP 1.0". HTTP 1.0 did include request headers for content negotiation, a.k.a. "MIME, someday, maybe."

Tony went on:

> An alternative I was considering was:
>
> ```
> <A HREF="..." INCLUDE>See photo</A>
> ```
>
> I don't much like adding more functionality to the <A> tag, but the idea here is to maintain compatibility with browsers that can not honour the INCLUDE parameter. The intention is that browsers which do understand INCLUDE, replace the anchor text (in this case "See photo") with the included document (picture), while older or dumber browsers ignore the INCLUDE tag completely.

This proposal was never implemented, although the idea of providing text if an image is missing is an important accessibility technique that was missing from Marc's initial <IMG> proposal. Many years later, this feature was bolted on as the <img alt> attribute, which Netscape promptly broke by erroneously treating it as a tooltip.

A few hours after Tony posted his message, Tim Berners-Lee responded:

> I had imagined that figures would be represented as
>
> ```
> <a name=fig1 href="fghjkdfghj" REL="EMBED, PRESENT">Figure </a>
> ```
>
> where the relationship values mean
>
> ```
> EMBED     Embed this here when presenting it
> PRESENT   Present this whenever the source document is presented
> ```
>
> Note that you can have various combinations of these, and if the browser doesn't support either one, it doesn't break.
>
> [I] see that using this as a method for selectable icons means nesting anchors. Hmmm. But I hadn't wanted a special tag.

This proposal was never implemented, but the `rel` attribute is still around (see "Friends and (Link) Relations" on page 36).

Jim Davis added:

> It would be nice if there was a way to specify the content type, e.g.
>
> `<IMG HREF="http://nsa.gov/pub/sounds/gorby.au" CONTENT-TYPE=audio/basic>`
>
> But I am completely willing to live with the requirement that I specify the content type by file extension.

This proposal was never implemented, but Netscape did later add support for arbitrary embedding of media objects with the `<embed>` element.

Jay C. Weber asked:

> While images are at the top of my list of desired medium types in a WWW browser, I don't think we should add idiosyncratic hooks for media one at a time. Whatever happened to the enthusiasm for using the MIME typing mechanism?

Marc Andreessen replied:

> This isn't a substitute for the upcoming use of MIME as a standard document mechanism; this provides a necessary and simple implementation of functionality that's needed independently from MIME.

Jay C. Weber responded:

> Let's temporarily forget about MIME, if it clouds the issue. My objection was to the discussion of "how are we going to support embedded images" rather than "how are we going to support embedded objections in various media."
>
> Otherwise, next week someone is going to suggest "let's put in a new tag `<AUD SRC="file://foobar.com/foo/bar/blargh.snd">`" for audio.
>
> There shouldn't be much cost in going with something that generalizes.

With the benefit of hindsight, it appears that Jay's concerns were well founded. It took a little more than a week, but HTML5 did finally add new `<video>` and `<audio>` elements.

Responding to Jay's original message, Dave Raggett said:

> True indeed! I want to consider a whole range of possible image/line art types, along with the possibility of format negotiation. Tim's note on supporting clickable areas within images is also important.

Later in 1993, Dave proposed HTML+ as an evolution of the HTML standard. The proposal was never implemented, and it was superseded by HTML 2.0. HTML 2.0 was a "retro-spec," which means it formalized features already in common use: "This specification brings together, clarifies, and formalizes a set of features that roughly corresponds to the capabilities of HTML in common use prior to June 1994."

Dave later wrote HTML 3.0, based on his earlier HTML+ draft. Outside of the W3C's own reference implementation, Arena, HTML 3.0 was never implemented. It was superseded by HTML 3.2, which was also a "retro-spec": "HTML 3.2 adds widely deployed features such as tables, applets and text flow around images, while providing full backward compatibility with the existing standard HTML 2.0."

Dave later coauthored HTML 4.0, developed HTML Tidy, and went on to help with XHTML, XForms, MathML, and other modern W3C specifications.

Getting back to 1993, Marc replied to Dave:

> Actually, maybe we should think about a general-purpose procedural graphics language within which we can embed arbitrary hyperlinks attached to icons, images, or text, or anything. Has anyone else seen Intermedia's capabilities with regard to this?

Intermedia was a hypertext project from Brown University. It was developed from 1985 to 1991 and ran on A/UX, a Unix-like operating system for early Macintosh computers.

The idea of a "general-purpose procedural graphics language" did eventually catch on. Modern browsers support both SVG (declarative markup with embedded scripting) and <canvas> (a procedural direct-mode graphics API), although the latter started as a proprietary extension before being "retro-specced" by the WHAT Working Group.

Bill Janssen replied:

> Other systems to look at which have this (fairly valuable) notion are Andrew and Slate. Andrew is built with _insets_, each of which has some interesting type, such as text, bitmap, drawing, animation, message, spreadsheet, etc. The notion of arbitrary recursive embedding is present, so that an inset of any kind can be embedded in any other kind which supports embedding. For example, an inset can be embedded at any point in the text of the text widget, or in any rectangular area in the drawing widget, or in any cell of the spreadsheet.

"Andrew" is a reference to the Andrew User Interface System, although at that time it was simply known as the Andrew Project.

Meanwhile, Thomas Fine had a different idea:

> Here's my opinion. The best way to do images in WWW is by using MIME. I'm sure postscript is already a supported subtype in MIME, and it deals very nicely with mixing text and graphics.
>
> But it isn't clickable, you say? Yes, you're right. I suspect there is already an answer to this in display postscript. Even if there isn't the addition to standard postscript is trivial. Define an anchor command which specifies the URL and uses the current path as a closed region for the button. Since postscript deals so well with paths, this makes arbitrary button shapes trivial.

Display PostScript was an onscreen rendering technology codeveloped by Adobe and NeXT.

This proposal was never implemented, but the idea that the best way to fix HTML is to replace it with something else altogether still pops up from time to time.

On March 2, 1993, Tim Berners-Lee commented:

> HTTP2 allows a document to contain any type which the user has said he can handle, not just registered MIME types. So one can experiment. Yes I think there is a case for postscript with hypertext. I don't know whether display postscript has enough. I know Adobe are trying to establish their own postscript-based "PDF" which will have links, and be readable by their proprietary brand of viewers.

> I thought that a generic overlaying language for anchors (HyTime based?) would allow the hypertext and the graphics/video standards to evolve separately, which would help both.

> Let the `IMG` tag be `INCLUDE` and let it refer to an arbitrary document type. Or `EMBED` if `INCLUDE` sounds like a cpp include which people will expect to provide SGML source code to be parsed inline—not what was intended.

HyTime was an early, SGML-based hypertext document system. It loomed large in many early discussions of HTML, and later XML.

Tim's proposal for an `<INCLUDE>` tag was never implemented, although you can see echoes of it in `<object>`, `<embed>`, and the `<iframe>` element.

Finally, on March 12, 1993, Marc Andreessen revisited the thread:

> Back to the inlined image thread again—I'm getting close to releasing Mosaic v0.10, which will support inlined GIF and XBM images/bitmaps, as mentioned previously. [...]

> We're not prepared to support `INCLUDE`/`EMBED` at this point. [...] So we're probably going to go with `<IMG SRC="url">` (not `ICON`, since not all inlined images can be meaningfully called icons). For the time being, inlined images won't be explicitly content-type'd; down the road, we plan to support that (along with the general adaptation of MIME). Actually, the image reading routines we're currently using figure out the image format on the fly, so the filename extension won't even be significant.

An Unbroken Line

I am extraordinarily fascinated with all aspects of this almost 17-year-old conversation that led to the creation of an HTML element that has been used on virtually every web page ever published. Consider this:

- HTTP still exists. It successfully evolved from 0.9 into 1.0 and later 1.1, and still it evolves (*http://www.ietf.org/dyn/wg/charter/httpbis-charter.html*).
- HTML still exists. That rudimentary data format (it didn't even support inline images!) successfully evolved into 2.0, 3.2, and 4.0. HTML is an unbroken line. A twisted, knotted, snarled line, to be sure—there were plenty of "dead branches" in the evolutionary tree, places where standards-minded people got ahead of themselves (and ahead of authors and implementors)—but still, here we are in 2010, and web pages from 1990 still render in modern browsers. I just loaded one up in the browser of my state-of-the-art Android mobile phone, and I didn't even get prompted to "please wait while importing legacy format..."

- HTML has always been a conversation between browser makers, authors, standards wonks, and other people who just showed up and liked to talk about angle brackets. Most of the successful versions of HTML have been "retro-specs," catching up to the world while simultaneously trying to nudge it in the right direction. Anyone who tells you that HTML should be kept "pure" (presumably by ignoring browser makers, or ignoring authors, or both) is simply misinformed. HTML has never been pure, and all attempts to purify it have been spectacular failures, matched only by the attempts to replace it.

- None of the browsers in use in 1993 still exist in any recognizable form. Netscape Navigator was abandoned in 1998 and rewritten from scratch to create the Mozilla Suite, which was then forked to create Firefox. Internet Explorer had its humble "beginnings" in "Microsoft Plus! for Windows 95," where it was bundled with some desktop themes and a pinball game; but of course, that browser can be traced back further too.

- Some of the operating systems from 1993 still exist, but none of them are relevant to the modern Web. Most people today who "experience" the Web do so on a PC running Windows 2000 or later, a Mac running Mac OS X, a PC running some flavor of Linux, or a handheld device like an iPhone. In 1993, Windows was at Version 3.1 (and competing with OS/2), Macs were running System 7, and Linux was distributed via Usenet. (Want to have some fun? Find a graybeard and whisper "Trumpet Winsock" or "MacPPP.")

- Some of the same *people* are still around and still involved in what we now simply call "web standards." That's after almost 20 years. And some were involved in predecessors of HTML, going back into the 1980s and before.

- Speaking of predecessors.... With the eventual popularity of HTML and the Web, it is easy to forget the contemporary formats and systems that informed their design. Before you read this chapter, had you ever heard of Andrew? Intermedia? HyTime? And HyTime was not some rinky-dink academic research project; it was an ISO standard approved for military use. It was Big Business. And you can read about it yourself at *http://www.sgmlsource.com/history/hthist.htm*.

But none of this answers the original question: why do we have an `<img>` element? Why not an `<icon>` element? Or an `<include>` element? Why not a hyperlink with an `include` attribute, or some combination of `rel` values? Why an `<img>` element? Quite simply, because Marc Andreessen shipped one, and shipping code wins.

That's not to say that *all* shipping code wins; after all, Andrew and Intermedia and HyTime shipped code too. Code is necessary but not sufficient for success. And I *certainly* don't mean to say that shipping code before a standard will produce the best solution. Marc's `<img>` element didn't mandate a common graphics format; it didn't define how text flowed around it; it didn't support text alternatives or fallback content for older browsers. And 17 years later, we're still struggling with content sniffing, and it's still a source of crazy security vulnerabilities. You can trace that through the Great

Browser Wars, all the way back to February 25, 1993, when Marc Andreessen off-handedly remarked, "MIME, someday, maybe," and then shipped his code anyway.

A Timeline of HTML Development from 1997 to 2004

In December 1997, the World Wide Web Consortium (W3C) published HTML 4.0 and promptly shut down the HTML Working Group. Less than two months later, a separate W3C Working Group published XML 1.0. A mere three months after that, the W3C held a workshop called "Shaping the Future of HTML" to answer the question, "Has W3C given up on HTML?" This was the answer:

> In discussions, it was agreed that further extending HTML 4.0 would be difficult, as would converting 4.0 to be an XML application. The proposed way to break free of these restrictions is to make a fresh start with the next generation of HTML based upon a suite of XML tag-sets.

The W3C rechartered the HTML Working Group to create this "suite of XML tag-sets." The members' first step, in December 1998, was to draft an interim specification that simply reformulated HTML in XML without adding any new elements or attributes. This specification later became known as "XHTML 1.0". It defined a new MIME type for XHTML documents, `application/xhtml+xml`. However, to ease the migration of existing HTML 4 pages, it also included Appendix C, which "summarizes design guidelines for authors who wish their XHTML documents to render on existing HTML user agents." Appendix C said you were allowed to author so-called "XHTML" pages but still serve them with the `text/html` MIME type.

The next target was web forms. In August 1999, the same HTML Working Group published a first draft of XHTML Extended Forms. Its members set the expectations in the very first sentences of this draft document (*http://www.w3.org/TR/1999/WD -xhtml-forms-req-19990830#intro*):

> After careful consideration, the HTML Working Group has decided that the goals for the next generation of forms are incompatible with preserving backward compatibility with browsers designed for earlier versions of HTML. It is our objective to provide a clean new forms model ("XHTML Extended Forms") based on a set of well-defined requirements. The requirements described in this document are based on experience with a very broad spectrum of form applications.

A few months later, "XHTML Extended Forms" was renamed "XForms" and moved to its own Working Group. That group worked in parallel with the HTML Working Group and finally published the first edition of XForms 1.0 in October 2003.

Meanwhile, with the transition to XML complete, the members of the HTML Working Group set their sights on creating "the next generation of HTML." In May 2001, they published the first edition of XHTML 1.1, which added only a few minor features on top of XHTML 1.0 but eliminated the "Appendix C" loophole. Starting with Version 1.1, all XHTML documents were to be served with a MIME type of `application/xhtml+xml`.

Everything You Know About XHTML Is Wrong

Why are MIME types important? Why do I keep coming back to them? Three words: draconian error handling. Browsers have always been "forgiving" with HTML. If you create an HTML page but forget to give it a `<title>`, browsers will display the page anyway, even though the `<title>` element has always been required in every version of HTML. Certain tags are not allowed within other tags, but if you create a page that puts them inside anyway, browsers will just deal with it (somehow) and move on without displaying an error message.

As you might expect, the fact that "broken" HTML markup still worked in web browsers led authors to create broken HTML pages. A lot of broken pages. By some estimates, over 99 percent of HTML pages on the Web today have at least one error in them. But because these errors don't cause browsers to display visible error messages, nobody ever fixes them.

The W3C saw this as a fundamental problem with the Web, and set out to correct it. XML, published in 1997, broke from the tradition of forgiving clients and mandated that all programs that consumed XML must treat so-called "well-formedness" errors as fatal. This concept of failing on the first error became known as "draconian error handling," after the Greek leader Draco, who instituted the death penalty for relatively minor infractions of his laws. When the W3C reformulated HTML as an XML vocabulary, the people in charge mandated that all documents served with the new `application/xhtml+xml` MIME type would be subject to draconian error handling. If there was even a single error in your XHTML page, web browsers would have no choice but to stop processing and display an error message to the end user.

This idea was not universally popular. With an estimated error rate of 99 percent on existing pages, the ever-present possibility of displaying errors to the end user, and the dearth of new features in XHTML 1.0 and 1.1 to justify the cost, web authors basically ignored `application/xhtml+xml`. But that doesn't mean they ignored XHTML altogether. Oh, most definitely not. Appendix C of the XHTML 1.0 specification gave the web authors of the world a loophole: "Use something that looks kind of like XHTML syntax, but keep serving it with the `text/html` MIME type." And that's exactly what thousands of web developers did: they "upgraded" to XHTML syntax but kept serving it with a `text/html` MIME type.

Even today, while many web pages claim to be XHTML—they start with the XHTML doctype on the first line, use lowercase tag names, use quotes around attribute values, and add a trailing slash after empty elements like `<br />` and `<hr />`—only a tiny fraction of these pages are served with the `application/xhtml+xml` MIME type that would trigger XML's draconian error handling. Any page served with a MIME type of `text/html`, regardless of its doctype, syntax, or coding style, will be parsed using a "forgiving" HTML parser, silently ignoring any markup errors and never alerting end users (or anyone else), even if the page is technically broken.

XHTML 1.0 included this loophole, but XHTML 1.1 closed it, and the never-finalized XHTML 2.0 continued the tradition of requiring draconian error handling. And that's why there are billions of pages that claim to be XHTML 1.0, and only a handful that claim to be XHTML 1.1 (or XHTML 2.0). So, are you really using XHTML? Check your MIME type. (Actually, if you don't know what MIME type you're using, I can pretty much guarantee that you're still using `text/html`.) Unless you're serving your pages with a MIME type of `application/xhtml+xml`, your so-called "XHTML" is XML in name only.

A Competing Vision

In June 2004, the W3C held the Workshop on Web Applications and Compound Documents. Present at this workshop were representatives of several browser vendors, web development companies, and other W3C members. A group of interested parties, including the Mozilla Foundation and Opera Software, gave a presentation on their competing visions of the future of the Web: an evolution of the existing HTML 4 standard to include new features for modern web application developers (*http://www .w3.org/2004/04/webapps-cdf-ws/papers/opera.html*):

> The following seven principles represent what we believe to be the most critical requirements for this work:
>
> *Backward compatibility, clear migration path*
>> Web application technologies should be based on technologies authors are familiar with, including HTML, CSS, DOM, and JavaScript.
>>
>> Basic Web application features should be implementable using behaviors, scripting, and style sheets in IE6 today so that authors have a clear migration path. Any solution that cannot be used with the current high-market-share user agent without the need for binary plug-ins is highly unlikely to be successful.
>
> *Well-defined error handling*
>> Error handling in Web applications must be defined to a level of detail where User Agents (UAs) do not have to invent their own error handling mechanisms or reverse engineer other User Agents'.
>
> *Users should not be exposed to authoring errors*
>> Specifications must specify exact error recovery behaviour for each possible error scenario. Error handling should for the most part be defined in terms of graceful error recovery (as in CSS), rather than obvious and catastrophic failure (as in XML).
>
> *Practical use*
>> Every feature that goes into the Web Applications specifications must be justified by a practical use case. The reverse is not necessarily true: every use case does not necessarily warrant a new feature.
>>
>> Use cases should preferably be based on real sites where the authors previously used a poor solution to work around the limitation.

Scripting is here to stay
> But should be avoided where more convenient declarative markup can be used. Scripting should be device and presentation neutral unless scoped in a device-specific way (e.g., unless included in XBL).

Device-specific profiling should be avoided
> Authors should be able to depend on the same features being implemented in desktop and mobile versions of the same UA.

Open process
> The Web has benefited from being developed in an open environment. Web Applications will be core to the Web, and its development should also take place in the open. Mailing lists, archives and draft specifications should continuously be visible to the public.

In a straw poll, the workshop participants were asked, "Should the W3C develop declarative extensions to HTML and CSS and imperative extensions to DOM, to address medium level Web Application requirements, as opposed to sophisticated, fully-fledged OS-level APIs?" The vote was 11 to 8 against. In their summary of the workshop (*http://www.w3.org/2004/04/webapps-cdf-ws/summary*), the W3C's members wrote, "At present, W3C does not intend to put any resources into the third straw-poll topic: extensions to HTML and CSS for Web Applications, other than technologies being developed under the charter of current W3C Working Groups."

Faced with this decision, the people who had proposed evolving HTML and HTML forms had only two choices: give up, or continue their work outside of the W3C. They chose the latter, registered the whatwg.org domain, and in June 2004, the WHAT Working Group was born.

What Working Group?

What the heck is the WHAT Working Group? I'll let it explain for itself (*http://www .whatwg.org/news/start*):

> The Web Hypertext Applications Technology Working Group is a loose, unofficial, and open collaboration of Web browser manufacturers and interested parties. The group aims to develop specifications based on HTML and related technologies to ease the deployment of interoperable Web Applications, with the intention of submitting the results to a standards organisation. This submission would then form the basis of work on formally extending HTML in the standards track.

> The creation of this forum follows from several months of work by private e-mail on specifications for such technologies. The main focus up to this point has been extending HTML4 Forms to support features requested by authors, without breaking backward compatibility with existing content. This group was created to ensure that future development of these specifications will be completely open, through a publicly-archived, open mailing list.

The key phrase here is "without breaking backward compatibility." XHTML (minus the Appendix C loophole) is not backward compatible with HTML. It requires an entirely new MIME type, and it mandates draconian error handling for all content served with that MIME type. XForms is not backward compatible with HTML forms, because it can only be used in documents that are served with the new XHTML MIME type, which means that XForms also mandates draconian error handling. All roads lead to MIME.

Instead of scrapping over a decade's worth of investment in HTML and making 99 percent of existing web pages unusable, the WHAT Working Group decided to take a different approach: documenting the "forgiving" error handling algorithms that browsers actually used. Web browsers have always been forgiving of HTML errors, but nobody had ever bothered to write down exactly how they did it. NCSA Mosaic had its own algorithms for dealing with broken pages, and Netscape tried to match them. Then Internet Explorer tried to match Netscape. Then Opera and Firefox tried to match Internet Explorer. Then Safari tried to match Firefox. And so on, right up to the present day. Along the way, developers burned thousands and thousands of hours trying to make their products compatible with those of their competitors.

If that sounds like an insane amount of work, that's because it is. Or rather, it was. It took several years, but (modulo a few obscure edge cases) the WHAT Working Group successfully documented how to parse HTML in a way that is compatible with existing web content. Nowhere in the final algorithm is there a step that mandates that the HTML consumer should stop processing and display an error message to the end user.

While all that reverse-engineering was going on, the WHAT Working Group was quietly working on a few other things, too. One of them was a specification, initially dubbed Web Forms 2.0, that added new types of controls to HTML forms. (You'll learn more about web forms in Chapter 9.) Another was a draft specification called "Web Applications 1.0" that included major new features, like a direct-mode drawing canvas (see Chapter 4) and native support for audio and video without plug-ins (see Chapter 5).

Back to the W3C

For several years, the W3C and the WHAT Working Group largely ignored each other. While the WHAT Working Group focused on web forms and new HTML features, the W3C HTML Working Group was busy with Version 2.0 of XHTML. But by October 2006, it was clear that the WHAT Working Group had picked up serious momentum, while XHTML 2 was still languishing in draft form, unimplemented by any major browser. In October 2006, Tim Berners-Lee, the founder of the W3C itself, announced that the W3C would work together with the WHAT Working Group (*http://dig.csail .mit.edu/breadcrumbs/node/166*) to evolve HTML:

> Some things are clearer with hindsight of several years. It is necessary to evolve HTML incrementally. The attempt to get the world to switch to XML, including quotes around attribute values and slashes in empty tags and namespaces all at once didn't work. The

large HTML-generating public did not move, largely because the browsers didn't complain. Some large communities did shift and are enjoying the fruits of well-formed systems, but not all. It is important to maintain HTML incrementally, as well as continuing a transition to a well-formed world, and developing more power in that world.

The plan is to charter a completely new HTML group. Unlike the previous one, this one will be chartered to do incremental improvements to HTML, and also in parallel XHTML. It will have a different chair and staff contact. It will work on HTML and XHTML together. We have strong support for this group, from many people we have talked to, including browser makers.

There will also be work on forms. This is a complex area, as existing HTML forms and XForms are both form languages. HTML forms are ubiquitously deployed, and there are many implementations and users of XForms. Meanwhile, the Webforms submission has suggested sensible extensions to HTML forms. The plan is, informed by Webforms, to extend HTML forms.

One of the first things the newly rechartered W3C HTML Working Group decided was to rename "Web Applications 1.0" to "HTML5." And here we are, diving into HTML5.

Postscript

In October 2009, the W3C shut down the XHTML 2 Working Group and issued this statement to explain the decision (*http://www.w3.org/2009/06/xhtml-faq.html*):

> When W3C announced the HTML and XHTML 2 Working Groups in March 2007, we indicated that we would continue to monitor the market for XHTML 2. W3C recognizes the importance of a clear signal to the community about the future of HTML.

> While we recognize the value of the XHTML 2 Working Group's contributions over the years, after discussion with the participants, W3C management has decided to allow the Working Group's charter to expire at the end of 2009 and not to renew it.

The ones that win are the ones that ship.

Further Reading

- "The History of the Web" (*http://hixie.ch/commentary/web/history*), an old draft by Ian Hickson
- "HTML/History" (*http://esw.w3.org/topic/HTML/history*), by Michael Smith, Henri Sivonen, and others
- "A Brief History of HTML" (*http://www.atendesigngroup.com/blog/brief-history-of -html*), by Scott Reynen

## CHAPTER 2

Detecting HTML5 Features

Diving In

You may well ask, "How can I start using HTML5 if older browsers don't support it?" But the question itself is misleading. HTML5 is not one big thing; it is a collection of individual features. So, you can't detect "HTML5 support," because that doesn't make any sense. But you *can* detect support for individual features, like canvas, video, or geolocation.

Detection Techniques

When your browser renders a web page, it constructs a Document Object Model (DOM), a collection of objects that represent the HTML elements on the page. Every element—every `<p>`, every `<div>`, every `<span>`—is represented in the DOM by a different object. (There are also global objects, like `window` and `document`, that aren't tied to specific elements.)

All DOM objects share a set of common properties, but some objects have more than others. In browsers that support HTML5 features, certain objects will have unique properties. A quick peek at the DOM will tell you which features are supported.

There are four basic techniques for detecting whether a browser supports a particular feature. From simplest to most complex:

1. Check if a certain property exists on a global object (such as `window` or `navigator`).

   For an example of testing for geolocation support, see "Geolocation" on page 24.

2. Create an element, then check if a certain property exists on that element.

   For an example of testing for canvas support, see "Canvas" on page 16.

3. Create an element, check if a certain method exists on that element, then call the method and check the value it returns.

For an example of testing which video formats are supported, see "Video Formats" on page 19.

4. Create an element, set a property to a certain value, then check if the property has retained its value.

For an example of testing which `<input>` types are supported, see "Input Types" on page 25.

Modernizr: An HTML5 Detection Library

Modernizr (*http://www.modernizr.com*) is an open source, MIT-licensed JavaScript library that detects support for many HTML5 and CSS3 features. At the time of writing, the latest version is 1.1. You should always use the latest version. To do so, include the following `<script>` element at the top of your page:

```html
<!DOCTYPE html>
<html>
<head>
  <meta charset="utf-8">
  <title>Dive into HTML5</title>
  <script src="modernizr.min.js"></script>
</head>
<body>
  ...
</body>
</html>
```

Modernizr runs automatically. There is no `modernizr_init()` function to call. When it runs, it creates a global object called `Modernizr` that contains a set of Boolean properties for each feature it can detect. For example, if your browser supports the canvas API (see Chapter 4), the `Modernizr.canvas` property will be `true`. If your browser does not support the canvas API, the `Modernizr.canvas` property will be `false`:

```javascript
if (Modernizr.canvas) {
  // let's draw some shapes!
} else {
  // no native canvas support available :(
}
```

Canvas

HTML5 defines the `<canvas>` element (*http://bit.ly/9JHzOf*) as "a resolution-dependent bitmap canvas which can be used for rendering graphs, game graphics, or other visual images on the fly." A canvas is a rectangle in your page within which you can use JavaScript to draw anything you want. HTML5 defines a set of functions ("the canvas API") for drawing shapes, defining paths, creating gradients, and applying transformations.

Checking for canvas API support uses detection technique #2 (see "Detection Techniques" on page 15). If your browser supports the canvas API, the DOM object it creates to represent a `<canvas>` element will have a `getContext()` method (see "Simple Shapes" on page 58). If your browser doesn't support the canvas API, the DOM object it creates for a `<canvas>` element will have only the set of common properties, not anything canvas-specific. You can check for canvas support using this function:

```
function supports_canvas() {
  return !!document.createElement('canvas').getContext;
}
```

This function starts by creating a dummy `<canvas>` element:

```
return !!document.createElement('canvas').getContext;
```

This element is never attached to your page, so no one will ever see it. It's just floating in memory, going nowhere and doing nothing, like a canoe on a lazy river.

As soon as you create the dummy `<canvas>` element, you test for the presence of a `getContext()` method. This method will only exist if your browser supports the canvas API:

```
return !!document.createElement('canvas').getContext;
```

Finally, you use the double-negative trick to force the result to a Boolean value (`true` or `false`):

```
return !!document.createElement('canvas').getContext;
```

This function will detect support for most of the canvas API, including shapes (see "Simple Shapes" on page 58), paths (see "Paths" on page 61), gradients (see "Gradients" on page 67), and patterns. It will not detect the third-party `explorercanvas` library (see "What About IE?" on page 73) that implements the canvas API in Microsoft Internet Explorer.

Instead of writing this function yourself, you can use Modernizr (introduced in the preceding section) to detect support for the canvas API:

```
if (Modernizr.canvas) {
  // let's draw some shapes!
} else {
  // no native canvas support available :(
}
```

There is a separate test for the canvas text API, which I will demonstrate next.

Canvas Text

Even if your browser supports the canvas API, it might not support the canvas text API. The canvas API grew over time, and the text functions were added late in the game. Some browsers shipped with canvas support before the text API was complete.

Checking for canvas text API support again uses detection technique #2 (see "Detection Techniques" on page 15). If your browser supports the canvas API, the DOM object it creates to represent a <canvas> element will have the getContext() method (see "Simple Shapes" on page 58). If your browser doesn't support the canvas API, the DOM object it creates for a <canvas> element will have only the set of common properties, not anything canvas-specific. You can check for canvas text support using this function:

```
function supports_canvas_text() {
  if (!supports_canvas()) { return false; }
  var dummy_canvas = document.createElement('canvas');
  var context = dummy_canvas.getContext('2d');
  return typeof context.fillText == 'function';
}
```

The function starts by checking for canvas support, using the supports_canvas() function introduced in the previous section:

```
if (!supports_canvas()) { return false; }
```

If your browser doesn't support the canvas API, it certainly won't support the canvas text API!

Next, you create a dummy <canvas> element and get its drawing context. This is guaranteed to work, because the supports_canvas() function already checked that the getContext() method exists on all canvas objects:

```
var dummy_canvas = document.createElement('canvas');
var context = dummy_canvas.getContext('2d');
```

Finally, you check whether the drawing context has a fillText() function. If it does, the canvas text API is available:

```
return typeof context.fillText == 'function';
```

Instead of writing this function yourself, you can use Modernizr (see "Modernizr: An HTML5 Detection Library" on page 16) to detect support for the canvas text API:

```
if (Modernizr.canvastext) {
  // let's draw some text!
} else {
  // no native canvas text support available :(
}
```

Video

HTML5 defines a new element called <video> for embedding video in your web pages. Embedding video used to be impossible without third-party plug-ins such as Apple QuickTime or Adobe Flash.

The `<video>` element is designed to be usable without any detection scripts. You can specify multiple video files, and browsers that support HTML5 video will choose one based on what video formats they support.[*]

Browsers that don't support HTML5 video will ignore the `<video>` element completely, but you can use this to your advantage and tell them to play video through a third-party plug-in instead. Kroc Camen has designed a solution called Video for Everybody! (*http://camendesign.com/code/video_for_everybody*) that uses HTML5 video where available, but falls back to QuickTime or Flash in older browsers. This solution uses no JavaScript whatsoever, and it works in virtually every browser, including mobile browsers.

If you want to do more with video than plop it on your page and play it, you'll need to use JavaScript. Checking for video support uses detection technique #2 (see "Detection Techniques" on page 15). If your browser supports HTML5 video, the DOM object it creates to represent a `<video>` element will have a `canPlayType()` method. If your browser doesn't support HTML5 video, the DOM object it creates for a `<video>` element will have only the set of properties common to all elements. You can check for video support using this function:

```
function supports_video() {
  return !!document.createElement('video').canPlayType;
}
```

Instead of writing this function yourself, you can use Modernizr (see "Modernizr: An HTML5 Detection Library" on page 16) to detect support for HTML5 video:

```
if (Modernizr.video) {
  // let's play some video!
} else {
  // no native video support available :(
  // maybe check for QuickTime or Flash instead
}
```

There is a separate test for detecting which video formats your browser can play, which I will demonstrate next.

Video Formats

Video formats are like written languages. An English newspaper may convey the same information as a Spanish newspaper, but if you can only read English, only one of them will be useful to you! To play a video, your browser needs to understand the "language" in which the video was written.

---

[*] See "A gentle introduction to video encoding, part 1: container formats" (*http://diveintomark.org/archives/2008/12/18/give-part-1-container-formats*) and "part 2: lossy video codecs" (*http://diveintomark.org/archives/2008/12/19/give-part-2-lossy-video-codecs*) to learn about different video formats.

The "language" of a video is called a "codec"—this is the algorithm used to encode the video into a stream of bits. There are dozens of codecs in use all over the world. Which one should you use? The unfortunate reality of HTML5 video is that browsers can't agree on a single codec. However, they seem to have narrowed it down to two. One codec costs money (because of patent licensing), but it works in Safari and on the iPhone. (This one also works in Adobe Flash, if you use a solution like Video for Everybody!.) The other codec is free and works in open source browsers like Chromium and Mozilla Firefox.

Checking for video format support uses detection technique #3 (see "Detection Techniques" on page 15). If your browser supports HTML5 video, the DOM object it creates to represent a `<video>` element will have a `canPlayType()` method. This method will tell you whether the browser supports a particular video format.

This function checks for the patent-encumbered format supported by Macs and iPhones:

```
function supports_h264_baseline_video() {
  if (!supports_video()) { return false; }
  var v = document.createElement("video");
  return v.canPlayType('video/mp4; codecs="avc1.42E01E, mp4a.40.2"');
}
```

The function starts by checking for HTML5 video support, using the `supports_video()` function from the previous section:

```
if (!supports_video()) { return false; }
```

If your browser doesn't support HTML5 video, it certainly won't support any video formats!

Next, the function creates a dummy `<video>` element (but doesn't attach it to the page, so it won't be visible) and calls the `canPlayType()` method. This method is guaranteed to be there, because the `supports_video()` function just checked for it:

```
var v = document.createElement("video");
return v.canPlayType('video/mp4; codecs="avc1.42E01E, mp4a.40.2"');
```

A "video format" is really a combination of several different things. In technical terms, you're asking the browser whether it can play H.264 Baseline video and AAC LC audio in an MPEG-4 container.[†]

The `canPlayType()` function doesn't return `true` or `false`. In recognition of how complex video formats are, the function returns a string:

`"probably"`
 If the browser is fairly confident it can play this format

---

† I'll explain what all that means in Chapter 5. You might also be interested in reading "A gentle introduction to video encoding" (*http://diveintomark.org/tag/give*).

"maybe"

If the browser thinks it might be able to play this format

"" *(an empty string)*

If the browser is certain it can't play this format

This second function checks for the open video format supported by Mozilla Firefox and other open source browsers. The process is exactly the same; the only difference is the string you pass in to the `canPlayType()` function. In technical terms, you're asking the browser whether it can play Theora video and Vorbis audio in an Ogg container:

```
function supports_ogg_theora_video() {
  if (!supports_video()) { return false; }
  var v = document.createElement("video");
  return v.canPlayType('video/ogg; codecs="theora, vorbis"');
}
```

Finally, WebM (*http://www.webmproject.org*) is a newly open-sourced (and non-patent-encumbered) video codec that will be included in the next version of major browsers, including Chrome, Firefox, and Opera. You can use the same technique to detect support for open WebM video:

```
function supports_webm_video() {
  if (!supports_video()) { return false; }
  var v = document.createElement("video");
  return v.canPlayType('video/webm; codecs="vp8, vorbis"');
}
```

Instead of writing this function yourself, you can use Modernizr to detect support for several different HTML5 video formats (note that Modernizr does not yet have support for detecting support for the open WebM video format):

```
if (Modernizr.video) {
  // let's play some video! but what kind?
  if (Modernizr.video.ogg) {
    // try Ogg Theora + Vorbis in an Ogg container
  } else if (Modernizr.video.h264){
    // try H.264 video + AAC audio in an MP4 container
  }
}
```

Local Storage

HTML5 Storage (*http://dev.w3.org/html5/webstorage/*) provides a way for websites to store information on your computer and retrieve it later. The concept is similar to cookies, but it's designed for larger quantities of information. Cookies are limited in size, and your browser sends them back to the web server every time it requests a new page (which takes extra time and precious bandwidth). HTML5 Storage stays on your computer, and websites can access it with JavaScript after the page is loaded.

Checking for HTML5 Storage support uses detection technique #1 (see "Detection Techniques" on page 15). If your browser supports HTML5 Storage, there will be a `localStorage` property on the global `window` object. If your browser doesn't support HTML5 Storage, the `localStorage` property will be undefined. You can check for local storage support using this function:

```
function supports_local_storage() {
  return ('localStorage' in window) && window['localStorage'] !== null;
}
```

Instead of writing this function yourself, you can use Modernizr (see "Modernizr: An HTML5 Detection Library" on page 16) to detect support for HTML5 local storage:

```
if (Modernizr.localstorage) {
  // window.localStorage is available!
} else {
  // no native support for local storage :(
  // maybe try Gears or another third-party solution
}
```

Note that JavaScript is case-sensitive. The Modernizr attribute is called `localstorage` (all lowercase), but the DOM property is called `window.localStorage` (mixed case).

Web Workers

Web workers (*http://bit.ly/9jheof*) provide a standard way for browsers to run JavaScript in the background. With web workers, you can spawn multiple "threads" that all run at the same time, more or less. (Think of how your computer can run multiple applications at the same time, and you're most of the way there.) These "background threads" can do complex mathematical calculations, make network requests, or access local storage while the main web page responds to the user scrolling, clicking, or typing.

Checking for web workers uses detection technique #1 (see "Detection Techniques" on page 15). If your browser supports the Web Worker API, there will be a `Worker` property on the global `window` object. If your browser doesn't support the Web Worker API, the `Worker` property will be undefined. This function checks for web worker support:

```
function supports_web_workers() {
  return !!window.Worker;
}
```

Instead of writing this function yourself, you can use Modernizr (see "Modernizr: An HTML5 Detection Library" on page 16) to detect support for web workers:

```
if (Modernizr.webworkers) {
  // window.Worker is available!
} else {
  // no native support for web workers :(
  // maybe try Gears or another third-party solution
}
```

Note that JavaScript is case-sensitive. The Modernizr attribute is called `webworkers` (all lowercase), but the DOM object is called `window.Worker` (with a capital "W" in "Worker").

Offline Web Applications

Reading static web pages offline is easy: connect to the Internet, load a web page, disconnect from the Internet, drive to a secluded cabin, and read the web page at your leisure. (To save time, you may wish to skip the step about the cabin.) But what about using web applications like Gmail or Google Docs when you're offline? Thanks to HTML5, anyone (not just Google!) can build a web application that works offline.

Offline web applications start out as online web applications. The first time you visit an offline-enabled website, the web server tells your browser which files it needs in order to work offline. These files can be anything—HTML, JavaScript, images, even videos (see "Video" on page 18). Once your browser downloads all the necessary files, you can revisit the website even if you're not connected to the Internet. Your browser will notice that you're offline and use the files it has already downloaded. When you get back online, any changes you've made can be uploaded to the remote web server.

Checking for offline support uses detection technique #1 (see "Detection Techniques" on page 15). If your browser supports offline web applications, there will be an `applicationCache` property on the global `window` object. If your browser doesn't support offline web applications, the `applicationCache` property will be undefined. You can check for offline support with the following function:

```
function supports_offline() {
  return !!window.applicationCache;
}
```

Instead of writing this function yourself, you can use Modernizr (see "Modernizr: An HTML5 Detection Library" on page 16) to detect support for offline web applications:

```
if (Modernizr.applicationcache) {
  // window.applicationCache is available!
} else {
  // no native support for offline :(
  // maybe try Gears or another third-party solution
}
```

Note that JavaScript is case-sensitive. The Modernizr attribute is called `applicationcache` (all lowercase), but the DOM object is called `window.applicationCache` (mixed case).

Geolocation

Geolocation is the art of figuring out where you are in the world and (optionally) sharing that information with people you trust. There are many ways to figure out where you are—your IP address, your wireless network connection, which cell tower your phone is talking to, or dedicated GPS hardware that receives latitude and longitude information from satellites in the sky.

Ask Professor Markup

Q: Is geolocation part of HTML5? Why are you talking about it?

A: Geolocation support is being added to browsers right now, along with support for new HTML5 features. Strictly speaking, geolocation is being standardized by the Geolocation Working Group (*http://www.w3.org/2008/geolocation/*), which is separate from the HTML5 Working Group. But I'm going to talk about geolocation in this book anyway, because it's part of the evolution of the Web that's happening now.

Checking for geolocation support uses detection technique #1 (see "Detection Techniques" on page 15). If your browser supports the geolocation API, there will be a `geolocation` property on the global `navigator` object. If your browser doesn't support the geolocation API, the `geolocation` property will be undefined. Here's how to check for geolocation support:

```
function supports_geolocation() {
  return !!navigator.geolocation;
}
```

Instead of writing this function yourself, you can use Modernizr (see "Modernizr: An HTML5 Detection Library" on page 16) to detect support for the geolocation API:

```
if (Modernizr.geolocation) {
  // let's find out where you are!
} else {
  // no native geolocation support available :(
  // maybe try Gears or another third-party solution
}
```

If your browser does not support the geolocation API natively, there is still hope. Gears (*http://tools.google.com/gears/*) is an open source browser plug-in from Google that works on Windows, Mac, Linux, Windows Mobile, and Android. It provides a number of features for older browsers that do not support all the fancy new stuff we've discussed in this chapter. One of the features that Gears provides is a geolocation API. It's not the same as the `navigator.geolocation` API, but it serves the same purpose.

There are also device-specific geolocation APIs on several mobile phone platforms, including BlackBerry, Nokia, Palm, and OMTP BONDI.

Chapter 6 will go into excruciating detail about how to use all of these different APIs.

Input Types

You know all about web forms, right? Make a `<form>`, add a few `<input type="text">` elements and maybe an `<input type="password">`, and finish it off with an `<input type="submit">` button.

You don't know the half of it. HTML5 defines over a dozen new input types that you can use in your forms:

`<input type="search">`
> See *http://bit.ly/9mQt5C* for search boxes

`<input type="number">`
> See *http://bit.ly/aPZHjD* for spinboxes

`<input type="range">`
> See *http://bit.ly/dmLiRr* for sliders

`<input type="color">`
> See *http://bit.ly/bwRcMO* for color pickers

`<input type="tel">`
> See *http://bit.ly/amkWLq* for telephone numbers

`<input type="url">`
> See *http://bit.ly/cjKb3a* for web addresses

```
<input type="email">
```
See *http://bit.ly/aaDrgS* for email addresses
```
<input type="date">
```
See *http://bit.ly/c8hL58* for calendar date pickers
```
<input type="month">
```
See *http://bit.ly/cDgHRI* for months
```
<input type="week">
```
See *http://bit.ly/bR3r58* for weeks
```
<input type="time">
```
See *http://bit.ly/bfMCMn* for timestamps
```
<input type="datetime">
```
See *http://bit.ly/c46zVW* for precise, absolute date/timestamps
```
<input type="datetime-local">
```
See *http://bit.ly/aziNkE* for local dates and times

Checking for HTML5 input types uses detection technique #4 (see "Detection Techniques" on page 15). First, you create a dummy `<input>` element in memory:

```
var i = document.createElement("input");
```

The default input type for all `<input>` elements is `"text"`. This will prove to be vitally important.

Next, set the `type` attribute on the dummy `<input>` element to the input type you want to detect:

```
i.setAttribute("type", "color");
```

If your browser supports that particular input type, the `type` property will retain the value you set. If your browser doesn't support that particular input type, it will ignore the value you set and the `type` property will still be `"text"`:

```
return i.type !== "text";
```

Instead of writing 13 separate functions yourself, you can use Modernizr (see "Modernizr: An HTML5 Detection Library" on page 16) to detect support for all the new input types defined in HTML5. Modernizr reuses a single `<input>` element to efficiently detect support for all 13 input types. Then it builds a hash called `Modernizr.input types`, which contains 13 keys (the HTML5 `type` attributes) and 13 Boolean values (`true` if supported, `false` if not):

```
if (!Modernizr.inputtypes.date) {
  // no native support for <input type="date"> :(
  // maybe build one yourself with
  // Dojo
  // or jQueryUI
}
```

Placeholder Text

Besides new input types, HTML5 includes several small tweaks to existing forms. One improvement is the ability to set placeholder text in an input field. Placeholder text is displayed inside the input field as long as the field is empty and not focused. As soon as you click on (or tab to) the input field, the placeholder text disappears. "Placeholder Text" on page 147 has screenshots if you're having trouble visualizing it.

Checking for placeholder support uses detection technique #2 (see "Detection Techniques" on page 15). If your browser supports placeholder text in input fields, the DOM object it creates to represent an `<input>` element will have a `placeholder` property (even if you don't include a `placeholder` attribute in your HTML). If your browser doesn't support placeholder text, the DOM object it creates for an `<input>` element will not have a `placeholder` property. Here's how to check for placeholder support:

```
function supports_input_placeholder() {
  var i = document.createElement('input');
  return 'placeholder' in i;
}
```

Instead of writing this function yourself, you can use Modernizr (see "Modernizr: An HTML5 Detection Library" on page 16) to detect support for placeholder text:

```
if (Modernizr.input.placeholder) {
  // your placeholder text should already be visible!
} else {
  // no placeholder support :(
  // fall back to a scripted solution
}
```

Form Autofocus

Many websites use JavaScript to focus the first input field of a web form automatically. For example, the home page of Google.com will autofocus the input box so you can type your search keywords without having to position the cursor in the search box. While this is convenient for most people, it can be annoying for power users or people with special needs. If you press the space bar expecting to scroll the page, the page will not scroll because the focus is already in a form input field. (Instead, you'll type a space in the field.) If you focus a different input field while the page is still loading, the site's autofocus script may "helpfully" move the focus back to the original input field upon completion, disrupting your flow and causing you to type in the wrong place.

Because the autofocusing is done with JavaScript, it can be tricky to handle all of these edge cases, and there is little recourse for people who don't want a web page to "steal" the focus.

To solve this problem, HTML5 introduces an **autofocus** attribute on all web form controls. The **autofocus** attribute does exactly what it says on the tin: it moves the focus to a particular input field. But because it's just markup instead of a script, the behavior will be consistent across all websites. Also, browser vendors (or extension authors) can offer users a way to disable the autofocusing behavior.

Checking for autofocus support uses detection technique #2 (see "Detection Techniques" on page 15). If your browser supports autofocusing web form controls, the DOM object it creates to represent an `<input>` element will have an **autofocus** property (even if you don't include the **autofocus** attribute in your HTML). If your browser doesn't support autofocusing web form controls, the DOM object it creates for an `<input>` element will not have an **autofocus** property. You can detect autofocus support with this function:

```
function supports_input_autofocus() {
  var i = document.createElement('input');
  return 'autofocus' in i;
}
```

Instead of writing this function yourself, you can use Modernizr (see "Modernizr: An HTML5 Detection Library" on page 16) to detect support for autofocused form fields:

```
if (Modernizr.input.autofocus) {
  // autofocus works!
} else {
  // no autofocus support :(
  // fall back to a scripted solution
}
```

Microdata

Microdata (*http://bit.ly/ckt9Rj*) is a standardized way to provide additional semantics in your web pages. For example, you can use microdata to declare that a photograph is available under a specific Creative Commons license. As you'll see in Chapter 10, you can also use microdata to mark up an "About Me" page. Browsers, browser extensions, and search engines can convert your HTML5 microdata markup into a vCard, a standard format for sharing contact information. You can also define your own microdata vocabularies.

The HTML5 microdata standard includes both HTML markup (primarily for search engines) and a set of DOM functions (primarily for browsers). There's no harm in including microdata markup in your web pages; it's nothing more than a few well-placed attributes, and search engines that don't understand the microdata attributes will just ignore them. But if you need to access or manipulate microdata through the DOM, you'll need to check whether the browser supports the microdata DOM API.

Checking for HTML5 microdata API support uses detection technique #1 (see "Detection Techniques" on page 15). If your browser supports the HTML5 microdata API, there will be a `getItems()` function on the global `document` object. If your browser doesn't support microdata, the `getItems()` function will be undefined. You can check for support as follows:

```
function supports_microdata_api() {
  return !!document.getItems;
}
```

Modernizr does not yet support checking for the microdata API, so you'll need to use a function like this one.

Further Reading

Specifications and standards:

- The `<canvas>` element (*http://bit.ly/9JHzOf*)
- The `<video>` element (*http://bit.ly/a3kpiq*)
- `<input>` types (*http://bit.ly/akweH4*)
- The `<input placeholder>` attribute (*http://bit.ly/caGl8N*)
- The `<input autofocus>` attribute (*http://bit.ly/db1Fj4*)
- HTML5 Storage (*http://dev.w3.org/html5/webstorage/*)
- Web workers (*http://bit.ly/9jheof*)
- Offline web applications (*http://bit.ly/d8ZgzX*)
- The geolocation API (*http://www.w3.org/TR/geolocation-API/*)

JavaScript libraries:

- Modernizr (*http://www.modernizr.com/*), an HTML5 detection library
- *geo.js* (*http://code.google.com/p/geo-location-javascript/*), a geolocation API wrapper

Other articles and tutorials:

- Video for Everybody! (*http://camendesign.com/code/video_for_everybody*)
- "A gentle introduction to video encoding" (*http://diveintomark.org/tag/give*)
- "Video type parameters" (*http://wiki.whatwg.org/wiki/Video_type_parameters*)
- The Appendix of this book

## CHAPTER 3

What Does It All Mean?

Diving In

This chapter will take an HTML page that has absolutely nothing wrong with it, and improve it. Parts of it will become shorter. Parts will become longer. All of it will become more semantic. It'll be awesome.

Here is the page in question: *http://diveintohtml5.org/examples/blog-original.html*. Learn it. Live it. Love it. Open it in a new tab and don't come back until you've hit "View Source" at least once.

The Doctype

From the top:

```
<!DOCTYPE html
        PUBLIC "-//W3C//DTD XHTML 1.0 Strict//EN"
        "http://www.w3.org/TR/xhtml1/DTD/xhtml1-strict.dtd">
```

This is called the *doctype*. There's a long history—and a black art—behind the doctype. During the development of Internet Explorer 5 for Mac, Microsoft found itself with a surprising problem. The upcoming version of its browser had improved its standards support so much, older pages no longer rendered properly. Or rather, they rendered properly (according to specifications), but people expected them to render *improperly*. The pages themselves had been authored based on the quirks of the dominant browsers of the day, primarily Netscape 4 and Internet Explorer 4. IE5/Mac was so advanced, it actually broke the Web.

Microsoft came up with a novel solution. Before rendering a page, IE5/Mac looked at the "doctype," which is typically the first line of the HTML source (even before the <html> element). Older pages (that relied on the rendering quirks of older browsers) generally didn't have a doctype at all. IE5/Mac rendered these pages like older browsers did. In order to "activate" the new standards support, web page authors had to opt in by supplying the right doctype before the <html> element.

This idea spread like wildfire, and soon all major browsers had two modes: "quirks mode" and "standards mode." Of course, this being the Web, things quickly got out of hand. When Mozilla tried to ship Version 1.1 of its browser, it discovered that there were pages being rendered in standards mode that were actually relying on one specific quirk. Mozilla had just fixed its rendering engine to eliminate this quirk, and thousands of pages broke all at once. Thus was created—and I am not making this up—"almost standards mode".

In his seminal work, "Activating Browser Modes with Doctype" (*http://hsivonen.iki.fi/doctype/*), Henri Sivonen summarizes the different modes:

Quirks Mode
    In the Quirks mode, browsers violate contemporary Web format specifications in order to avoid "breaking" pages authored according to practices that were prevalent in the late 1990s.

Standards Mode
    In the Standards mode, browsers try to give conforming documents the specification-wise correct treatment to the extent implemented in a particular browser. HTML5 calls this mode the "no quirks mode."

Almost Standards Mode
    Firefox, Safari, Chrome, Opera (since 7.5) and IE8 also have a mode known as the "Almost Standards mode," which implements the vertical sizing of table cells traditionally and not rigorously according to the CSS2 specification. HTML5 calls this mode the "limited quirks mode."

 You should read the rest of Henri's article, because I'm simplifying immensely here. Even in IE5/Mac, there were a few older doctypes that didn't count as far as opting into standards support. Over time, the list of quirks grew, and so did the list of doctypes that triggered quirks mode. The last time I tried to count, there were 5 doctypes that triggered almost standards mode, and 73 that triggered quirks mode. But I probably missed some, and I'm not even going to talk about the stuff that Internet Explorer 8 does to switch between its four—four!—different rendering modes. There's a flowchart at *http://hsivonen.iki.fi/doctype/ie8-mode .png*. Kill it. Kill it with fire.

Now then. Where were we? Ah yes, the doctype:

```
<!DOCTYPE html
          PUBLIC "-//W3C//DTD XHTML 1.0 Strict//EN"
          "http://www.w3.org/TR/xhtml1/DTD/xhtml1-strict.dtd">
```

This happens to be one of the 15 doctypes that trigger standards mode in all modern browsers. There is nothing wrong with it. If you like it, you can keep it. Or you can change it to the HTML5 doctype, which is shorter and sweeter and also triggers standards mode in all modern browsers.

This is the HTML5 doctype:

```
<!DOCTYPE html>
```

That's it. Just 15 characters. It's so easy, you can type it by hand and not screw it up.

Professor Markup Says

Your doctype needs to be on the first line of your HTML file. If there's anything else before it—*even a single blank line*—certain browsers will treat your page as if it has no doctype at all. Without a doctype, the browser will render your page in quirks mode. This can be a very difficult error to catch. Extra whitespace usually doesn't matter in HTML, so my eyes tend to just skip over it, but in this case it's very important!

The Root Element

An HTML page is a series of nested elements. The entire structure of the page is like a tree. Some elements are "siblings," like two branches that extend from the same tree trunk. Some elements can be "children" of other elements, like a smaller branch that extends from a larger branch. (It works the other way too; an element that contains other elements is called the "parent" node of its immediate child elements, and the "ancestor" of its grandchildren.) Elements that have no children are called "leaf" nodes. The outermost element, which is the ancestor of all other elements on the page, is called the "root element." The root element of an HTML page is always `<html>`.

In our example page (*http://diveintohtml5.org/examples/blog-original.html*), the root element looks like this: •*info*

```
<html xmlns="http://www.w3.org/1999/xhtml"
      lang="en"
      xml:lang="en">
```

There is nothing wrong with this markup. Again, if you like it, you can keep it. It is valid HTML5. But parts of it are no longer necessary in HTML5, so you can save a few bytes by removing them.

The first thing to discuss is the `xmlns` attribute. This is a vestige of XHTML 1.0. It says that elements in this page are in the XHTML namespace, `http://www.w3.org/1999/xhtml`. But elements in HTML5 are always in this namespace, so you no longer need to declare it explicitly. Your HTML5 page will work exactly the same in all modern browsers, whether this attribute is present or not.

Dropping the `xmlns` attribute leaves us with this root element:

```
<html lang="en" xml:lang="en">
```

The two attributes here, lang and xml:lang, both define the language of this HTML page. en stands for "English."* Why two attributes for the same thing? Again, this is a vestige of XHTML. Only the lang attribute has any effect in HTML5. You can keep the xml:lang attribute if you like, but if you do, you need to ensure that it contains the same value as the lang attribute:

> To ease migration to and from XHTML, authors may specify an attribute in no name-space with no prefix and with the literal localname "xml:lang" on HTML elements in HTML documents, but such attributes must only be specified if a lang attribute in no namespace is also specified, and both attributes must have the same value when compared in an ASCII case-insensitive manner. The attribute in no namespace with no prefix and with the literal localname "xml:lang" has no effect on language processing.

Are you ready to drop it? It's OK, just let it go. Going, going…gone! That leaves us with this root element:

```
<html lang="en">
```

And that's all I have to say about that.

The <head> Element

The first child of the root element is usually the <head> element. The <head> element contains metadata—information *about* the page, rather than the body of the page itself. (The body of the page is, unsurprisingly, contained in the <body> element.) The <head> element itself is rather boring, and it hasn't changed in any interesting way in HTML5. The good stuff is what's *inside* the <head> element. And for that, we turn once again to our example page:

```
<head>
  <meta http-equiv="Content-Type" content="text/html; charset=utf-8" />
  <title>My Weblog</title>
  <link rel="stylesheet" type="text/css" href="style-original.css" />
  <link rel="alternate" type="application/atom+xml"
                         title="My Weblog feed"
                         href="/feed/" />
  <link rel="search" type="application/opensearchdescription+xml"
                         title="My Weblog search"
                         href="opensearch.xml"  />
  <link rel="shortcut icon" href="/favicon.ico" />
</head>
```

First up: the <meta> element.

---

* Not writing in English? Find your language code at *http://www.w3.org/International/questions/qa-choosing-language-tags*.

Character Encoding

When you think of "text," you probably think of "characters and symbols I see on my computer screen." But computers don't deal in characters and symbols; they deal in bits and bytes. Every piece of text you've ever seen on a computer screen is actually stored in a particular *character encoding*. There are many different character encodings, some optimized for particular languages like Russian or Chinese or English, and others that can be used for multiple languages. Very roughly speaking, the character encoding provides a mapping between the stuff you see on your screen and the stuff your computer actually stores in memory and on disk.

In reality, it's more complicated than that. Many characters are common to multiple encodings, but each encoding may use a different sequence of bytes to actually store those characters in memory or on disk. So, you can think of the character encoding as a kind of decryption key for the text. Whenever someone gives you a sequence of bytes and claims it's "text," you need to know what character encoding he used so you can decode the bytes into characters and display them (or process them, or whatever).

So, how does your browser actually determine the character encoding of the stream of bytes that a web server sends? I'm glad you asked. If you're familiar with HTTP headers, you may have seen a header like this:

```
Content-Type: text/html; charset="utf-8"
```

Briefly, this says that the web server thinks it's sending you an HTML document, and that it thinks the document uses the UTF-8 character encoding. Unfortunately, in the whole magnificent soup of the World Wide Web, very few authors actually have control over their HTTP servers. Think Blogger (*http://www.blogger.com*): the content is provided by individuals, but the servers are run by Google. So HTML 4 provided a way to specify the character encoding in the HTML document itself. You've probably seen this too:

```
<meta http-equiv="Content-Type" content="text/html; charset=utf-8">
```

Briefly, this says that the web author thinks she has authored an HTML document using the UTF-8 character encoding.

Both of these techniques still work in HTML5. The HTTP header is the preferred method, and it overrides the <meta> tag if present. But not everyone can set HTTP headers, so the <meta> tag is still around. In fact, it got a little easier in HTML5. Now it looks like this:

```
<meta charset="utf-8" />
```

This works in all browsers. How did this shortened syntax come about? Here is the best explanation I could find (*http://lists.w3.org/Archives/Public/public-html/2007Jul/0550.html*):

> The rationale for the `<meta charset="">` attribute combination is that UAs already implement it, because people tend to leave things unquoted, like:
>
> `<META HTTP-EQUIV=Content-Type CONTENT=text/html; charset=ISO-8859-1>`

There are even a few `<meta charset>` test cases (*http://simon.html5.org/test/html/parsing/encoding*), if you don't believe that browsers already do this.

Ask Professor Markup

Q: I never use funny characters. Do I still need to declare my character encoding?

A: Yes! You should *always* specify a character encoding on every HTML page you serve. Not specifying an encoding can lead to security vulnerabilities (*http://code.google.com/p/doctype/wiki/ArticleUtf7*).

To sum up: character encoding is complicated, and it has not been made any easier by several decades of poorly written software used by copy-and-paste–educated authors. You should *always* specify a character encoding on *every* HTML document, or bad things will happen. You can do it with the HTTP `Content-Type` header, the `<meta http-equiv>` declaration, or the shorter `<meta charset>` declaration, but please do it. The Web thanks you.

Friends and (Link) Relations

Regular links (`<a href>`) simply point to another page. Link relations are a way to explain *why* you're pointing to another page. They finish the sentence "I'm pointing to this other page because…"

- …it's a stylesheet containing CSS rules that your browser should apply to this document.
- …it's a feed that contains the same content as this page, but in a standard subscribable format.
- …it's a translation of this page into another language.
- …it's the same content as this page, but in PDF format.
- …it's the next chapter of an online book of which this page is also a part.

And so on. HTML5 breaks link relations into two categories (*http://bit.ly/d2cbiR*):

> Two categories of links can be created using the link element. **Links to external resources** are links to resources that are to be used to augment the current document, and **hyperlink links** are links to other documents. [...]

The exact behavior for links to external resources depends on the exact relationship, as defined for the relevant link type.

Of the examples I just gave, only the first (`rel="stylesheet"`) is a link to an external resource. The rest are hyperlinks to other documents. You may wish to follow those links, or you may not, but they're not required in order to view the current page.

Most often, link relations are seen on `<link>` elements within the `<head>` of a page. Some link relations can also be used on `<a>` elements, but this is uncommon even when allowed. HTML5 also allows some relations on `<area>` elements, but this is even *less* common. (HTML 4 did not allow a `rel` attribute on `<area>` elements.) See the full chart of link relations (*http://bit.ly/a3nsqi*) to check where you can use specific `rel` values.

Ask Professor Markup

Q: *Can I make up my own link relations?*

A: There seems to be an infinite supply of ideas for new link relations. In an attempt to prevent people from just making stuff up, the WHAT Working Group maintains a registry of proposed `rel` values (*http://wiki.whatwg.org/wiki/RelExtensions*) and defines the process for getting them accepted (*http://bit.ly/da3pse*).

---

rel = stylesheet

Let's look at the first link relation in our example page:

```
<link rel="stylesheet" href="style-original.css" type="text/css" />
```

This is the most frequently used link relation in the world (literally). `<link rel="style sheet">` is for pointing to CSS rules that are stored in a separate file. One small optimization you can make in HTML5 is to drop the **type** attribute. There's only one stylesheet language for the Web, CSS, so that's the default value for the **type** attribute:

```
<link rel="stylesheet" href="style-original.css" />
```

This works in all browsers. (I suppose someone could invent a new stylesheet language someday, but if that happens, you can just add the **type** attribute back.)

rel = alternate

Continuing with our example page:

```
<link rel="alternate"
      type="application/atom+xml"
      title="My Weblog feed"
      href="/feed/" />
```

This link relation is also quite common. `<link rel="alternate">`, combined with either the RSS or Atom media type in the **type** attribute, enables something called "feed autodiscovery." It allows syndicated feed readers like Google Reader to discover that a site has a news feed of the latest articles. Most browsers also support feed autodiscovery by displaying a special icon next to the URL. (Unlike with `rel="stylesheet"`, the `type` attribute matters here. Don't drop it!)

The `rel="alternate"` link relation has always been a strange hybrid of use cases, even in HTML 4. In HTML5, its definition has been clarified and extended to more accurately describe existing web content. As you just saw, using `rel="alternate"` in conjunction with `type=application/atom+xml` indicates an Atom feed for the current page. But you can also use `rel="alternate"` in conjunction with other `type` attributes to indicate the same content in another format, like PDF.

HTML5 also puts to rest a long-standing confusion about how to link to translations of documents. HTML 4 says to use the `lang` attribute in conjunction with `rel="alter nate"` to specify the language of the linked document, but this is incorrect. The HTML 4 Errata lists four outright errors in the HTML 4 spec (along with several editorial nits); one of these outright errors is how to specify the language of a document linked with `rel="alternate"`. (The correct way, described in the HTML 4 Errata document and now in HTML5, is to use the `hreflang` attribute.) Unfortunately, these errata were never reintegrated into the HTML 4 spec, because no one in the W3C HTML Working Group was working on HTML anymore.

Other link relations in HTML5

`rel="archives"`
> (*http://bit.ly/clzlyG*) "indicates that the referenced document describes a collection of records, documents, or other materials of historical interest. A blog's index page could link to an index of the blog's past posts with `rel="archives"`."

`rel="author"`
> is used to link to information about the author of the page. This can be a `mailto:` address, though it doesn't have to be. It could simply link to a contact form or "about the author" page.

`rel="external"`
> (*http://bit.ly/dBVO09*) "indicates that the link is leading to a document that is not part of the site that the current document forms a part of." I believe it was first popularized by WordPress, which uses it on links left by commenters.

`rel="start"`, `rel="prev"`, *and* `rel="next"`
> (*http://www.w3.org/TR/html401/types.html#type-links*) to define relations between pages that are part of a series (like chapters of a book, or even posts on a blog). The only one that was ever used correctly was `rel="next"`. People used `rel="previous"` instead of `rel="prev"`; they used `rel="begin"` and `rel="first"` instead of `rel="start"`; they used `rel="end"` instead of `rel="last"`. Oh, and—all by themselves—they made up `rel="up"` to point to a "parent" page.
>
> HTML5 includes `rel="first"`, which was the most common variation of the different ways to say "first page in a series." (`rel="start"` is a nonconforming synonym, provided for backward compatibility.) It also includes `rel="prev"` and

`rel="next"`, just like HTML 4 (and supports `rel="previous"`, for backward compatibility), as well as `rel="last"` (the last in a series, mirroring `rel="first"`) and `rel="up"`.

The best way to think of `rel="up"` is to look at your breadcrumb navigation (or at least imagine it). Your home page is probably the first page in your breadcrumbs, and the current page is at the tail end. `rel="up"` points to the next-to-last page in the breadcrumbs.

`rel="icon"`

(*http://bit.ly/diAJUP*) is the second most popular link relation (*http://code.google .com/webstats/2005-12/linkrels.html*), after `rel="stylesheet"`. It is usually found together with `shortcut`, like so:

```
<link rel="shortcut icon" href="/favicon.ico">
```

All major browsers support this usage to associate a small icon with the page. Usually it's displayed in the browser's location bar next to the URL, or in the browser tab, or both.

Also new in HTML5: the `sizes` attribute can be used in conjunction with the `icon` relationship to indicate the size of the referenced icon (*http://bit.ly/diAJUP*).

`rel="license"`

(*http://bit.ly/9n9Xfv*) was invented by the microformats community. It "indicates that the referenced document provides the copyright license terms under which the current document is provided."

`rel="nofollow"`

(*http://bit.ly/cGjSPi*) "indicates that the link is not endorsed by the original author or publisher of the page, or that the link to the referenced document was included primarily because of a commercial relationship between people affiliated with the two pages." It was invented by Google and standardized within the microformats community. The thinking was that if "nofollow" links did not pass on PageRank, spammers would give up trying to post spam comments on blogs. That didn't happen, but `rel="nofollow"` persists. Many popular blogging systems default to adding `rel="nofollow"` to links added by commenters.

`rel="noreferrer"`

(*http://bit.ly/cQMSJg*) "indicates that no referrer information is to be leaked when following the link." No shipping browser currently supports this, but support was recently added to WebKit nightlies, so it will eventually show up in Safari, Google Chrome, and other WebKit-based browsers. You can find a `rel="noreferrer"` test case at *http://wearehugh.com/public/2009/04/rel-noreferrer.html*.

`rel="pingback"`

(*http://bit.ly/cIAGXB*) specifies the address of a "pingback" server. As explained in the Pingback specification (*http://hixie.ch/specs/pingback/pingback-1.0*), "The pingback system is a way for a blog to be automatically notified when other websites link to it. [...] It enables reverse linking—a way of going back up a chain of links rather than merely drilling down." Blogging systems, notably WordPress, implement the pingback mechanism to notify authors that you have linked to them when creating a new blog post.

rel="prefetch"
(*http://bit.ly/9o0nMS*) "indicates that preemptively fetching and caching the specified resource is likely to be beneficial, as it is highly likely that the user will require this resource." Search engines sometimes add `<link rel="prefetch" href="<empha sis>URL OF TOP SEARCH RESULT</emphasis>">` to the search results page if they feel that the top result is wildly more popular than any other. For example: using Firefox, search Google for CNN, view the page source, and search for the keyword `prefetch`. Mozilla Firefox is the only current browser that supports `rel="prefetch"`.

rel="search"
(*http://bit.ly/aApkaP*) "indicates that the referenced document provides an interface specifically for searching the document and its related resources." Specifically, if you want `rel="search"` to do anything useful, it should point to an Open Search document that describes how a browser could construct a URL to search the current site for a given keyword. OpenSearch (and `rel="search"` links that point to OpenSearch description documents) has been supported in Microsoft Internet Explorer since Version 7 and in Mozilla Firefox since Version 2.

rel="sidebar"
(*http://bit.ly/azTA9D*) "indicates that the referenced document, if retrieved, is intended to be shown in a secondary browsing context (if possible), instead of in the current browsing context." What does that mean? In Opera and Mozilla Firefox, it means "when I click this link, prompt the user to create a bookmark that, when selected from the Bookmarks menu, opens the linked document in a browser sidebar." (Opera actually calls it the "panel" instead of the "sidebar.") Internet Explorer, Safari, and Chrome ignore `rel="sidebar"` and just treat it as a regular link. You can find a `rel="sidebar"` test case at *http://wearehugh.com/public/2009/04/rel -sidebar.html*.

rel="tag"
(*http://bit.ly/9bYlfa*) "indicates that the tag that the referenced document represents applies to the current document." Marking up "tags" (category keywords) with the `rel` attribute was invented by Technorati to help in the categorization of blog posts. Early blogs and tutorials thus referred to them as "Technorati tags." (You read that right: a commercial company convinced the entire world to add metadata that made the company's job easier. Nice work if you can get it!) The syntax was later standardized within the microformats community, where it was simply called `rel="tag"`. Most blogging systems that allow associating categories, keywords, or tags with individual posts will mark them up with `rel="tag"` links. Browsers do not do anything special with them; they're really designed for search engines to use as a signal of what the page is about.

New Semantic Elements in HTML5

HTML5 is not just about making existing markup shorter (although it does a fair amount of that). It also defines a number of new semantic elements. The following elements are defined by the HTML5 specification:

`<section>` The `section` element represents a generic section of a document or application. A section, in this context, is a thematic grouping of content, typically with a heading. Examples of sections would be chapters, the various tabbed pages in a tabbed dialog box, or the numbered sections of a thesis. A website's home page could be split into different sections for the introduction, news items, and contact information.

`<nav>` The `nav` element represents a section of a page that links to other pages or to parts within the page: a section with navigation links. Not all groups of links on a page need to be in a `nav` element—only sections that consist of major navigation blocks are appropriate for the `nav` element. In particular, it is common for footers to have a short list of links to various pages of a site, such as the terms of service, home page, and copyright page. The `footer` element alone is sufficient for such cases, without a `nav` element.

`<article>` The `article` element represents a self-contained composition in a document, page, application, or site that is intended to be independently distributable or reusable, e.g., in syndication. This could be a forum post, a magazine or newspaper article, a blog entry, a user-submitted comment, an interactive widget or gadget, or any other independent item of content.

`<aside>` The `aside` element represents a section of a page that consists of content that is tangentially related to the content around the `aside` element, and that could be considered separate from that content. Such sections are often represented as sidebars in printed typography. The element can be used for typographical effects like pull quotes or sidebars, for advertising, for groups of `nav` elements, and for other content that is considered separate from the main content of the page.

`<hgroup>` The `hgroup` element represents the heading of a section. The element is used to group a set of h1–h6 elements when the heading has multiple levels, such as subheadings, alternative titles, or taglines.

`<header>` The `header` element represents a group of introductory or navigational aids. A `header` element is usually intended to contain the section's heading (an h1–h6 element or an hgroup element), but this is not required. The `header` element can also be used to wrap a section's table of contents, a search form, or any relevant logos.

`<footer>` The `footer` element represents a footer for its nearest ancestor sectioning content or sectioning root element. A footer typically contains information about its section such as who wrote it, links to related documents, copyright data, and the like. Footers don't necessarily have to appear at the end of a section, though they usually do. When the `footer` element contains entire sections, they represent appendixes, indexes, long colophons, verbose license agreements, and other such content.

`<time>` The `time` element represents either a time on a 24-hour clock or a precise date in the proleptic Gregorian calendar, optionally with a time and a timezone offset.

`<mark>` The `mark` element represents a run of text in one document marked or highlighted for reference purposes.

I know you're anxious to start using these new elements, or you wouldn't be reading this chapter. But first we need to take a little detour.

A Long Digression into How Browsers Handle Unknown Elements

Every browser has a master list of HTML elements that it supports. For example, Mozilla Firefox's list is stored in *nsElementTable.cpp* (*http://mxr.mozilla.org/seamon key/source/parser/htmlparser/src/nsElementTable.cpp*). Elements not in this list are treated as "unknown elements." There are two fundamental questions regarding unknown elements:

How should the element be styled?

By default, `<p>` has spacing on the top and bottom, `<blockquote>` is indented with a left margin, and `<h1>` is displayed in a larger font.

What should the element's DOM look like?

Mozilla's *nsElementTable.cpp* includes information about what kinds of other elements each element can contain. If you include markup like `<p><p>`, the second paragraph element implicitly closes the first one, so the elements end up as siblings, not parent and child. But if you write `<p><span>`, the span does not close the paragraph, because Firefox knows that `<p>` is a block element that can contain the inline element `<span>`. So the `<span>` ends up as a child of the `<p>` in the DOM.

Different browsers answer these questions in different ways. (Shocking, I know.) Of the major browsers, Microsoft Internet Explorer's answer to both questions is the most problematic.

The first question should be relatively simple to answer: don't give any special styling to unknown elements. Just let them inherit whatever CSS properties are in effect wherever they appear on the page, and let the page author specify all styling with CSS. Unfortunately, Internet Explorer (prior to Version 9) does not allow styling on unknown elements. For example, if you had this markup:

```
<style type="text/css">
  article { display: block; border: 1px solid red }
</style>
...
<article>
<h1>Welcome to Initech</h1>
<p>This is your <span>first day</span>.</p>
</article>
```

Internet Explorer (up to and including IE 8) will not put a red border around the article. As I write this, Internet Explorer 9 is still in beta, but Microsoft has stated (and developers have verified) that Internet Explorer 9 will not have this problem.

The second problem is the DOM that browsers create when they encounter unknown elements. Again, the most problematic browser is Internet Explorer. If IE doesn't explicitly recognize the element name, it will insert the element into the DOM *as an empty node with no children.* All the elements that you would expect to be direct children of the unknown element will actually be inserted as siblings instead.

Here is some ASCII art to showcase the difference. This is the DOM that HTML5 dictates:

```
article
|
+--h1 (child of article)
|   |
|   +--text node "Welcome to Initech"
|
+--p (child of article, sibling of h1)
    |
    +--text node "This is your "
    |
    +--span
    |   |
    |   +--text node "first day"
    |
    +--text node "."
```

But this is the DOM that Internet Explorer actually creates:

```
article (no children)
h1 (sibling of article)
|
+--text node "Welcome to Initech"
p (sibling of h1)
|
+--text node "This is your "
|
+--span
|   |
|   +--text node "first day"
|
+--text node "."
```

There is a wondrous workaround for this problem. If you create a dummy `<article>` element with JavaScript before you use it in your page, Internet Explorer will magically recognize the `<article>` element and let you style it with CSS. There is no need to ever insert the dummy element into the DOM. Simply creating the element once (per page) is enough to teach IE to style the element it doesn't recognize. For example:

```
<html>
<head>
<style>
  article { display: block; border: 1px solid red }
</style>
<script>document.createElement("article");</script>
</head>
<body>
<article>
<h1>Welcome to Initech</h1>
<p>This is your <span>first day</span>.</p>
```

```
      </article>
    </body>
  </html>
```

This works in all versions of Internet Explorer, all the way back to IE 6! We can extend this technique to create dummy copies of all the new HTML5 elements at once—again, they're never inserted into the DOM, so you'll never see these dummy elements—and then just start using them without having to worry too much about non-HTML5-capable browsers.

Remy Sharp has done just that, with his aptly named "HTML5 enabling script" (*http: //remysharp.com/2009/01/07/html5-enabling-script*). The script has gone through several revisions, but this is the basic idea:

```
<!--[if lt IE 9]>
<script>
  var e = ("abbr,article,aside,audio,canvas,datalist,details," +
    "figure,footer,header,hgroup,mark,menu,meter,nav,output," +
    "progress,section,time,video").split(',');
  for (var i = 0; i < e.length; i++) {
    document.createElement(e[i]);
  }
</script>
<![endif]-->
```

The `<!--[if lt IE 9]>` and `<![endif]-->` bits are conditional comments. Internet Explorer interprets them like an `if` statement: "if the current browser is a version of Internet Explorer less than Version 9, then execute this block." Every other browser will treat the entire block as an HTML comment. The net result is that Internet Explorer (up to and including Version 8) will execute this script, but other browsers will ignore it altogether. This makes your page load faster in browsers that don't need this hack.

The JavaScript code itself is relatively straightforward. The variable `e` ends up as an array of strings like `"abbr"`, `"article"`, `"aside"`, and so on. Then we loop through this array and create each of the named elements by calling `document.createElement()`. But since we ignore the return value, the elements are never inserted into the DOM. Still, this is enough to get Internet Explorer to treat these elements the way we want them to be treated when we actually use them later in the page.

That "later" bit is important. This script needs to be at the top of your page—preferably in your `<head>` element—not at the bottom. That way, Internet Explorer will execute the script *before* it parses your tags and attributes. If you put this script at the bottom of your page, it will be too late. Internet Explorer will have already misinterpreted your markup and constructed the wrong DOM, and it won't go back and adjust it just because of this script.

Remy Sharp has "minified" this script and hosted it on Google Project Hosting (*http:// code.google.com/p/html5shiv/*). (In case you were wondering, the script itself is open source and MIT-licensed, so you can use it in any project.) If you like, you can even "hotlink" the script by pointing directly to the hosted version, like this:

```
<head>
  <meta charset="utf-8" />
  <title>My Weblog</title>
  <!--[if lt IE 9]>
  <script src="http://html5shiv.googlecode.com/svn/trunk/html5.js"></script>
  <![endif]-->
</head>
```

Now we're ready to start using the new semantic elements in HTML5.

Headers

Let's go back to our example page. Specifically, let's look at the headers:

```
<div id="header">
  <h1>My Weblog</h1>
  <p class="tagline">A lot of effort went into making this effortless.</p>
</div>

...

<div class="entry">
  <h2>Travel day</h2>
</div>

...

<div class="entry">
  <h2>I'm going to Prague!</h2>
</div>
```

There is nothing wrong with this markup. If you like it, you can keep it. It is valid HTML5. But HTML5 provides some additional semantic elements for headers and sections.

First off, let's get rid of that `<div id="header">`. This is a very common pattern, but it doesn't mean anything. The `div` element has no defined semantics, and the `id` attribute has no defined semantics. (User agents are not allowed to infer any meaning from the value of the `id` attribute.) You could change this to `<div id="shazbot">` and it would have the same semantic value, i.e., nothing.

HTML5 defines a `<header>` element for this purpose. The HTML5 specification has a number of real-world examples of using the `<header>` element. Here is what it would look like on our example page:

```
<header>
  <h1>My Weblog</h1>
  <p class="tagline">A lot of effort went into making this effortless.</p>
  ...
</header>
```

That's good. It tells anyone who wants to know that this is a header. But what about that tagline? Another common pattern, which up until now had no standard markup.

It's a difficult thing to mark up. A tagline is like a subheading, but it's "attached" to the primary heading. That is, it's a subheading that doesn't create its own section.

Header elements like `<h1>` and `<h2>` give your page structure. Taken together, they create an outline that you can use to visualize (or navigate) your page. Screenreaders use document outlines to help blind users navigate through your page. There are online tools (*http://gsnedders.html5.org/outliner/*) and browser extensions (*http://chrispederick .com/work/web-developer/*) that can help you visualize your document's outline.

In HTML 4, `<h1>`–`<h6>` elements were the *only* way to create a document outline. The outline on the example page looks like this:

```
My Weblog (h1)
|
+--Travel day (h2)
|
+--I'm going to Prague! (h2)
```

That's fine, but it means that there's no way to mark up the tagline "A lot of effort went into making this effortless." If we tried to mark it up as an `<h2>`, it would add a phantom node to the document outline:

```
My Weblog (h1)
|
+--A lot of effort went into making this effortless. (h2)
|
+--Travel day (h2)
|
+--I'm going to Prague! (h2)
```

But that's not the structure of the document. The tagline does not represent a section; it's just a subheading.

Perhaps we could mark up the tagline as an `<h2>` and mark up each article title as an `<h3>`? No, that's even worse:

```
My Weblog (h1)
|
+--A lot of effort went into making this effortless. (h2)
   |
   +--Travel day (h3)
   |
   +--I'm going to Prague! (h3)
```

Now we still have a phantom node in our document outline, but it has "stolen" the children that rightfully belong to the root node. And herein lies the problem: HTML 4 does not provide a way to mark up a subheading without adding it to the document outline. No matter how we try to shift things around, "A lot of effort went into making this effortless" is going to end up in that graph. And that's why we ended up with semantically meaningless markup like `<p class="tagline">`.

HTML5 provides a solution for this: the `<hgroup>` element. The `<hgroup>` element acts as a wrapper for two or more *related* heading elements. What does "related" mean? It means that, taken together, they create a single node in the document outline.

Given this markup:

```
<header>
  <hgroup>
    <h1>My Weblog</h1>
    <h2>A lot of effort went into making this effortless.</h2>
  </hgroup>
  ...
</header>

...

<div class="entry">
  <h2>Travel day</h2>
</div>

...

<div class="entry">
  <h2>I'm going to Prague!</h2>
</div>
```

This is the document outline that is created:

```
My Weblog (h1 of its hgroup)
|
+--Travel day (h2)
|
+--I'm going to Prague! (h2)
```

You can test your own pages in the HTML5 Outliner to ensure that you're using the heading elements properly.

Articles

Continuing with our example page, let's see what we can do about this markup:

```
<div class="entry">
  <p class="post-date">October 22, 2009</p>
  <h2>
    <a href="#"
       rel="bookmark"
       title="link to this post">
       Travel day
    </a>
  </h2>
  ...
</div>
```

Again, this is valid HTML5. But HTML5 provides a more specific element for the common case of marking up an article on a page—the aptly named `<article>` element:

```
<article>
  <p class="post-date">October 22, 2009</p>
  <h2>
    <a href="#"
       rel="bookmark"
       title="link to this post">
       Travel day
    </a>
  </h2>
  ...
</article>
```

Ah, but it's not quite that simple. There is one more change you should make. I'll show it to you first, then explain it:

```
<article>
  <header>
    <p class="post-date">October 22, 2009</p>
    <h1>
      <a href="#"
         rel="bookmark"
         title="link to this post">
         Travel day
      </a>
    </h1>
  </header>
  ...
</article>
```

Did you catch that? I changed the `<h2>` element to an `<h1>`, and wrapped it inside a `<header>` element. You've already seen the `<header>` element in action. Its purpose is to wrap all the elements that form the article's header (in this case, the article's publication date and title). But...but...but...shouldn't you only have one `<h1>` per document? Won't this screw up the document outline? No, but to understand why not, we need to back up a step.

In HTML 4, the *only* way to create a document outline was with the `<h1>`–`<h6>` elements. If you only wanted one root node in your outline, you had to limit yourself to one `<h1>` in your markup. But the HTML5 specification defines an algorithm for generating a document outline that incorporates the new semantic elements in HTML5. The HTML5 algorithm says that an `<article>` element creates a new section, that is, a new node in the document outline. And in HTML5, each section can have its own `<h1>` element.

This is a drastic change from HTML 4, and here's why it's a good thing. Many web pages are really generated by templates. A bit of content is taken from one source and inserted into the page up here; a bit of content is taken from another source and inserted into the page down there. Many tutorials are structured the same way. "Here's some HTML markup. Just copy it and paste it into your page." That's fine for small bits of content, but what if the markup you're pasting is an entire section? In that case, the tutorial will read something like this: "Here's some HTML markup. Just copy it, paste it into a text editor, and fix the heading tags so they match the nesting level of the corresponding heading tags in the page you're pasting it into."

Let me put it another way. HTML 4 has no *generic* heading element. It has six strictly numbered heading elements, `<h1>`–`<h6>`, which must be nested in exactly that order. That kind of sucks, especially if your page is "assembled" instead of "authored." And this is the problem that HTML5 solves with the new sectioning elements and the new rules for the existing heading elements. If you're using the new sectioning elements, I can give you this markup:

```
<article>
  <header>
    <h1>A syndicated post</h1>
  </header>
  <p>Lorem ipsum blah blah...</p>
</article>
```

and you can copy it and paste it *anywhere in your page* without modification. The fact that it contains an `<h1>` element is not a problem, because the entire thing is contained within an `<article>`. The `<article>` element defines a self-contained node in the document outline, the `<h1>` element provides the title for that outline node, and all the other sectioning elements on the page will remain at whatever nesting level they were at before.

Professor Markup Says

As with all things on the Web, reality is a little more complicated than I'm letting on. The new "explicit" sectioning elements (like `<h1>` wrapped in `<article>`) may interact in unexpected ways with the old "implicit" sectioning elements (`<h1>`–`<h6>` by themselves). Your life will be simpler if you use one or the other, but not both. If you must use both on the same page, be sure to check the result in the HTML5 Outliner and verify that your document outline makes sense.

Dates and Times

This is exciting, right? I mean, it's not "skiing down Mount Everest naked while reciting the Star Spangled Banner backward" exciting, but it's pretty exciting as far as semantic markup goes. Let's continue with our example page. The next line I want to highlight is this one:

```
<div class="entry">
  <p class="post-date">October 22, 2009</p>
  <h2>Travel day</h2>
</div>
```

Same old story, right? A common pattern—designating the publication date of an article—that has no semantic markup to back it up, so authors resort to generic markup with custom `class` attributes. Again, this is valid HTML5. You're not *required* to change it. But HTML5 does provide a specific solution for this case—the `<time>` element:

```
<time datetime="2009-10-22" pubdate>October 22, 2009</time>
```

There are three parts to a `<time>` element:

- A machine-readable timestamp
- Human-readable text content
- An optional `pubdate` flag

In this example, the `datetime` attribute only specifies a date, not a time. The format is a four-digit year, two-digit month, and two-digit day, separated by dashes:

```
<time datetime="2009-10-22" pubdate>October 22, 2009</time>
```

If you want to include a time too, add the letter `T` after the date, then the time in 24-hour format, then a timezone offset:

```
<time datetime="2009-10-22T13:59:47-04:00" pubdate>
  October 22, 2009 1:59pm EDT
</time>
```

The date/time format is pretty flexible. The HTML5 specification contains a number of examples of valid date/time strings.

Notice I changed the text content—the stuff between `<time>` and `</time>`—to match the machine-readable timestamp. This is not actually required. The text content can be anything you like, as long as you provide a machine-readable date/timestamp in the `datetime` attribute. So this is valid HTML5:

```
<time datetime="2009-10-22">last Thursday</time>
```

And this is also valid HTML5:

```
<time datetime="2009-10-22"></time>
```

The final piece of the puzzle here is the `pubdate` attribute. It's a Boolean attribute, so just add it if you need it, like this:

```
<time datetime="2009-10-22" pubdate>October 22, 2009</time>
```

If you dislike "naked" attributes, this is also equivalent:

```
<time datetime="2009-10-22" pubdate="pubdate">October 22, 2009</time>
```

What does the `pubdate` attribute mean? It means one of two things. If the `<time>` element is in an `<article>` element, it means that this timestamp is the publication date of the article. If the `<time>` element is not in an `<article>` element, it means that this timestamp is the publication date of the entire document.

Here's the entire article, reformulated to take full advantage of HTML5:

```
<article>
  <header>
    <time datetime="2009-10-22" pubdate>
      October 22, 2009
    </time>
    <h1>
      <a href="#"
        rel="bookmark"
        title="link to this post">
        Travel day
      </a>
    </h1>
  </header>
  <p>Lorem ipsum dolor sit amet...</p>
</article>
```

Navigation

One of the most important parts of any website is the navigation bar. CNN.com has "tabs" along the top of each page that link to the different news sections—"Tech," "Health," "Sports," etc. Google search results pages have a similar strip at the top of the page enabling you to try your search in different Google services—"Images," "Video," "Maps," etc. And our example page has a navigation bar in the header that includes links to different sections of our hypothetical site—"home," "blog," "gallery," and "about."

This is how the navigation bar was originally marked up:

```
<div id="nav">
  <ul>
    <li><a href="#">home</a></li>
    <li><a href="#">blog</a></li>
    <li><a href="#">gallery</a></li>
    <li><a href="#">about</a></li>
  </ul>
</div>
```

Again, this is valid HTML5. But while it's marked up as a list of four items, there is nothing about the list that tells you that it's part of the site navigation. Visually, you could guess that by the fact that it's part of the page header, and by reading the text of the links. But semantically, there is nothing to distinguish this list of links from any other.

Who cares about the semantics of site navigation? For one, people with disabilities (*http://diveintoaccessibility.org*). Why is that? Consider this scenario: your motion is limited, and using a mouse is difficult or impossible. To compensate, you might use a browser add-on that allows you to jump to (or jump past) major navigation links. Or consider this: your sight is limited, and you use a dedicated program called a "screen-reader" that uses text-to-speech to speak and summarize web pages. Once you get past the page title, the next important pieces of information about a page are the major navigation links. If you want to navigate quickly, you'll tell your screenreader to jump to the navigation bar and start reading. If you want to browse quickly, you might tell your screenreader to jump *over* the navigation bar and start reading the main content. Either way, being able to determine navigation links programmatically is important.

So, while there's nothing wrong with using `<div id="nav">` to mark up your site navigation, there's nothing particularly right about it either. It's suboptimal in ways that affect real people. HTML5 provides a semantic way to mark up navigation sections—the `<nav>` element:

```
<nav>
  <ul>
    <li><a href="#">home</a></li>
    <li><a href="#">blog</a></li>
    <li><a href="#">gallery</a></li>
    <li><a href="#">about</a></li>
  </ul>
</nav>
```

Ask Professor Markup

Q: *Are skip links compatible with the* `<nav>` *element? Do I still need skip links in HTML5?*

A: Skip links allow readers to skip over navigation sections. They are helpful for disabled users who use third-party software to read a web page aloud and navigate it without a mouse. Learn how and why to provide skip links at *http://www.webaim.org/techniques/ skipnav*.

Once screenreaders are updated to recognize the `<nav>` element, skip links will become obsolete, since the screenreader software will be able to automatically offer to skip over a navigation section marked up with the `<nav>` element. However, it will be a while before all the disabled users on the Web upgrade to HTML5-savvy screenreader software, so you should continue to provide your own skip links to jump over `<nav>` sections.

Footers

At long last, we have arrived at the end of our example page. The last thing I want to talk about is the last thing on the page: the footer. The footer was originally marked up like this:

```
<div id="footer">
  <p>&#167;</p>
  <p>&#169; 2001&#8211;9 <a href="#">Mark Pilgrim</a></p>
</div>
```

This is valid HTML5. If you like it, you can keep it. But HTML5 provides a more specific element for this—the `<footer>` element:

```
<footer>
  <p>&#167;</p>
  <p>&#169; 2001&#8211;9 <a href="#">Mark Pilgrim</a></p>
</footer>
```

What's appropriate to put in a `<footer>` element? Probably whatever you're putting in a `<div id="footer">` now. OK, that's a circular answer. But really, that's it. The HTML5 specification says: "A footer typically contains information about its section such as who wrote it, links to related documents, copyright data, and the like." That's what's in this example page's footer: a short copyright statement and a link to an about-the-author page. Looking around at some popular sites, I see lots of footer potential:

- CNN has a footer that contains a copyright statement, links to translations, and links to terms of service, privacy, "about us," "contact us," and "help" pages. All totally appropriate `<footer>` material.

- Google has a famously sparse home page, but at the bottom of it are links to "Advertising Programs," "Business Solutions," and "About Google"; a copyright statement; and a link to Google's privacy policy. All of that could be wrapped in a `<footer>`.

- My weblog (*http://diveintomark.org*) has a footer with links to my other sites, plus a copyright statement. Definitely appropriate for a `<footer>` element. (Note that the links themselves should *not* be wrapped in a `<nav>` element, because they are not site navigation links; they are just a collection of links to my other projects on other sites.)

Fat footers (*http://ui-patterns.com/pattern/FatFooter*) are all the rage these days. Take a look at the footer on the W3C site (*http://www.w3.org*). It contains three columns, labeled "Navigation," "Contact W3C," and "W3C Updates." The markup looks like this, more or less:

```
<div id="w3c_footer">
  <div class="w3c_footer-nav">
    <h3>Navigation</h3>
    <ul>
      <li><a href="/">Home</a></li>
      <li><a href="/standards/">Standards</a></li>
      <li><a href="/participate/">Participate</a></li>
      <li><a href="/Consortium/membership">Membership</a></li>
      <li><a href="/Consortium/">About W3C</a></li>
    </ul>
  </div>
  <div class="w3c_footer-nav">
    <h3>Contact W3C</h3>
    <ul>
      <li><a href="/Consortium/contact">Contact</a></li>
      <li><a href="/Help/">Help and FAQ</a></li>
      <li><a href="/Consortium/sup">Donate</a></li>
```

```
      <li><a href="/Consortium/siteindex">Site Map</a></li>
    </ul>
  </div>
  <div class="w3c_footer-nav">
    <h3>W3C Updates</h3>
    <ul>
      <li><a href="http://twitter.com/W3C">Twitter</a></li>
      <li><a href="http://identi.ca/w3c">Identi.ca</a></li>
    </ul>
  </div>
  <p class="copyright">Copyright © 2009 W3C</p>
</div>
```

To convert this to semantic HTML5, I would make the following changes:

- Convert the outer `<div id="w3c_footer">` to a `<footer>` element.

- Convert the first two instances of `<div class="w3c_footer-nav">` to `<nav>` elements, and the third instance to a `<section>` element.

- Convert the `<h3>` headers to `<h1>`, since each will now be inside a sectioning element. The `<nav>` element creates a section in the document outline, just like the `<article>` element (see "Articles" on page 47).

The final markup might look something like this:

```
<footer>
  <nav>
    <h1>Navigation</h1>
    <ul>
      <li><a href="/">Home</a></li>
      <li><a href="/standards/">Standards</a></li>
      <li><a href="/participate/">Participate</a></li>
      <li><a href="/Consortium/membership">Membership</a></li>
      <li><a href="/Consortium/">About W3C</a></li>
    </ul>
  </nav>
  <nav>
    <h1>Contact W3C</h1>
    <ul>
      <li><a href="/Consortium/contact">Contact</a></li>
      <li><a href="/Help/">Help and FAQ</a></li>
      <li><a href="/Consortium/sup">Donate</a></li>
      <li><a href="/Consortium/siteindex">Site Map</a></li>
    </ul>
  </nav>
  <section>
    <h1>W3C Updates</h1>
    <ul>
      <li><a href="http://twitter.com/W3C">Twitter</a></li>
      <li><a href="http://identi.ca/w3c">Identi.ca</a></li>
    </ul>
  </section>
  <p class="copyright">Copyright © 2009 W3C</p>
</footer>
```

Further Reading

Example pages used throughout this chapter:

- Original (HTML 4) (*http://diveintohtml5.org/examples/blog-original.html*)
- Modified (HTML5) (*http://diveintohtml5.org/examples/blog-html5.html*)

On character encoding:

- "The Absolute Minimum Every Software Developer Absolutely, Positively Must Know About Unicode and Character Sets (No Excuses!)" (*http://www.joelonsoft ware.com/articles/Unicode.html*), by Joel Spolsky
- "On the Goodness of Unicode" (*http://www.tbray.org/ongoing/When/200x/2003/ 04/06/Unicode*), "On Character Strings" (*http://www.tbray.org/ongoing/When/ 200x/2003/04/13/Strings*), and "Characters vs. Bytes" (*http://www.tbray.org/ongo ing/When/200x/2003/04/26/UTF*), by Tim Bray

On enabling new HTML5 in Internet Explorer:

- "How to style unknown elements in IE" (*http://xopus.com/devblog/2008/style-un known-elements.html*), by Sjoerd Visscher
- HTML5 shiv (*http://ejohn.org/blog/html5-shiv/*), by John Resig
- HTML5 enabling script (*http://remysharp.com/2009/01/07/html5-enabling -script/*), by Remy Sharp

On standards modes and doctype sniffing:

- "Activating Browser Modes with Doctype" (*http://hsivonen.iki.fi/doctype/*), by Henri Sivonen. This is the only article you should read on the subject. There are many other articles, but they are either out of date, incomplete, or wrong.

HTML5-aware validator:

- Validator.nu (X)HTML5 Validator (*http://html5.validator.nu*)

## CHAPTER 4

Let's Call It a Draw(ing Surface)

Diving In

HTML5 defines the `<canvas>` element (*http://bit.ly/9JHzOf*) as "a resolution-dependent bitmap canvas which can be used for rendering graphs, game graphics, or other visual images on the fly." A canvas is a rectangle on your page in which you can use JavaScript to draw anything you want. The following table shows which browsers offer basic canvas support at the time of this writing:

IE[a]	Firefox	Safari	Chrome	Opera	iPhone	Android
7.0+	3.0+	3.0+	3.0+	10.0+	1.0+	1.0+

a Internet Explorer support requires the third-party explorercanvas library.

So what does a canvas look like? Nothing, really. A `<canvas>` element has no content and no border of its own. The markup looks like this:

```
<canvas width="300" height="225"></canvas>
```

Figure 4-1 shows the canvas with a dotted border so we can see what we're dealing with.

You can have several `<canvas>` elements on the same page. Each canvas will show up in the DOM, and each canvas maintains its own state. If you give each canvas an `id` attribute, you can access them just like you would any other element.

Let's expand that markup to include an `id` attribute:

```
<canvas id="a" width="300" height="225"></canvas>
```

Now we can easily find that `<canvas>` element in the DOM:

```
var a_canvas = document.getElementById("a");
```

Figure 4-1. Canvas with border

Simple Shapes

IE[a]	Firefox	Safari	Chrome	Opera	iPhone	Android
7.0+	3.0+	3.0+	3.0+	10.0+	1.0+	1.0+

a Internet Explorer support requires the third-party explorercanvas library.

Every canvas starts out blank. That's boring! Let's draw something. You can use the `onclick` handler to call a function that draws a rectangle (see *http://diveintohtml5.org/canvas.html* for an interactive example):

```
function draw_b() {
  var b_canvas = document.getElementById("b");
  var b_context = b_canvas.getContext("2d");
  b_context.fillRect(50, 25, 150, 100);
}
```

The first line of the function is nothing special; it just finds the `<canvas>` element in the DOM. The second line is where it gets more interesting. Every canvas has a drawing context, which is where all the fun stuff happens. Once you've found a `<canvas>` element in the DOM (by using `document.getElementById()` or any other method you like), you can call its `getContext()` method. You *must* pass the string `"2d"` to the `getContext()` method:

```
function draw_b() {
  var b_canvas = document.getElementById("b");
  var b_context = b_canvas.getContext("2d");
  b_context.fillRect(50, 25, 150, 100);
}
```

So, you have a `<canvas>` element, and you have its drawing context. The drawing context is where all the drawing methods and properties are defined. There's a whole group of properties and methods devoted to drawing rectangles:

- The `fillStyle` property can be a CSS color, a pattern, or a gradient. (More on gradients shortly.) The default `fillStyle` is solid black, but you can set it to whatever you like. Each drawing context remembers its own properties as long as the page is open, unless you do something to reset it.
- `fillRect(x, y, width, height)` draws a rectangle filled with the current fill style.
- The `strokeStyle` property is like `fillStyle`—it can be a CSS color, a pattern, or a gradient.
- `strokeRect(x, y, width, height)` draws a rectangle with the current stroke style. `strokeRect` doesn't fill in the middle; it just draws the edges.
- `clearRect(x, y, width, height)` clears the pixels in the specified rectangle.

Getting back to that code in the previous example:

```
var b_canvas = document.getElementById("b");
var b_context = b_canvas.getContext("2d");
b_context.fillRect(50, 25, 150, 100);
```

Calling the `fillRect()` method draws the rectangle and fills it with the current fill style, which is black until you change it. The rectangle is bounded by its upper-left corner (`50`, `25`), its width (`150`), and its height (`100`). To get a better picture of how that works, let's look at the canvas coordinate system.

Canvas Coordinates

The canvas is a two-dimensional grid. The coordinate (0, 0) is at the upper-left corner of the canvas. Along the x-axis, values increase toward the right edge of the canvas. Along the y-axis, values increase toward the bottom edge of the canvas.

The coordinate diagram in Figure 4-2 was drawn with a `<canvas>` element. It comprises:

- A set of off-white vertical lines
- A set of off-white horizontal lines
- Two black horizontal lines
- Two small black diagonal lines that form an arrow
- Two black vertical lines
- Two small black diagonal lines that form another arrow
- The letter "x"
- The letter "y"
- The text "(0, 0)" near the upper-left corner
- The text "(500, 375)" near the lower-right corner
- A dot in the upper-left corner, and another in the lower-right corner

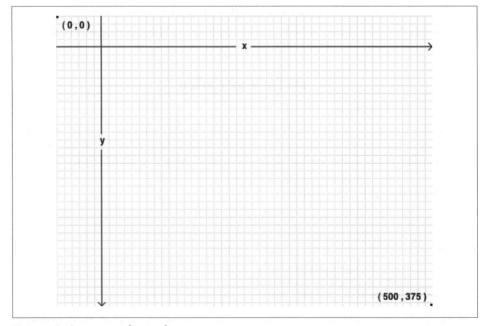

Figure 4-2. Canvas coordinates diagram

In the following sections, we'll explore how to create the effect shown in this figure. First, we need to define the `<canvas>` element itself. The `<canvas>` element defines the `width` and `height` of the rectangle, and the `id` so we can find it later:

```
<canvas id="c" width="500" height="375"></canvas>
```

Then we need a script to find the `<canvas>` element in the DOM and get its drawing context:

```
var c_canvas = document.getElementById("c");
var context = c_canvas.getContext("2d");
```

Now we can start drawing lines.

Paths

IEª	Firefox	Safari	Chrome	Opera	iPhone	Android
7.0+	3.0+	3.0+	3.0+	10.0+	1.0+	1.0+

a Internet Explorer support requires the third-party explorercanvas library.

Imagine you're drawing a picture in ink. You don't want to just dive in and start drawing, because you might make a mistake. Instead, you sketch the lines and curves with a pencil, and once you're happy with it, you trace over your sketch in ink.

Each canvas has a *path*. Defining the path is like drawing with a pencil. You can draw whatever you like, but it won't be part of the finished product until you pick up the quill and trace over your path in ink.

To draw straight lines in pencil, you use the following two methods:

- `moveTo(x, y)` moves the pencil to the specified starting point.
- `lineTo(x, y)` draws a line to the specified ending point.

The more you call `moveTo()` and `lineTo()`, the bigger the path gets. These are "pencil" methods—you can call them as often as you like, but you won't see anything on the canvas until you call one of the "ink" methods.

Let's begin by drawing the off-white grid:

```
for (var x = 0.5; x < 500; x += 10) {
  context.moveTo(x, 0);
  context.lineTo(x, 375);
}

for (var y = 0.5; y < 375; y += 10) {
  context.moveTo(0, y);
  context.lineTo(500, y);
}
```

Those were all "pencil" methods. Nothing has actually been drawn on the canvas yet. We need an "ink" method to make it permanent:

```
context.strokeStyle = "#eee";
context.stroke();
```

stroke() is one of the "ink" methods. It takes the complex path you defined with all those moveTo() and lineTo() calls, and actually draws it on the canvas. The strokeStyle controls the color of the lines. Figure 4-3 shows the result.

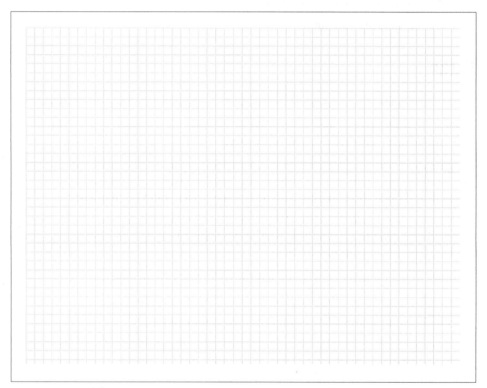

Figure 4-3. A grid drawn on a canvas

Ask Professor Markup

Q: Why did you start x and y at 0.5? Why not 0?

A: Imagine each pixel as a large square. The whole-number coordinates (0, 1, 2...) are the edges of the squares. If you draw a one-unit-wide line between whole-number coordinates, it will overlap opposite sides of the pixel square, and the resulting line will be drawn two pixels wide. To draw a line that is only one pixel wide, you need to shift the coordinates by 0.5 perpendicular to the line's direction.

Now let's draw the horizontal arrow. All the lines and curves on a path are drawn in the same color (or gradient—yes, we'll get to those soon). We want to draw the arrow in a different color ink—black instead of off-white—so we need to start a new path:

```
context.beginPath();
context.moveTo(0, 40);
context.lineTo(240, 40);
context.moveTo(260, 40);
context.lineTo(500, 40);
context.moveTo(495, 35);
context.lineTo(500, 40);
context.lineTo(495, 45);
```

The vertical arrow looks much the same. Since the vertical arrow is the same color as the horizontal arrow, we do *not* need to start another new path. The two arrows will be part of the same path:

```
context.moveTo(60, 0);
context.lineTo(60, 153);
context.moveTo(60, 173);
context.lineTo(60, 375);
context.moveTo(65, 370);
context.lineTo(60, 375);
context.lineTo(55, 370);
```

I said these arrows were going to be black, but the `strokeStyle` is still off-white. (The `fillStyle` and `strokeStyle` don't get reset when you start a new path.) That's OK, because we've just run a series of "pencil" methods. But before we draw it for real, in "ink," we need to set the `strokeStyle` to black. Otherwise, these two arrows will be off-white, and we'll hardly be able to see them! The following lines change the color to black and draw the lines on the canvas:

```
context.strokeStyle = "#000";
context.stroke();
```

Figure 4-4 shows the result.

Text

IE[a]	Firefox[b]	Safari	Chrome	Opera	iPhone	Android
7.0+	3.0+	3.0+	3.0+	10.0+	1.0+	1.0+

a Internet Explorer support requires the third-party explorercanvas library.

b Mozilla Firefox 3.0 support requires a compatibility shim.

In addition to drawing lines on a canvas, you can also draw text on a canvas. Unlike text on the surrounding web page, there is no box model. That means none of the familiar CSS layout techniques are available: no floats, no margins, no padding, no word wrapping. (Maybe you think that's a good thing!) You can set a few font attributes, then you pick a point on the canvas and draw your text there.

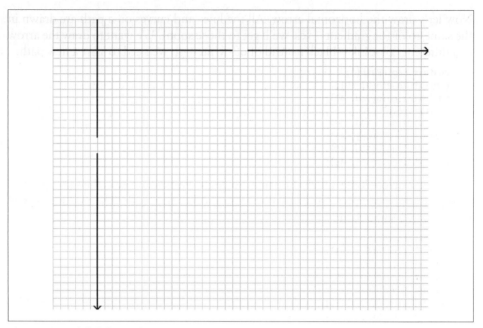

Figure 4-4. Unlabeled axes drawn on a canvas

The following font attributes are available on the drawing context (see "Simple Shapes" on page 58):

- `font` can be anything you would put in a CSS `font` rule. That includes font style, font variant, font weight, font size, line height, and font family.
- `textAlign` controls text alignment. It is similar (but not identical) to a CSS `text-align` rule. Possible values are `start`, `end`, `left`, `right`, and `center`.
- `textBaseline` controls where the text is drawn relative to the starting point. Possible values are `top`, `hanging`, `middle`, `alphabetic`, `ideographic`, and `bottom`.

`textBaseline` is tricky, because text is tricky. (Well, English text isn't tricky, but you can draw any Unicode character you like on a canvas, and Unicode is tricky.) The HTML5 specification explains the different text baselines:[*]

> The top of the em square is roughly at the top of the glyphs in a font, the hanging baseline is where some glyphs like आ are anchored, the middle is half-way between the top of the em square and the bottom of the em square, the alphabetic baseline is where characters like Á, ÿ, f, and Ω are anchored, the ideographic baseline is where glyphs like 私 and 達 are anchored, and the bottom of the em square is roughly at the bottom of the glyphs in a font. The top and bottom of the bounding box can be far from these baselines, due to glyphs extending far outside the em square (see Figure 4-5).

---

[*] *http://bit.ly/aHCdDO*

Figure 4-5. Text baselines

For simple alphabets like English, you can safely stick with top, middle, or bottom for the textBaseline property.

Let's draw some text! Text drawn inside the canvas inherits the font size and style of the <canvas> element itself, but you can override this by setting the font property on the drawing context:

```
context.font = "bold 12px sans-serif";
context.fillText("x", 248, 43);
context.fillText("y", 58, 165);
```

The fillText() method draws the actual text:

```
context.font = "bold 12px sans-serif";
context.fillText("x", 248, 43);
context.fillText("y", 58, 165);
```

Ask Professor Markup

Q: Can I use relative font sizes to draw text on a canvas?

A: Yes. Like every other HTML element on your page, the <canvas> element itself has a computed font size based on your page's CSS rules. If you set the context.font property to a relative font size like 1.5em or 150%, your browser multiplies this by the computed font size of the <canvas> element itself.

For the text in the upper-left corner, say we want the top of the text to be at y=5. But we're lazy—we don't want to measure the height of the text and calculate the baseline. Instead, we can set textBaseline to top and pass in the upper-left coordinate of the text's bounding box:

```
context.textBaseline = "top";
context.fillText("( 0 , 0 )", 8, 5);
```

Now for the text in the lower-right corner. Let's say we want the bottom-right corner of the text to be at coordinates (492,370)—just a few pixels away from the bottom-right corner of the canvas—but again, we don't want to measure the width or height of the text. We can set textAlign to right and textBaseline to bottom, then call fillText() with the bottom-right coordinates of the text's bounding box:

```
context.textAlign = "right";
context.textBaseline = "bottom";
context.fillText("( 500 , 375 )", 492, 370);
```

Figure 4-6 shows the result.

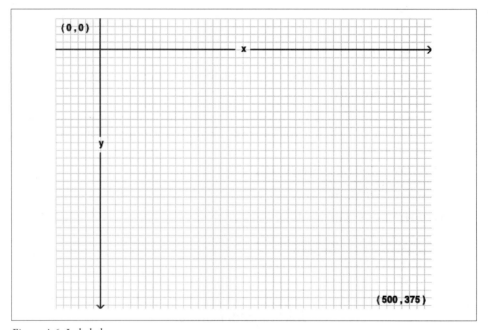

Figure 4-6. Labeled axes on a canvas

Oops! We forgot the dots in the corners. We'll see how to draw circles a little later; for now we'll cheat a little and draw them as rectangles (see "Simple Shapes" on page 58):

```
context.fillRect(0, 0, 3, 3);
context.fillRect(497, 372, 3, 3);
```

And that's all she wrote! Figure 4-7 shows the final product.

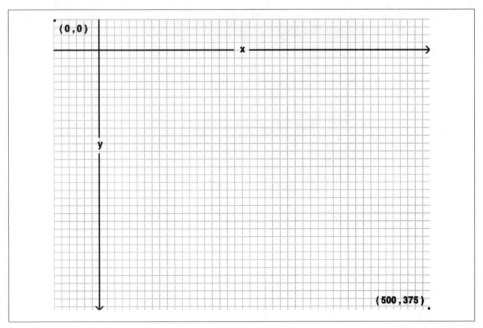

Figure 4-7. A canvas coordinates diagram on a canvas

Gradients

	IE[a]	Firefox	Safari	Chrome	Opera	iPhone	Android
Linear gradients	7.0+	3.0+	3.0+	3.0+	10.0+	1.0+	1.0+
Radial gradients	·	3.0+	3.0+	3.0+	10.0+	1.0+	1.0+

a Internet Explorer support requires the third-party explorercanvas library.

Earlier in this chapter, you learned how to draw a rectangle filled with a solid color (see "Simple Shapes" on page 58), then a line stroked with a solid color (see "Paths" on page 61). But shapes and lines aren't limited to solid colors. You can do all kinds of magic with gradients. Figure 4-8 shows an example.

The markup looks the same as any other canvas:

```
<canvas id="d" width="300" height="225"></canvas>
```

First, we need to find the `<canvas>` element and its drawing context:

```
var d_canvas = document.getElementById("d");
var context = d_canvas.getContext("2d");
```

Figure 4-8. A left-to-right linear gradient

Once we have the drawing context, we can start to define a gradient. A gradient is a smooth transition between two or more colors. The canvas drawing context supports two types of gradients:

- `createLinearGradient(`*x0, y0, x1, y1*`)` paints along a line from (*x0, y0*) to (*x1, y1*).
- `createRadialGradient(`*x0, y0, r0, x1, y1, r1*`)` paints along a cone between two circles. The first three parameters represent the starting circle, with origin (*x0, y0*) and radius *r0*. The last three parameters represent the ending circle, with origin (*x1, y1*) and radius *r1*.

Let's make a linear gradient. Gradients can be any size, but we'll make this gradient 300 pixels wide, like the canvas:

```
var my_gradient = context.createLinearGradient(0, 0, 300, 0);
```

Because the `y` values (the second and fourth parameters) are both `0`, this gradient will shade evenly from left to right.

Once we have a gradient object, we can define the gradient's colors. A gradient has two or more color stops. Color stops can be anywhere along the gradient. To add a color stop, you need to specify its position along the gradient. Gradient positions can be anywhere between 0 and 1.

Let's define a gradient that shades from black to white:

```
my_gradient.addColorStop(0, "black");
my_gradient.addColorStop(1, "white");
```

Defining a gradient doesn't draw anything on the canvas. It's just an object tucked away in memory somewhere. To draw a gradient, you set your `fillStyle` to the gradient and draw a shape, like a rectangle or a line:

```
context.fillStyle = my_gradient;
context.fillRect(0, 0, 300, 225);
```

Figure 4-9 shows the result.

Figure 4-9. A left-to-right linear gradient

Suppose you want a gradient that shades from top to bottom. When you create the gradient object, keep the x values (the first and third parameters) constant, and make the y values (the second and fourth parameters) range from 0 to the height of the canvas:

```
var my_gradient = context.createLinearGradient(0, 0, 0, 225);
my_gradient.addColorStop(0, "black");
my_gradient.addColorStop(1, "white");
context.fillStyle = my_gradient;
context.fillRect(0, 0, 300, 225);
```

Figure 4-10 shows the result.

Figure 4-10. A top-to-bottom linear gradient

You can also create gradients along a diagonal. For example:

```
var my_gradient = context.createLinearGradient(0, 0, 300, 225);
my_gradient.addColorStop(0, "black");
my_gradient.addColorStop(1, "white");
context.fillStyle = my_gradient;
context.fillRect(0, 0, 300, 225);
```

Figure 4-11 shows the result.

Figure 4-11. A diagonal linear gradient

Images

IE[a]	Firefox	Safari	Chrome	Opera	iPhone	Android
7.0+	3.0+	3.0+	3.0+	10.0+	1.0+	1.0+

a Internet Explorer support requires the third-party explorercanvas library.

Figure 4-12 shows an image of a cat displayed with the `<img>` element.

Figure 4-12. Cat with an <img> element

Figure 4-13 shows the same cat, drawn on a canvas.

Figure 4-13. Cat with a <canvas> element

The canvas drawing context defines several methods for drawing an image on a canvas:

- drawImage(*image*, *dx*, *dy*) takes an image and draws it on the canvas. The given coordinates (*dx*, *dy*) will be the upper-left corner of the image. Coordinates (0, 0) would draw the image at the upper-left corner of the canvas.

- drawImage(*image*, *dx*, *dy*, *dw*, *dh*) takes an image, scales it to a width of *dw* and a height of *dh*, and draws it on the canvas at coordinates (*dx*, *dy*).

- drawImage(*image*, *sx*, *sy*, *sw*, *sh*, *dx*, *dy*, *dw*, *dh*) takes an image, clips it to the rectangle (*sx*, *sy*, *sw*, *sh*), scales it to dimensions (*dw*, *dh*), and draws it on the canvas at coordinates (*dx*, *dy*).

The HTML5 specification explains the drawImage() parameters (*http://bit.ly/9WTZAp*):

> The source rectangle is the rectangle [within the source image] whose corners are the four points (*sx*, *sy*), (*sx+sw*, *sy*), (*sx+sw*, *sy+sh*), (*sx*, *sy+sh*).

> The destination rectangle is the rectangle [within the canvas] whose corners are the four points (*dx*, *dy*), (*dx+dw*, *dy*), (*dx+dw*, *dy+dh*), (*dx*, *dy+dh*).

Figure 4-14 gives a visual representation of these parameters.

To draw an image on a canvas, you need an image. The image can be an existing <img> element, or you can create an Image object with JavaScript. Either way, you need to ensure that the image is fully loaded before you can draw it on the canvas.

If you're using an existing <img> element, you can safely draw it on the canvas during the window.onload event:

```
<img id="cat" src="images/cat.png" alt="sleeping cat" width="177" height="113">
<canvas id="e" width="177" height="113"></canvas>
<script>
window.onload = function() {
  var canvas = document.getElementById("e");
  var context = canvas.getContext("2d");
  var cat = document.getElementById("cat");
  context.drawImage(cat, 0, 0);
};
</script>
```

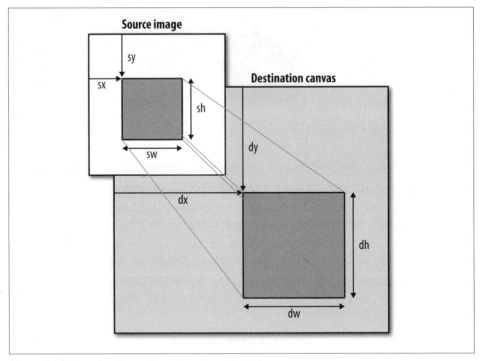

Figure 4-14. How drawImage() maps an image to a canvas

If you're creating the image object entirely in JavaScript, you can safely draw the image on the canvas during the `Image.onload` event:

```
<canvas id="e" width="177" height="113"></canvas>
<script>
  var canvas = document.getElementById("e");
  var context = canvas.getContext("2d");
  var cat = new Image();
  cat.src = "images/cat.png";
  cat.onload = function() {
    context.drawImage(cat, 0, 0);
  };
</script>
```

The optional third and fourth parameters to the `drawImage()` method control image scaling. Figure 4-15 shows the same image of a cat, scaled to half its width and height and drawn repeatedly at different coordinates within a single canvas:

Here is the script that produces the "multicat" effect:

```
cat.onload = function() {
  for (var x = 0, y = 0;
       x < 500 && y < 375;
       x += 50, y += 37) {
    context.drawImage(cat, x, y, 88, 56);
```

```
    }
  };
```

All this effort raises a legitimate question: why would you want to draw an image on a canvas in the first place? What does the extra complexity buy you over an `<img>` element and some CSS rules? Even the "multicat" effect could be replicated with 10 overlapping `<img>` elements.

The simple answer is that you'd do this for the same reason you might want to draw text on a canvas (see "Text" on page 63). Our canvas coordinates diagram (see "Canvas Coordinates" on page 60) included text, lines, and shapes; the text-on-a-canvas element was just one part of a larger work. A more complex diagram could easily use `drawImage()` to include icons, sprites, or other graphics.

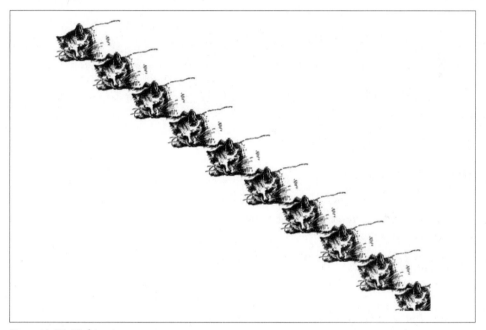

Figure 4-15. Multicat!

What About IE?

Microsoft Internet Explorer (up to and including Version 8, the current version at the time of writing) does not support the canvas API. However, Internet Explorer does support a Microsoft proprietary technology called VML, which can do many of the same things as the `<canvas>` element. And thus, *excanvas.js* was born.

ExplorerCanvas (*http://code.google.com/p/explorercanvas/*)—*excanvas.js*—is an open source, Apache-licensed JavaScript library that implements the canvas API in Internet Explorer. To use it, include the following `<script>` element at the top of your page:

```
<!DOCTYPE html>
<html>
<head>
  <meta charset="utf-8">
  <title>Dive Into HTML 5</title>
  <!--[if IE]>
    <script src="excanvas.js"></script>
  <![endif]-->
</head>
<body>
  ...
</body>
</html>
```

The `<!--[if IE]>` and `<![endif]-->` bits are conditional comments. Internet Explorer interprets them like an `if` statement: "if the current browser is any version of Internet Explorer, then execute this block." Every other browser will treat the entire block as an HTML comment. The net result is that Internet Explorer will download the *excanvas.js* script and execute it, but other browsers will ignore the script altogether (not download it, not execute it, not anything). This makes your page load faster in browsers that implement the canvas API natively.

Once you've included the *excanvas.js* script in the `<head>` of your page, you don't need to do anything else to accommodate Internet Explorer. You can just add `<canvas>` elements to your markup, or create them dynamically with JavaScript. Follow the instructions in this chapter to get the drawing context of a `<canvas>` element, and you can draw shapes, text, and patterns.

Well...not quite. There are a few limitations:

- Gradients (see "Gradients" on page 67) can only be linear. Radial gradients are not supported.
- Patterns must be repeating in both directions.
- Clipping regions are not supported.
- Nonuniform scaling does not correctly scale strokes.
- It's slow. This should not come as a raging shock to anyone, since Internet Explorer's JavaScript parser is slower than other browsers' to begin with. When you start drawing complex shapes via a JavaScript library that translates commands to a completely different technology, things are going to get bogged down. You won't notice the performance degradation in simple examples like drawing a few lines and transforming an image, but you'll see it right away once you start doing canvas-based animation and other crazy stuff.

There is one more caveat about using *excanvas.js*, and it's a problem that I ran into while creating the examples in this chapter. ExplorerCanvas initializes its own faux-canvas interface automatically whenever you include the *excanvas.js* script in your HTML page. But that doesn't mean that Internet Explorer is ready to use it immediately. In certain situations, you can run into a race condition where the faux-canvas interface is *almost*, but not quite, ready to use. The primary symptom of this state is that Internet Explorer will complain that "object doesn't support this property or method" whenever you try to do anything with a `<canvas>` element, such as get its drawing context.

The easiest solution to this is to defer all of your canvas-related manipulation until after the `onload` event fires. This may take a while—if your page has a lot of images or videos, they will delay the `onload` event—but it will give ExplorerCanvas time to work its magic.

A Complete Example

Halma is a centuries-old board game. Many variations exist. In this example, I've created a solitaire version of Halma with nine pieces on a 9 × 9 board. In the beginning of the game, the pieces form a 3 × 3 square in the bottom-left corner of the board. The object of the game is to move all the pieces so they form a 3 × 3 square in the upper-right corner of the board, in the least possible number of moves.

There are two types of legal moves in Halma:

- Take a piece and move it to any adjacent empty square. An "empty" square is one that does not currently have a piece in it. An "adjacent" square is immediately north, south, east, west, northwest, northeast, southwest, or southeast of the piece's current position. (The board does not wrap around from one side to the other. If a piece is in the leftmost column, it cannot move west, northwest, or southwest. If a piece is in the bottommost row, it cannot move south, southeast, or southwest.)

- Take a piece and hop over an adjacent piece, and possibly repeat. That is, if you hop over an adjacent piece, then hop over *another* piece adjacent to your new position, that counts as a single move. In fact, any number of hops still counts as a single move. (Since the goal is to minimize the total number of moves, doing well in Halma involves constructing, and then using, long chains of staggered pieces so that other pieces can hop over them in long sequences.)

Figure 4-16 is a screenshot of the game itself; you can also play it online (*http://divein tohtml5.org/examples/canvas-halma.html*) if you want to poke at it with your browser's developer tools.

So how does it work? I'm so glad you asked. I won't show *all* the code here (you can see it at *http://diveintohtml5.org/examples/halma.js*). I'll skip over most of the gameplay code itself, but I want to highlight a few parts of the code that deal with actually drawing on the canvas and responding to mouse clicks on the `<canvas>` element.

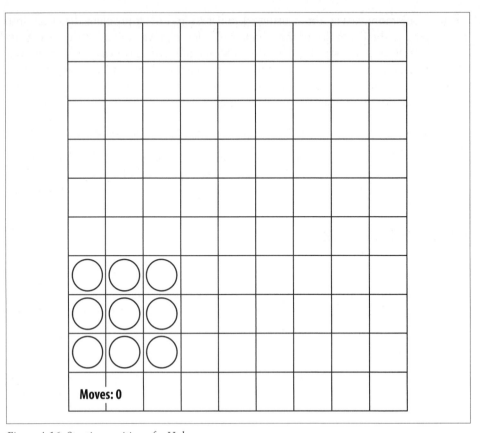

Figure 4-16. Starting position of a Halma game

During page load, we initialize the game by setting the dimensions of the `<canvas>` itself and storing a reference to its drawing context:

```
gCanvasElement.width = kPixelWidth;
gCanvasElement.height = kPixelHeight;
gDrawingContext = gCanvasElement.getContext("2d");
```

Then we do something you haven't seen yet—we add an event listener to the `<canvas>` element to listen for click events:

```
gCanvasElement.addEventListener("click", halmaOnClick, false);
```

The `halmaOnClick()` function gets called when the user clicks anywhere within the canvas. Its argument is a `MouseEvent` object that contains information about where the user clicked:

```
function halmaOnClick(e) {
    var cell = getCursorPosition(e);

    // the rest of this is just gameplay logic
    for (var i = 0; i < gNumPieces; i++) {
```

```
        if ((gPieces[i].row == cell.row) &&
            (gPieces[i].column == cell.column)) {
            clickOnPiece(i);
            return;
        }
    }
    clickOnEmptyCell(cell);
}
```

The next step is to take the MouseEvent object and calculate which square on the Halma board just got clicked. The Halma board takes up the entire canvas, so every click is *somewhere* on the board. We just need to figure out where. This is tricky, because mouse events are implemented differently in just about every browser:

```
function getCursorPosition(e) {
    var x;
    var y;
    if (e.pageX || e.pageY) {
      x = e.pageX;
      y = e.pageY;
    }
    else {
      x = e.clientX + document.body.scrollLeft +
          document.documentElement.scrollLeft;
      y = e.clientY + document.body.scrollTop +
          document.documentElement.scrollTop;
    }
```

At this point, we have x and y coordinates that are relative to the document (that is, the entire HTML page). But we want coordinates relative to the canvas. We can get them as follows:

```
x -= gCanvasElement.offsetLeft;
y -= gCanvasElement.offsetTop;
```

Now we have x and y coordinates that are relative to the canvas (see "Canvas Coordinates" on page 60). That is, if x is 0 and y is 0 at this point, we know that the user just clicked the top-left pixel of the canvas.

From here, we can calculate which Halma square the user clicked, and then act accordingly:

```
    var cell = new Cell(Math.floor(y/kPieceWidth),
                        Math.floor(x/kPieceHeight));
    return cell;
}
```

Whew! Mouse events are tough. But you can use the same logic (in fact, this exact code) in all of your own canvas-based applications. Remember: mouse click→document-relative coordinates→canvas-relative coordinates→application-specific code.

OK, let's look at the main drawing routine. Because the graphics are so simple, I've chosen to clear and redraw the board in its entirety every time anything changes within the game. This is not strictly necessary. The canvas drawing context will retain whatever you have previously drawn on it, even if the user scrolls the canvas out of view or changes to another tab and then comes back later. If you're developing a canvas-based application with more complicated graphics (such as an arcade game), you can optimize performance by tracking which regions of the canvas are "dirty" and redrawing just the dirty regions. But that is outside the scope of this book. Here's the board-clearing code:

```
gDrawingContext.clearRect(0, 0, kPixelWidth, kPixelHeight);
```

The board-drawing routine should look familiar. It's very similar to how we drew the canvas coordinates diagram (see "Canvas Coordinates" on page 60):

```
gDrawingContext.beginPath();

/* vertical lines */
for (var x = 0; x <= kPixelWidth; x += kPieceWidth) {
    gDrawingContext.moveTo(0.5 + x, 0);
    gDrawingContext.lineTo(0.5 + x, kPixelHeight);
}

/* horizontal lines */
for (var y = 0; y <= kPixelHeight; y += kPieceHeight) {
    gDrawingContext.moveTo(0, 0.5 + y);
    gDrawingContext.lineTo(kPixelWidth, 0.5 +  y);
}

/* draw it! */
gDrawingContext.strokeStyle = "#ccc";
gDrawingContext.stroke();
```

The real fun begins when we go to draw each of the individual pieces. A piece is a circle, something we haven't drawn before. Furthermore, if the user selects a piece in anticipation of moving it, we want to draw that piece as a filled-in circle. Here, the argument p represents a piece, which has row and column properties that denote the piece's current location on the board. We use some in-game constants to translate (column, row) into canvas-relative (x, y) coordinates, then draw a circle, then (if the piece is selected) fill in the circle with a solid color:

```
function drawPiece(p, selected) {
    var column = p.column;
    var row = p.row;
    var x = (column * kPieceWidth) + (kPieceWidth/2);
    var y = (row * kPieceHeight) + (kPieceHeight/2);
    var radius = (kPieceWidth/2) - (kPieceWidth/10);
```

That's the end of the game-specific logic. Now we have (x, y) coordinates, relative to the canvas, for the center of the circle we want to draw. There is no circle() method in the canvas API, but there is an arc() method. And really, what is a circle but an arc that goes all the way around? Do you remember your basic geometry? The arc() method takes a center point (x, y), a radius, a start and end angle (in radians), and a direction flag (false for clockwise, true for counterclockwise). We can use the Math module that's built into JavaScript to calculate radians:

```
gDrawingContext.beginPath();
gDrawingContext.arc(x, y, radius, 0, Math.PI * 2, false);
gDrawingContext.closePath();
```

But wait! Nothing has been drawn yet. Like moveTo() and lineTo(), the arc() method is a "pencil" method (see "Paths" on page 61). To actually draw the circle, we need to set the strokeStyle and call stroke() to trace it in "ink":

```
gDrawingContext.strokeStyle = "#000";
gDrawingContext.stroke();
```

What if the piece is selected? We can reuse the same path we created to draw the outline of the piece to fill in the circle with a solid color:

```
if (selected) {
    gDrawingContext.fillStyle = "#000";
    gDrawingContext.fill();
}
```

And that's...well, that's pretty much it. The rest of the program is game-specific logic—distinguishing between valid and invalid moves, keeping track of the number of moves, detecting whether the game is over. With nine circles, a few straight lines, and an onclick handler, we've created an entire game in <canvas>. Huzzah!

Further Reading

- Canvas tutorial (*https://developer.mozilla.org/en/Canvas_tutorial*) on the Mozilla Developer Center
- "HTML5 canvas—the basics" (*http://dev.opera.com/articles/view/html-5-canvas-the-basics/*), by Mihai Sucan
- Canvas Demos (*http://www.canvasdemos.com*): demos, tools, and tutorials for the HTML <canvas> element
- "The canvas element" (*http://bit.ly/9JHzOf*) in the HTML5 draft standard

## CHAPTER 5

Video on the Web

Diving In

Anyone who has visited YouTube.com in the past four years knows that you can embed video in a web page. But prior to HTML5, there was no standards-based way to do this. Virtually all the video you've ever watched "on the Web" has been funneled through a third-party plug-in—maybe QuickTime, maybe RealPlayer, maybe Flash. (YouTube uses Flash.) These plug-ins integrate with your browser well enough that you may not even be aware that you're using them—until you try to watch a video on a platform that doesn't support that plug-in, that is.

HTML5 defines a standard way to embed video in a web page, using a `<video>` element. Support for the `<video>` element is still evolving, which is a polite way of saying it doesn't work yet (at least, it doesn't work everywhere). But don't despair! There are alternatives and fallbacks and options galore. Table 5-1 shows which browsers support the `<video>` element at the time of writing.

Table 5-1. <video> element support

IE9	IE8	IE7	Firefox 3.5	Firefox 3.0	Safari 4	Safari 3	Chrome	Opera
✓	·	·	✓	·	✓	✓	✓	✓

Support for the `<video>` element itself is really only a small part of the story. Before we can talk about HTML5 video, you first need to understand a little about video itself. (If you know about video already, you can skip ahead to "What Works on the Web" on page 88.)

Video Containers

You may think of video files as "AVI files" or "MP4 files." In reality, "AVI" and "MP4" are just container formats. Just as a ZIP file can contain any sort of file within it, video container formats only define *how* to store things within them, not *what* kind of data is stored. (It's a little more complicated than that, because not all video streams are compatible with all container formats, but never mind that for now.)

A video file usually contains multiple tracks: a video track (without audio), plus one or more audio tracks (without video). Tracks are usually interrelated. An audio track contains markers within it to help synchronize the audio with the video. Individual tracks can have metadata, such as the aspect ratio of a video track or the language of an audio track. Containers can also have metadata, such as the title of the video itself, cover art for the video, episode numbers (for television shows), and so on.

There are *lots* of video container formats. Some of the most popular include:

MPEG-4
> Usually with an *.mp4* or *.m4v* extension. The MPEG-4 container is based on Apple's older QuickTime container (*.mov*). Movie trailers on Apple's website still use the older QuickTime container, but movies that you rent from iTunes are delivered in an MPEG-4 container.

Flash Video
> Usually with an *.flv* extension. Flash Video is, unsurprisingly, used by Adobe Flash. Prior to Flash 9.0.60.184 (a.k.a. Flash Player 9 Update 3), this was the only container format that Flash supported. More recent versions of Flash also support the MPEG-4 container.

Ogg
> Usually with an *.ogv* extension. Ogg is an open standard that is open source–friendly and is unencumbered by any known patents. Firefox 3.5, Chrome 4, and Opera 10.5 offer native support, without platform-specific plug-ins, for the Ogg container format, Ogg video (called "Theora"), and Ogg audio (called "Vorbis"). On the desktop, Ogg is supported out-of-the-box by all major Linux distributions, and you can use it on Mac and Windows by installing the QuickTime components or DirectShow filters, respectively. It is also playable with the excellent VLC (*http://www.videolan.org/vlc/*) on all platforms.

WebM
> With a *.webm* extension. WebM is a new container format that is technically very similar to another format called Matroska. WebM was announced at Google I/O 2010. It is designed to be used exclusively with the VP8 video codec and the Vorbis audio codec. (More on these in a minute.) It will be supported natively, without platform-specific plug-ins, in the next versions of Chromium, Google Chrome, Mozilla Firefox, and Opera. Adobe has also announced that the next version of Flash will support WebM video.

Audio Video Interleave
> Usually with an *.avi* extension. The AVI container format was invented by Microsoft in a simpler time, when the fact that computers could play video at all was considered pretty amazing. It does not officially support many of the features of

more recent container formats. It does not officially support any sort of video metadata. It does not even officially support most of the modern video and audio codecs in use today. Over time, various companies have tried to extend it in generally incompatible ways to support this or that, and it is still the default container format for popular encoders such as MEncoder (*http://www.mplayerhq.hu/DOCS/HTML/en/encoding-guide.html*).

Video Codecs

When you talk about "watching a video," you're probably talking about a combination of one video stream and one audio stream. But you don't have two different files; you just have "the video." Maybe it's an AVI file, or an MP4 file. As described in the preceding section, these are just container formats, like a ZIP file that contains multiple kinds of files within it. The container format defines how to store the video and audio streams in a single file.

When you "watch a video," your video player is doing several things at once:

- Interpreting the container format to find out which video and audio tracks are available, and how they are stored within the file so that it can find the data it needs to decode next
- Decoding the video stream and displaying a series of images on the screen
- Decoding the audio stream and sending the sound to your speakers

A *video codec* is an algorithm by which a video stream is encoded. That is, it specifies how to do #2 above. (The word "codec" is a portmanteau, a combination of the words "coder" and "decoder.") Your video player *decodes* the video stream according to the video codec, then displays a series of images, or "frames," on the screen. Most modern video codecs use all sorts of tricks to minimize the amount of information required to display one frame after the next. For example, instead of storing each individual frame (like screenshots), they only store the differences between frames. Most videos don't actually change all that much from one frame to the next, so this allows for high compression rates, which results in smaller file sizes.

There are *lossy* and *lossless* video codecs. Lossless video is much too big to be useful on the Web, so I'll concentrate on lossy codecs. With a lossy video codec, information is irretrievably lost during encoding. Like copying an audio cassette tape, every time you encode you're losing information about the source video and degrading the quality. Instead of the "hiss" of an audio cassette, a re-re-re-encoded video may look blocky, especially during scenes with a lot of motion. (Actually, this can happen even if you encode straight from the original source if you choose a poor video codec or pass it the wrong set of parameters.) On the bright side, lossy video codecs can offer amazing compression rates, and many offer ways to "cheat" and smooth over that blockiness during playback to make the loss less noticeable to the human eye.

There are *tons* of video codecs. The three most relevant codecs are H.264, Theora, and VP8.

H.264

H.264 (*http://en.wikipedia.org/wiki/H.264*) is also known as "MPEG-4 part 10," a.k.a. "MPEG-4 AVC," a.k.a. "MPEG-4 Advanced Video Coding." H.264 was developed by the MPEG group and standardized in 2003. It aims to provide a single codec for low-bandwidth, low-CPU devices (cell phones); high-bandwidth, high-CPU devices (modern desktop computers); and everything in between. To accomplish this, the H.264 standard is split into "profiles", each defining a set of optional features that trade complexity for file size. Higher profiles use more optional features, offer better visual quality at smaller file sizes, take longer to encode, and require more CPU power to decode in real time.

To give you a rough idea of the range of profiles, Apple's iPhone supports the Baseline profile, the AppleTV set-top box supports the Baseline and Main profiles, and Adobe Flash on a desktop PC supports the Baseline, Main, and High profiles. YouTube (owned by Google, my employer) now uses H.264 to encode high-definition videos playable through Adobe Flash; YouTube also provides H.264-encoded video to mobile devices, including Apple's iPhone and phones running Google's Android mobile operating system. Also, H.264 is one of the video codecs mandated by the Blu-ray specification; Blu-ray discs that use it generally use the High profile.

Most nonPC devices that play H.264 video (including iPhones and standalone Blu-ray players) actually do the decoding on a dedicated chip, since their main CPUs are nowhere near powerful enough to decode the video in real time. Many desktop graphics cards also support decoding H.264 in hardware. There are a number of competing H.264 encoders, including the open source x264 library. *The H.264 standard is patent-encumbered*; licensing is brokered through the MPEG LA group. H.264 video can be embedded in most popular container formats (see "Video Containers" on page 81), including MP4 (used primarily by Apple's iTunes Store) and MKV (used primarily by noncommercial video enthusiasts).

Theora

Theora (*http://en.wikipedia.org/wiki/Theora*) evolved from the VP3 codec and has subsequently been developed by the Xiph.org Foundation. *Theora is a royalty-free codec and is not encumbered by any known patents* other than the original VP3 patents, which have been licensed royalty-free. Although the standard has been "frozen" since 2004, the Theora project (which includes an open source reference encoder and decoder) only released Version 1.0 in November 2008 and Version 1.1 in September 2009.

Theora video can be embedded in any container format, although it is most often seen in an Ogg container. All major Linux distributions support Theora out of the box, and

Mozilla Firefox 3.5 includes native support for Theora video in an Ogg container. By "native," I mean "available on all platforms without platform-specific plug-ins." You can also play Theora video on Windows or on Mac OS X after installing Xiph.org's open source decoder software.

VP8

VP8 (*http://en.wikipedia.org/wiki/VP8*) is another video codec from On2, the same company that originally developed VP3 (later Theora). Technically, it is similar in quality to H.264 Baseline, with lots of potential for future improvements.

In 2010, Google acquired On2 and published the video codec specification and a sample encoder and decoder as open source. As part of this, Google also "opened" all the patents that On2 had filed on VP8 by licensing them royalty-free. (This is the best you can hope for with patents—you can't actually "release" them or nullify them once they've been issued. To make them open source–friendly, you license them royalty-free, and then anyone can use the technologies the patents cover without paying anything or negotiating patent licenses.) As of May 19, 2010, *VP8 is a royalty-free, modern codec and is not encumbered by any known patents*, other than the patents that On2 (now Google) has already licensed royalty-free.

Audio Codecs

Unless you're going to stick to films made before 1927 or so, you're going to want an audio track in your video. Like video codecs, *audio codecs* are encoding algorithms, in this case used for audio streams. As with video codecs, there are *lossy* and *lossless* audio codecs. And like lossless video, lossless audio is really too big to put on the Web, so I'll concentrate on lossy audio codecs.

Actually, we can narrow the focus even further, because there are different categories of lossy audio codecs. Audio is used in many places where video is not (telephony, for example), and there is an entire category of audio codecs optimized for encoding speech. You wouldn't rip a music CD with these codecs, because the result would sound like a four-year-old singing into a speakerphone. But you *would* use them in an Asterisk PBX, because bandwidth is precious, and these codecs can compress human speech into a fraction of the size of general-purpose codecs. However, due to lack of support in both native browsers and third-party plug-ins, speech-optimized audio codecs never really took off on the Web. So I'll concentrate on *general-purpose lossy audio codecs*.

As I mentioned in "Video Codecs" on page 83, when you "watch a video," your computer is doing several things at once:

1. Interpreting the container format
2. Decoding the video stream

3. Decoding the audio stream and sending the sound to your speakers

The *audio codec* specifies how to do #3—decoding the audio stream and turning it into digital waveforms that your speakers then turn into sound. As with video codecs, there are all sorts of tricks to minimize the amount of information stored in the audio stream. And since we're talking about *lossy* audio codecs, information is being lost during the recording→encoding→decoding→listening lifecycle. Different audio codecs throw away different things, but they all have the same purpose: to trick your ears into not noticing the parts that are missing.

One concept that audio has that video does not is *channels*. We're sending sound to your speakers, right? Well, how many speakers do you have? If you're sitting at your computer, you may only have two: one on the left and one on the right. My desktop has three: left, right, and one more on the floor. So-called "surround sound" systems can have six or more speakers, strategically placed around the room. Each speaker is fed a particular *channel* of the original recording. The theory is that you can sit in the middle of the six speakers, literally surrounded by six separate channels of sound, and your brain synthesizes them and makes you feel like you're in the middle of the action. Does it work? A multi-billion-dollar industry seems to think so.

Most general-purpose audio codecs can handle two channels of sound. During recording, the sound is split into left and right channels; during encoding, both channels are stored in the same audio stream; and during decoding, both channels are decoded and each is sent to the appropriate speaker. Some audio codecs can handle more than two channels, and they keep track of which channel is which so your player can send the right sound to the right speaker.

There are *lots* of audio codecs. Did I say there were lots of video codecs? Forget that. There are gobs and gobs of audio codecs, but on the Web, there are really only three you need to know about: MP3, AAC, and Vorbis.

MPEG-1 Audio Layer 3

MPEG-1 Audio Layer 3 (*http://en.wikipedia.org/wiki/MPEG-1_Audio_Layer_3*) is colloquially known as "MP3." If you haven't heard of MP3s, I don't know what to do with you. Walmart sells portable music players and calls them "MP3 players." *Walmart.* Anyway...

MP3s can contain *up to two channels* of sound. They can be encoded at different *bitrates*: 64 kbps, 128 kbps, 192 kbps, and a variety of others, from 32 to 320. Higher bitrates mean larger file sizes and better-quality audio, although the ratio of audio quality to bitrate is not linear. (128 kbps sounds more than twice as good as 64 kbps, but 256 kbps doesn't sound twice as good as 128 kbps.) Furthermore, the MP3 format (standardized in 1991) allows for *variable bitrate encoding*, which means that some parts of the encoded stream are compressed more than others. For example, silence between notes can be encoded at a very low bitrate, then the bitrate can spike up a moment later when multiple instruments start playing a complex chord. MP3s can also be encoded with a constant bitrate, which, unsurprisingly, is called *constant bitrate encoding*.

The MP3 standard doesn't define exactly how to encode MP3s (although it does define exactly how to decode them); different encoders use different psychoacoustic models that produce wildly different results, but are all decodable by the same players. The open source LAME project is the best free encoder, and arguably the best encoder, period, for all but the lowest bitrates.

The MP3 format is patent-encumbered, which explains why Linux can't play MP3 files out of the box. Pretty much every portable music player supports standalone MP3 files, and MP3 audio streams can be embedded in any video container. Adobe Flash can play both standalone MP3 files and MP3 audio streams within an MP4 video container.

Advanced Audio Coding

Advanced Audio Coding (*http://en.wikipedia.org/wiki/Advanced_Audio_Coding*) is affectionately known as "AAC." Standardized in 1997, it lurched into prominence when Apple chose it as the default format for the iTunes Store. Originally, all AAC files "bought" from the iTunes Store were encrypted with Apple's proprietary DRM scheme, called FairPlay. Many songs in the iTunes Store are now available as unprotected AAC files, which Apple calls "iTunes Plus" because it sounds so much better than calling everything else "iTunes Minus." *The AAC format is patent-encumbered*; licensing rates are available online.

AAC was designed to provide better sound quality than MP3 at the same bitrate, and it can encode audio at any bitrate. (MP3 is limited to a fixed number of bitrates, with an upper bound of 320 kbps.) AAC can encode *up to 48 channels of sound*, although in practice no one does that. The AAC format also differs from MP3 in defining multiple *profiles*, in much the same way as H.264, and for the same reasons. The "low-complexity" profile is designed to be playable in real time on devices with limited CPU power, while higher profiles offer better sound quality at the same bitrate, at the expense of slower encoding and decoding.

All current Apple products, including iPods, AppleTV, and QuickTime, support certain profiles of AAC in standalone audio files and in audio streams in an MP4 video container. Adobe Flash supports all profiles of AAC in MP4, as do the open source MPlayer and VLC video players. For encoding, the FAAC library is the open source option; support for it is a compile-time option in *mencoder* and *ffmpeg*.

Vorbis

Vorbis (*http://en.wikipedia.org/wiki/Vorbis*) is often called "Ogg Vorbis," although this is technically incorrect—"Ogg" is just a container format (see "Video Containers" on page 81), and Vorbis audio streams can be embedded in other containers. *Vorbis is not encumbered by any known patents* and is therefore supported out of the box by all major Linux distributions and by portable devices running the open source Rock box firmware. Mozilla Firefox 3.5 supports Vorbis audio files in an Ogg container, or Ogg videos with a Vorbis audio track. Android mobile phones can also play standalone Vorbis audio files. Vorbis audio streams are usually embedded in an Ogg or WebM container, but they can also be embedded in an MP4 or MKV container, or, with some hacking, in AVI. Vorbis supports *an arbitrary number of sound channels*.

There are open source Vorbis encoders and decoders, including the OggConvert encoder, the *ffmpeg* decoder, the aoTuV encoder, and the libvorbis decoder. There are also QuickTime components for Mac OS X and DirectShow filters for Windows.

What Works on the Web

If your eyes haven't glazed over yet, you're doing better than most. As you can tell, video (and audio) is a complicated subject—and this was the abridged version! I'm sure you're wondering how all of this relates to HTML5. Well, HTML5 includes a `<video>` element for embedding video into a web page. There are no restrictions on the video codec, audio codec, or container format you can use for your video. One `<video>` element can link to multiple video files, and the browser will choose the first video file it can actually play. *It is up to you to know which browsers support which containers and codecs.*

As of this writing, this is the landscape of HTML5 video:

- Mozilla Firefox (3.5 and later) supports Theora video and Vorbis audio in an Ogg container.
- Opera (10.5 and later) supports Theora video and Vorbis audio in an Ogg container.
- Google Chrome (3.0 and later) supports Theora video and Vorbis audio in an Ogg container. It also supports H.264 video (all profiles) and AAC audio (all profiles) in an MP4 container.
- As of this writing (June 9, 2010), the "dev channel" of Google Chrome, nightly builds of Chromium, nightly builds of Mozilla Firefox, and experimental builds of Opera all support VP8 video and Vorbis audio in a WebM container. (Visit webm project.org for more up-to-date information and download links for WebM-compatible browsers.)
- Safari on Macs and Windows PCs (3.0 and later) will support anything that Quick-Time supports. In theory, you could require your users to install third-party Quick-Time plug-ins. In practice, very few users are going to do that. So you're left with the formats that QuickTime supports "out of the box." This is a long list, but it does not include Theora video, Vorbis audio, or the Ogg container. However, QuickTime *does* support H.264 video (Main profile) and AAC audio in an MP4 container.

- Mobile devices like Apple's iPhone and Google Android phones support H.264 video (Baseline profile) and AAC audio (low-complexity profile) in an MP4 container.
- Adobe Flash (9.0.60.184 and later) supports H.264 video (all profiles) and AAC audio (all profiles) in an MP4 container.
- Internet Explorer 9 will support some as-yet-unspecified profiles of H.264 video and AAC audio in an MP4 container.
- Internet Explorer 8 has no HTML5 video support at all, but virtually all Internet Explorer users will have the Adobe Flash plug-in. Later in this chapter, I'll show you how you can use HTML5 video but gracefully fall back to Flash.

Table 5-2 provides the above information in an easier-to-digest form.

Table 5-2. Video codec support in shipping browsers

Codecs/Container	IE	Firefox	Safari	Chrome	Opera	iPhone	Android
Theora+Vorbis+Ogg	·	3.5+	·	5.0+	10.5+	·	·
H.264+AAC+MP4	·	·	3.0+	5.0+	·	3.0+	2.0+
WebM	·	·	·	·	·	·	·

A year from now, the landscape will look significantly different: WebM will be implemented in multiple browsers, those browsers will ship nonexperimental WebM-enabled versions, and users will upgrade to those new versions. The anticipated codec support is shown in Table 5-3.

Table 5-3. Video codec support in upcoming browsers

Codecs/Container	IE	Firefox	Safari	Chrome	Opera	iPhone	Android
Theora+Vorbis+Ogg	·	3.5+	·	5.0+	10.5+	·	·
H.264+AAC+MP4	·	·	3.0+	5.0+	·	3.0+	2.0+
WebM	9.0+[a]	4.0+	·	6.0+	11.0+	·	[b]

[a] Internet Explorer 9 will only support WebM "when the user has installed a VP8 codec", which implies that Microsoft will not be shipping the codec itself.

[b] Google has committed to supporting WebM "in a future release" of Android, but there's no firm timeline yet.

And now for the knockout punch....

Professor Markup Says

There is no single combination of containers and codecs that works in all HTML5 browsers.

This is not likely to change in the near future.

To make your video watchable across all of these devices and platforms, you're going to need to encode your video more than once.

For maximum compatibility, here's what your video workflow will look like:

1. Make one version that uses Theora video and Vorbis audio in an Ogg container.

2. Make another version that uses WebM (VP8 + Vorbis).

3. Make another version that uses H.264 Baseline video and AAC low-complexity audio in an MP4 container.

4. Link to all three video files from a single `<video>` element, and fall back to a Flash-based video player.

Licensing Issues with H.264 Video

Before we continue, I need to point out that there is a cost to encoding your videos twice. That is, in addition to the obvious cost—that you have to encode your videos twice, which takes more computers and more time than just doing it once—there's another very real cost associated with H.264 video: licensing fees.

Remember when I first explained H.264 video (see "H.264" on page 84), and I mentioned that the video codec was patent-encumbered and licensing was brokered by the MPEG LA consortium? That turns out to be kind of important. To understand why it's important, I direct you to the H.264 Licensing Labyrinth:[*]

> MPEG LA splits the H.264 license portfolio into two sublicenses: one for manufacturers of encoders or decoders and the other for distributors of content. [...]
>
> The sublicense on the distribution side gets further split out to four key subcategories, two of which (subscription and title-by-title purchase or paid use) are tied to whether the end user pays directly for video services, and two of which ("free" television and Internet broadcast) are tied to remuneration from sources other than the end viewer. [...]
>
> The licensing fee for "free" television is based on one of two royalty options. The first is a one-time payment of $2,500 per AVC transmission encoder, which covers one AVC encoder "used by or on behalf of a Licensee in transmitting AVC video to the End User," who will decode and view it. If you're wondering whether this is a double charge, the answer is yes: A license fee has already been charged to the encoder manufacturer, and the broadcaster will in turn pay one of the two royalty options.
>
> The second licensing fee is an annual broadcast fee. [...] [T]he annual broadcast fee is broken down by viewership sizes:
>
> • $2,500 per calendar year per broadcast markets of 100,000–499,999 television households
>
> • $5,000 per calendar year per broadcast market of 500,000–999,999 television households
>
> • $10,000 per calendar year per broadcast market of 1,000,000 or more television households

---

[*] *http://www.streamingmedia.com/Articles/Editorial/Featured-Articles/The-H.264-Licensing-Labyrinth-65403 .aspx.*

[...] With all the issues around "free" television, why should someone involved in non-broadcast delivery care? As I mentioned before, the participation fees apply to any delivery of content. After defining that "free" television meant more than just [over-the-air], MPEG LA went on to define participation fees for Internet broadcasting as "AVC video that is delivered via the Worldwide Internet to an end user for which the end user does not pay remuneration for the right to receive or view." In other words, any public broadcast, whether it is [over-the-air], cable, satellite, or the Internet, is subject to participation fees. [...]

The fees are potentially somewhat steeper for Internet broadcasts, perhaps assuming that Internet delivery will grow much faster than OTA or "free" television via cable or satellite. Adding the "free television" broadcast-market fee together with an additional fee, MPEG LA grants a reprieve of sorts during the first license term, which ends on Dec. 31, 2010, and notes that "after the first term the royalty shall be no more than the economic equivalent of royalties payable during the same time for free television."

That last part—about the fee structure for Internet broadcasts—has already been amended. The MPEG LA recently announced that free Internet streaming would be extended through December 31, 2015. And after that...who knows?

Encoding Ogg Video with Firefogg

(In this section, I'm going to use "Ogg video" as a shorthand for "Theora video and Vorbis audio in an Ogg container." This is the combination of codecs+container that works natively in Mozilla Firefox and Google Chrome.)

Firefogg is an open source, GPL-licensed Firefox extension for encoding Ogg video. To use it, you'll need to install Mozilla Firefox 3.5 or later, then visit the Firefogg website, shown in Figure 5-1.

Click "Install Firefogg." Firefox will prompt whether you really want to allow the site to install an extension. Click "Allow" to continue (Figure 5-2).

Firefox will present the standard software installation window. Click "Install Now" to continue (Figure 5-3).

Click "Restart Firefox" to complete the installation (Figure 5-4).

Once Firefox has restarted, the Firefogg website will confirm that Firefogg was successfully installed (Figure 5-5).

Click "Make Ogg Video" to start the encoding process (Figure 5-6), then click "Select file" to select your source video (Figure 5-7).

Figure 5-1. Firefogg home page

Figure 5-2. Allow Firefogg to install

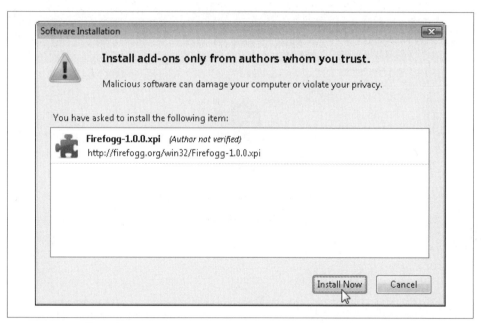

Figure 5-3. Install Firefogg

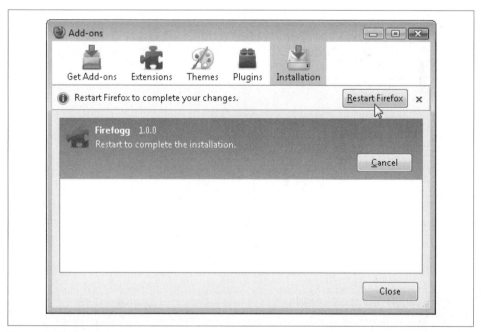

Figure 5-4. Restart Firefox

Figure 5-5. Installation successful

Figure 5-6. Let's make some video!

Figure 5-7. Select your video file

The main Firefogg interface has six "tabs" (shown in Figure 5-8):

Presets
> The default preset is "web video," which is fine for our purposes.

Encoding range
> Encoding video can take a long time. When you're first getting started, you may want to encode just part of your video (say, the first 30 seconds) until you find a combination of settings you like.

Basic quality and resolution control
> This is where most of the important options are.

Metadata
> I won't cover it here, but you can add metadata like title and author to your encoded video. You've probably added metadata to your music collection with iTunes or some other music manager. This is the same idea.

Advanced video encoding controls
> Don't mess with these unless you know what you're doing. (Firefogg offers interactive help on most of these options. Click the "i" symbol next to each option to learn more about it.)

Advanced audio encoding controls
> Again, don't mess with these unless you know what you're doing.

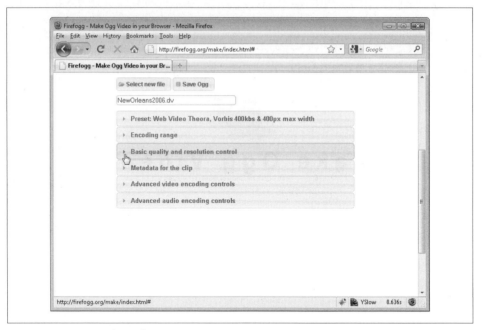

Figure 5-8. Let's encode a video

We're only going to look at the "Basic quality and resolution control" tab (Figure 5-9), which contains all the important options:

Video Quality
> This is measured on a scale of 0 (lowest quality) to 10 (highest quality). Higher numbers mean bigger file sizes, so you'll need to experiment to determine the best size/quality ratio for your needs.

Audio Quality
> This is measured on a scale of –1 (lowest quality) to 10 (highest quality). Higher numbers mean bigger file sizes, just like with the video quality setting.

Video Codec
> This should always be "theora."

Audio Codec
> This should always be "vorbis."

Video Width and Video Height
> These default to the actual width and height of your source video. If you want to resize the video during encoding, you can change the width or height here. Firefogg will automatically adjust the other dimension to maintain the original proportions, so your video won't end up smooshed or stretched.

In Figure 5-10, I resize the video to half its original width. Notice how Firefogg automatically adjusts the height to match.

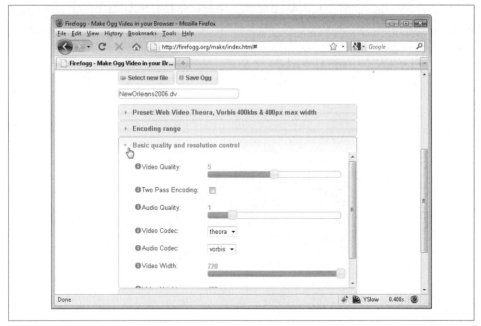

Figure 5-9. Basic quality and resolution control

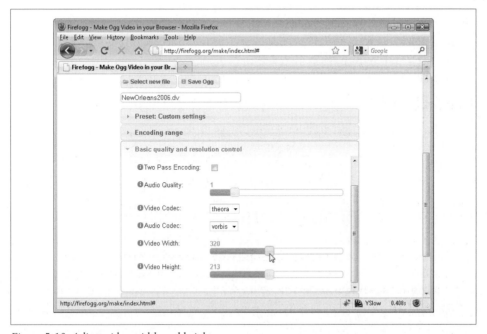

Figure 5-10. Adjust video width and height

Once you've fiddled with all the knobs, click "Save Ogg" to start the actual encoding process (Figure 5-11). Firefogg will prompt you for a filename for the encoded video.

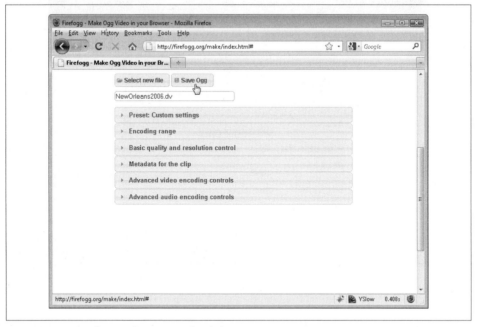

Figure 5-11. Start the encoding process by clicking "Save Ogg"

Firefogg will show a nice progress bar as it encodes your video (Figure 5-12). All you need to do is wait (and wait, and wait)!

Batch Encoding Ogg Video with ffmpeg2theora

(As in the previous section, in this section I'm going to use "Ogg video" as a shorthand for "Theora video and Vorbis audio in an Ogg container." This is the combination of codecs+container that works natively in Mozilla Firefox and Google Chrome.)

There are a number of offline encoders for Ogg video. If you're looking at batch encoding a lot of video files and you want to automate the process, you should definitely check out *ffmpeg2theora* (*http://v2v.cc/~j/ffmpeg2theora/*).

ffmpeg2theora is an open source, GPL-licensed application for encoding Ogg video. Prebuilt binaries are available for Mac OS X, Windows, and modern Linux distributions. It can take virtually any video file as input, including the DV video produced by many consumer-level camcorders.

To use *ffmpeg2theora*, you need to call it from the command line. (On Windows, go to Start Menu→Programs→Accessories→Command Prompt. On Mac OS X, open Applications→Utilities→Terminal.)

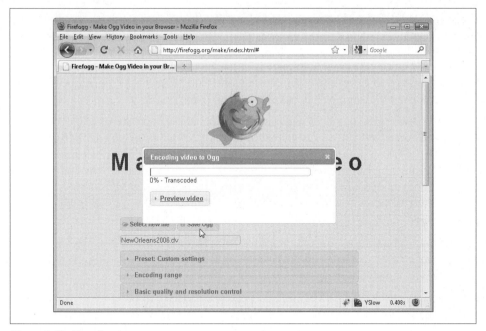

Figure 5-12. Encoding in progress

ffmpeg2theora can take a large number of command-line flags. (Type `ffmpeg2theora --help` to read about them all.) I'll focus on just three of them:

- `--video-quality` *Q*, where *Q* is a number from 0–10.
- `--audio-quality` *Q*, where *Q* is a number from –2–10.
- `--max_size=WxH`, where *W* and *H* are the maximum width and height you want for the video. (The x in between is really just the letter "x".) *ffmpeg2theora* will resize the video proportionally to fit within these dimensions, so the encoded video might be smaller than *WxH*. For example, encoding a 720 × 480 pixel video with `--max_size 320x240` will produce a video that is 320 pixels wide and 213 pixels high.

Thus, here is how you could encode a video with the same settings as we used in the previous section ("Encoding Ogg Video with Firefogg" on page 91):

```
you@localhost$ ffmpeg2theora --videoquality 5
                             --audioquality 1
                             --max_size 320x240
                             pr6.dv
```

The encoded video will be saved in the same directory as the original video, with an *.ogv* extension added. You can specify a different location and/or filename by passing an `--output=`*/path/to/encoded/video* command-line flag to *ffmpeg2theora*.

Encoding H.264 Video with HandBrake

(In this section, I'm going to use "H.264 video" as a shorthand for "H.264 Baseline profile video and AAC low-complexity profile audio in an MPEG-4 container." This is the combination of codecs+container that works natively in Safari, in Adobe Flash, on the iPhone, and on Google Android devices.)

Licensing issues aside (see "Licensing Issues with H.264 Video" on page 90), the easiest way to encode H.264 video is using HandBrake (*http://handbrake.fr*). HandBrake is an open source, GPL-licensed application for encoding H.264 video. (It used to do other video formats too, but in the latest version the developers have dropped support for most other formats and focused all their efforts on H.264 video.) Prebuilt binaries are available for Windows, Mac OS X, and modern Linux distributions (*http://handbrake .fr/downloads.php*).

HandBrake comes in two flavors: graphical and command line. I'll walk you through the graphical interface first, then we'll see how my recommended settings translate into the command-line version.

After you open the HandBrake application, the first thing to do is select your source video (Figure 5-13). Click "Source" and choose "Video File" from the drop-down menu to select a file. HandBrake can take virtually any video file as input, including DV video produced by many consumer-level camcorders.

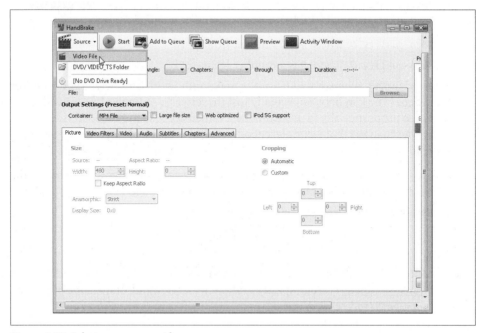

Figure 5-13. Select your source video

HandBrake will complain that you haven't set a default directory to save your encoded videos (Figure 5-14). You can safely ignore this warning, or you can open the options window (under the "Tools" menu) and set a default output directory.

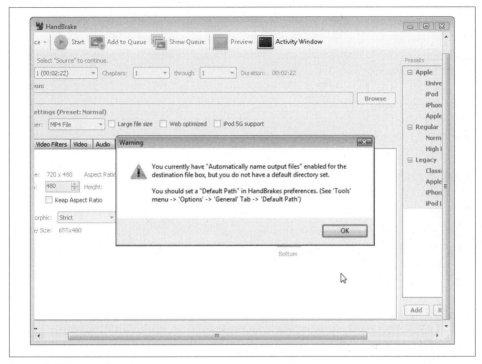

Figure 5-14. Ignore this warning

On the righthand side is a list of presets. Selecting the "iPhone & iPod Touch" preset, as in Figure 5-15, will set most of the options you need.

One important option that is off by default is the "Web optimized" option. Selecting this option, as shown in Figure 5-16, reorders some of the metadata within the encoded video so you can watch the start of the video while the rest is downloading in the background. I highly recommend always checking this option. It does not affect the quality or file size of the encoded video, so there's really no reason not to.

In the "Picture" tab, you can set the maximum width and height of the encoded video (Figure 5-17). You should also select the "Keep Aspect Ratio" option to ensure that HandBrake doesn't smoosh or stretch your video while resizing it.

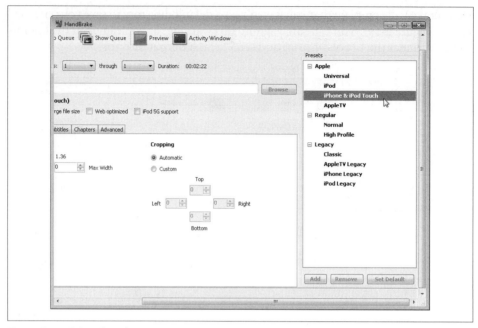

Figure 5-15. Select the iPhone preset

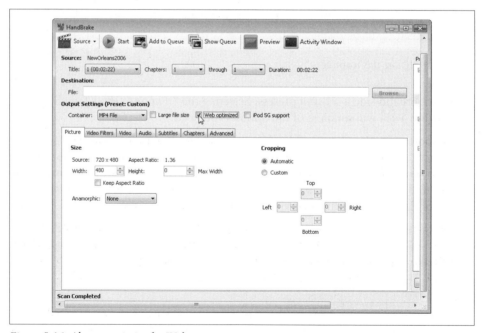

Figure 5-16. Always optimize for Web

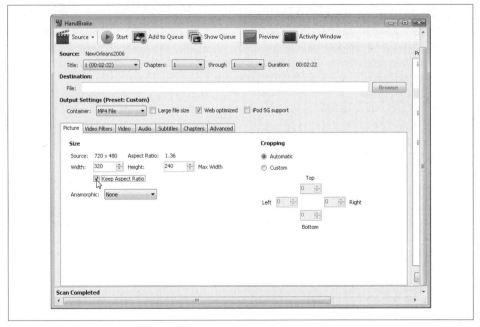

Figure 5-17. Set width and height

In the "Video" tab, shown in Figure 5-18, you can set several important options:

Video Codec
Make sure this is "H.264 (x264)".

2-Pass Encoding
If this is checked, HandBrake will run the video encoder twice. The first time, it just analyzes the video, looking for things like color composition, motion, and scene breaks. The second time, it actually encodes the video using the information it learned during the first pass. As you might expect, this takes about twice as long as single-pass encoding, but it results in better video without increasing file size. I always enable two-pass encoding for H.264 video. Unless you're building the next YouTube and encoding videos 24 hours a day, you should probably use two-pass encoding too.

Turbo First Pass
When you've enabled two-pass encoding, you can get a little bit of time back by enabling this option. It reduces the amount of work done in the first pass (analyzing the video), while only slightly degrading quality. I usually enable this option, but if quality is of the utmost importance to you, you should leave it disabled.

Quality
There are several different ways to specify the "quality" of your encoded video. You can set a target file size, and HandBrake will do its best to ensure that your encoded video is not larger than that. You can set an average "bitrate," which is

quite literally the number of bits required to store one second's worth of encoded video. (It's called an "average" bitrate because some seconds will require more bits than others.) Or you can specify a constant quality, on a scale of 0 to 100 percent. Higher numbers will result in better quality but larger files. There is no single right answer for what quality setting you should use.

Ask Professor Markup

Q: Can I use two-pass encoding on Ogg video too?

A: Yes, but due to fundamental differences in how the encoder works, you probably don't need to. Two-pass H.264 encoding almost always results in higher-quality video. Two-pass Ogg encoding of Ogg video is only useful if you're trying to get your encoded video to be a specific file size. (Maybe that is something you're interested in, but it's not what these examples show, and it's probably not worth the extra time for encoding web video.) For best Ogg video quality, use the video quality settings, and don't worry about two-pass encoding.

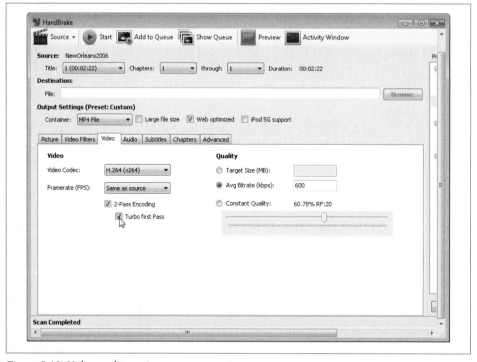

Figure 5-18. Video quality options

In this example, I've chosen an average bitrate of 600 kbps, which is quite high for a 320×240 encoded video. I've also enabled two-pass encoding with a "turbo" first pass.

In the "Audio" tab, shown in Figure 5-19, you probably don't need to change anything. If your source video has multiple audio tracks, you might need to select which one you want in the encoded video. If your video is mostly a person talking (as opposed to music or general ambient sounds), you can probably reduce the audio bitrate to 96 kbps or so. Other than that, the defaults you inherited from the "iPhone" preset should be fine.

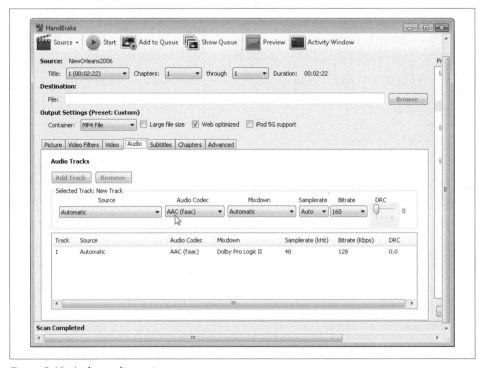

Figure 5-19. Audio quality options

Next, click the "Browse" button and choose a directory and filename to save your encoded video (Figure 5-20).

Finally, click "Start" to start encoding (Figure 5-21).

HandBrake will display some progress statistics while it encodes your video (Figure 5-22).

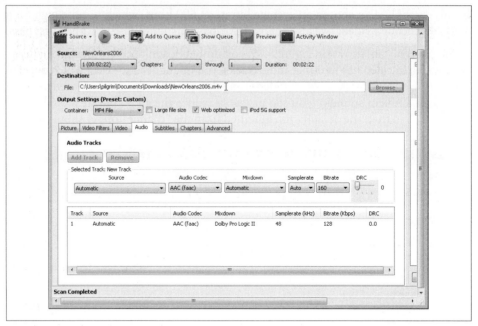

Figure 5-20. Set destination filename

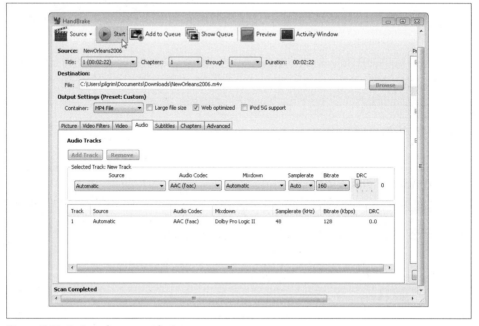

Figure 5-21. Let's make some video!

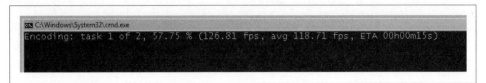

Figure 5-22. Patience, grasshopper

Batch Encoding H.264 Video with HandBrake

(As in the previous section, in this section I'm going to use "H.264 video" as a shorthand for "H.264 Baseline profile video and AAC low-complexity profile audio in an MPEG-4 container." This is the combination of codecs+container that works natively in Safari, in Adobe Flash, on the iPhone, and on Google Android devices.)

As I mentioned in the preceding section, HandBrake also comes in a command-line edition. As with the graphical edition, you should download a recent snapshot from *http://handbrake.fr/downloads2.php*.

Like *ffmpeg2theora* (see "Batch Encoding Ogg Video with ffmpeg2theora" on page 98), the command-line edition of HandBrake offers a dizzying array of options. (Type `HandBrakeCLI --help` in a Terminal window or at a command prompt to read about them.) I'll focus on just a few:

- `--preset "X"`, where `"X"` is the name of a HandBrake preset (it's important to put the name in quotes). The preset you want for H.264 web video is called "iPhone & iPod Touch".
- `--width W`, where `W` is the width of your encoded video. HandBrake will automatically adjust the height to maintain the original video's proportions.
- `--vb Q`, where `Q` is the average bitrate (measured in kilobits per second).
- `--two-pass`, which enables two-pass encoding.
- `--turbo`, which enables a turbo first pass during two-pass encoding.
- `--input F`, where `F` is the filename of your source video.
- `--output E`, where `E` is the destination filename for your encoded video.

Here is an example of calling HandBrake on the command line, with command-line flags that match the settings we chose with the graphical version of HandBrake:

```
you@localhost$ HandBrakeCLI --preset "iPhone & iPod Touch"
                            --width 320
                            --vb 600
                            --two-pass
                            --turbo
                            --input pr6.dv
                            --output pr6.mp4
```

From top to bottom, this command runs HandBrake with the "iPhone & iPod Touch" preset, resizes the video to 320 × 240, sets the average bitrate to 600 kbps, enables two-pass encoding with a turbo first pass, reads the file *pr6.dv*, and encodes it as *pr6.mp4*. Whew!

Encoding WebM Video with ffmpeg

I'm writing this on May 20, 2010. The WebM format was literally released yesterday. As such, there is not a lot of choice for encoding tools, and very few end-to-end guides are available. This will all get easier as tools are written (or updated) to provide one-click support for WebM. Until then, here are the tools you will need:

- *libvp8*, and a special version of *ffmpeg* with additional patches (to connect it with *libvp8*) that are not yet part of the official *ffmpeg* repository:
  - Instructions for Linux (*http://lardbucket.org/blog/archives/2010/05/19/vp8 -webm-and-ffmpeg/*), which I have personally tested on Ubuntu "Lucid" 10.04.
  - Instructions for Windows (*http://www.ioncannon.net/meta/1128/compiling -webm-ffmpeg-windows/*), which I have not personally tested.
- The latest version of *mkclean* (*http://www.matroska.org/downloads/mkclean.html*).

Ready? OK. On the command line, run *ffmpeg* with no parameters and verify that it was compiled with VP8 support:

```
you@localhost$ ffmpeg
FFmpeg version SVN-r23197, Copyright (c) 2000-2010 the FFmpeg developers
  built on May 19 2010 22:32:20 with gcc 4.4.3
  configuration: --enable-gpl --enable-version3 --enable-nonfree --enable-postproc
  --enable-pthreads --enable-libfaac --enable-libfaad --enable-libmp3lame
  --enable-libopencore-amrnb --enable-libopencore-amrwb --enable-libtheora
  --enable-libx264 --enable-libxvid --enable-x11grab --enable-libvpx-vp8
```

If you don't see the magic words `--enable-libvpx-vp8`, you don't have the right version of *ffmpeg*. (If you swear you just compiled it properly, check to see if you have two versions installed. That's fine, they won't conflict with each other—you'll just need to use the full path of the VP8-enabled version of *ffmpeg*.)

I'm going to show you how to do a two-pass encode (see "Encoding H.264 Video with HandBrake" on page 100). The first pass just scans through the input video file (`-i pr6.dv`) and writes out some statistics to a logfile (which will be autonamed *pr6.dv-0.log*). You specify the video codec with the `-vcodec` parameter:

```
you@localhost$ ffmpeg -pass 1 -passlogfile pr6.dv -threads 16 -token_partitions 4
                -altref 1 -lag 16 -keyint_min 0 -g 250 -mb_static_threshold 0
                -skip_threshold 0 -qmin 1 -qmax 51 -i pr6.dv -vcodec libvpx_vp8 -an
                -f rawvideo -y NUL
```

Most of the *ffmpeg* command line has nothing to do with VP8 or WebM. *libvp8* does support a number of VP8-specific options that you can pass to *ffmpeg*, but I don't yet know how any of them work. Once I find a good explanation of these options, I'll provide a link on this book's website.

For the second pass, *ffmpeg* will read the statistics it wrote during the first pass and actually do the encoding of the video and the audio. It will write out an MKV file, which we will convert to a WebM file later. (Eventually *ffmpeg* will be able to write WebM files directly, but that functionality is currently broken in a subtle and pernicious way.) Here's the command line for the second pass:

```
you@localhost$ ffmpeg -pass 2 -passlogfile pr6.dv -threads 16 -token_partitions 4
               -altref 1 -lag 16 -keyint_min 0 -g 250 -mb_static_threshold 0
               -skip_threshold 0 -qmin 1 -qmax 51 -i pr6.dv -vcodec libvpx_vp8
               -b 614400 -s 320x240 -aspect 4:3 -acodec vorbis -y pr6.mkv
```

There are five important parameters here:

-vcodec libvpx_vp8
> Specifies that we're encoding with the VP8 video codec. WebM always uses VP8 video.

-b 614400
> Specifies the bitrate. Unlike other formats, *libvp8* expects the bitrate in actual bits, not kilobits. If you want a 600-kbps video, multiply 600 by 1024 to get 614400.

-s 320x240
> Specifies the target size, width by height.

-aspect 4:3
> Specifies the aspect ratio of the video. Standard-definition video is usually 4:3, but most high-definition video is 16:9 or 16:10. In my testing, I found that I had to specify this explicitly on the command line, instead of relying on *ffmpeg* to auto-detect it.

-acodec vorbis
> Specifies that we're encoding with the Vorbis audio codec. WebM always uses Vorbis audio.

Now we have an MKV file with VP8 video and Vorbis audio. That's *really close* to what we want. The container format of WebM is technically very similar to MKV. In fact, it's a proper subset. We only need to twiddle a few bits to create our final WebM video file, using the *mkclean* utility I mentioned earlier:

```
you@localhost$ mkclean --doctype 4 pr6.mkv pr6.webm
```

And that's all she wrote!

At Last, the Markup

I'm pretty sure this was supposed to be an HTML book. So where's the markup?

HTML5 gives you two ways to include video on your web page. Both of them involve the `<video>` element. If you only have one video file, you can simply link to it in a `src` attribute. This is remarkably similar to including an image with an `<img src="...">` tag.

```
<video src="pr6.webm"></video>
```

Technically, that's all you need. But just like in an `<img>` tag, you should always include `width` and `height` attributes in your `<video>` tags. The `width` and `height` attributes can be the same as the maximum width and height you specified during the encoding process:

```
<video src="pr6.webm" width="320" height="240"></video>
```

Don't worry if one dimension of the video is a little smaller than that. Your browser will center the video inside the box defined by the `<video>` tag. It won't ever be smooshed or stretched out of proportion.

By default, the `<video>` element will not expose any sort of player controls. You can create your own controls with plain old HTML, CSS, and JavaScript. The `<video>` element has methods like `play()` and `pause()` and a read/write property called `currentTime`. There are also read/write `volume` and `muted` properties. So you really have everything you need to build your own interface.

If you don't want to build your own interface, you can tell the browser to display a built-in set of controls. To do this, just include the `controls` attribute in your `<video>` tag:

```
<video src="pr6.webm" width="320" height="240" controls></video>
```

There are two other optional attributes I want to mention before we go any further: `preload` and `autoplay`. Don't shoot the messenger; let me explain why these are useful. The `preload` attribute tells the browser that you would like it to start downloading the video file as soon as the page loads. This makes sense if the entire point of the page is to view the video. On the other hand, if it's just supplementary material that only a few visitors will watch, you can set `preload` to `none` to tell the browser to minimize network traffic.

Here's an example of a video that will start downloading (but not playing) as soon as the page loads:

```
<video src="pr6.webm" width="320" height="240" preload></video>
```

And here's an example of a video that will *not* start downloading as soon as the page loads:

```
<video src="pr6.webm" width="320" height="240" preload="none"></video>
```

The `autoplay` attribute does exactly what it sounds like: it tells the browser that you would like it to start downloading the video file as soon as the page loads, *and* that you would like it to start playing the video automatically as soon as possible. Some people love this; some people hate it. But let me explain why it's important to have an attribute like this in HTML5. Some people are going to want their videos to play automatically, even if it annoys their visitors. If HTML5 *didn't* define a standard way to autoplay videos, people would resort to JavaScript hacks to do it anyway, for example, by calling the video's `play()` method during the window's `load` event. This would be much harder for visitors to counteract. On the other hand, it's a simple matter to add an extension to your browser (or write one, if necessary) that allows you to say "ignore the `autoplay` attribute, I don't ever want videos to play automatically."

Here's an example of a video that will start downloading and playing as soon as possible after the page loads:

```
<video src="pr6.webm" width="320" height="240" autoplay></video>
```

And here is a Greasemonkey (*http://www.greasespot.net*) script that you can install in your local copy of Firefox that prevents HTML5 video from playing automatically. It uses the `autoplay` DOM attribute defined by HTML5, which is the JavaScript equivalent of the `autoplay` attribute in your HTML markup:

```
// ==UserScript==
// @name            Disable video autoplay
// @namespace       http://diveintomark.org/projects/greasemonkey/
// @description     Ensures that HTML5 video elements do not autoplay
// @include         *
// ==/UserScript==

var arVideos = document.getElementsByTagName('video');
for (var i = arVideos.length - 1; i >= 0; i--) {
    var elmVideo = arVideos[i];
    elmVideo.autoplay = false;
}
```

But wait a second. If you've been following along through this whole chapter, you know that you don't have just one video file; you have three. One is an *.ogv* file that you created with Firefogg (see "Encoding Ogg Video with Firefogg" on page 91) or *ffmpeg2theora* (see "Batch Encoding Ogg Video with ffmpeg2theora" on page 98). The second is an *.mp4* file that you created with HandBrake (see "Encoding H.264 Video with HandBrake" on page 100). The third is a *.webm* file that you created with *ffmpeg* (see "Encoding WebM Video with ffmpeg" on page 108). HTML5 provides a way to link to all three of them: the `<source>` element. Each `<video>` element can contain as many `<source>` elements as you need. Your browser will go down the list of video sources, in order, and play the first one it's able to play.

That raises another question: how does the browser know which video it can play? In the worst-case scenario, it loads each of the videos and tries to play them. That's a big waste of bandwidth, though. You'll save a lot of network traffic if you tell the browser up front about each video. You do this with the `type` attribute on the `<source>` element.

Here's the whole thing:

```
<video width="320" height="240" controls>
  <source src="pr6.mp4"  type='video/mp4; codecs="avc1.42E01E, mp4a.40.2"'>
  <source src="pr6.webm" type='video/webm; codecs="vp8, vorbis"'>
  <source src="pr6.ogv"  type='video/ogg; codecs="theora, vorbis"'>
</video>
```

Let's break that down. The `<video>` element specifies the width and height for the video, but it doesn't actually link to a video file. Inside the `<video>` element are two `<source>` elements. Each `<source>` element links to a single video file (with the `src` attribute) and gives information about the video format (in the `type` attribute).

The `type` attribute looks complicated—hell, it *is* complicated. It contains three pieces of information: the container format (see "Video Containers" on page 81), the video codec (see "Video Codecs" on page 83), and the audio codec (see "Audio Codecs" on page 85). Let's start from the bottom. For the *.ogv* video file, the container format is Ogg, represented here as `video/ogg`. (Technically speaking, that's the MIME type for Ogg video files.) The video codec is Theora, and the audio codec is Vorbis. That's simple enough, except the format of the attribute value is a little screwy. The `codecs` value itself has to include quotation marks, which means you'll need to use a different kind of quotation mark to surround the entire `type` value:

```
<source src="pr6.ogv" type='video/ogg; codecs="theora, vorbis"'>
```

The `<source>` element for the WebM file is much the same, but with a different MIME type (`video/webm` instead of `video/ogg`) and a different video codec (`vp8` instead of `theora`) listed within the `codecs` parameter:

```
<source src="pr6.webm" type='video/webm; codecs="vp8, vorbis"'>
```

The `<source>` element for the H.264 file is even more complicated. Remember when I said that both H.264 video (see "H.264" on page 84) and AAC audio (see "Advanced Audio Coding" on page 87) can come in different "profiles"? We encoded with the H.264 Baseline profile and the AAC low-complexity profile, then wrapped it all in an MPEG-4 container. All of that information is included in the `type` attribute:

```
<source src="pr6.mp4" type='video/mp4; codecs="avc1.42E01E, mp4a.40.2"'>
```

The benefit of going to all this trouble is that the browser will be able to check the `type` attribute first to see if it can play a particular video file. If a browser decides it can't play a particular video, *it won't download the file*. Not even part of the file. You'll save on bandwidth, and your visitors will see the video they came for, faster.

If you follow the instructions in this chapter for encoding your videos, you can just copy the `type` attribute values from this example. Otherwise, you'll need to work out the `type` parameters for yourself.

MIME Types Rear Their Ugly Head

There are so many pieces to the video puzzle, I hesitate to even bring this up. But it's important, because a misconfigured web server can lead to endless frustration as you try to debug why your videos play on your local computer but fail to play when you deploy them to your production site. If you run into this problem, the root cause is probably MIME types.

I mentioned MIME types in Chapter 1 (see "MIME Types" on page 1), but you probably glazed over that and didn't appreciate the significance. So here it is in all-caps.

What's the proper MIME type? You've already seen it; it's part of the value of the type attribute of a <source> element. But setting the type attribute in your HTML markup is not sufficient. You also need to ensure that your web server includes the proper MIME type in the Content-Type HTTP header.

If you're using the Apache web server or some derivative of Apache, you can use Add Type directives in your site-wide *httpd.conf* or in an *.htaccess* file in the directory where you store your video files. (If you use some other web server, consult your server's documentation on how to set the Content-Type HTTP header for specific file types.) The AddType directives you'll need to include are:

```
AddType video/ogg .ogv
AddType video/mp4 .mp4
AddType video/webm .webm
```

The first line is for videos in an Ogg container. The second line is for videos in an MPEG-4 container. The third is for WebM. Set these once, and forget them. If you don't, your videos *will* fail to play in some browsers, even if you include the MIME type in the type attribute in your HTML markup.

For even more gory details about configuring your web server, I direct your attention to an excellent Mozilla Developer Center article, "Configuring servers for Ogg media" (*https://developer.mozilla.org/en/Configuring_servers_for_Ogg_media*). (The advice in that article applies to MP4 and WebM video, too.)

What About IE?

As I write this, Microsoft has released a "developer preview" of Internet Explorer 9. It does not yet support the HTML5 `<video>` element, but Microsoft has publicly promised (*http://blogs.msdn.com/ie/archive/2010/03/16/html5-hardware-accelerated-first -ie9-platform-preview-available-for-developers.aspx*) that the final version of IE 9 will support H.264 video and AAC audio in an MPEG-4 container, just like Safari on desktop Macs and Mobile Safari on iOS.

But what about older versions of Internet Explorer? Like, you know, all shipping versions up to and including IE 8? Most people who use Internet Explorer also have the Adobe Flash plug-in installed. Modern versions of Adobe Flash (starting with 9.0.60.184) support H.264 video and AAC audio in an MPEG-4 container. Once you've encoded your H.264 video for Safari (see "Encoding H.264 Video with Hand-Brake" on page 100), you can play it in a Flash-based video player if you detect that your visitor doesn't have an HTML5-capable browser.

FlowPlayer (*http://flowplayer.org*) is an open source, GPL-licensed, Flash-based video player. (Commercial licenses are also available; see *http://flowplayer.org/download/.*) FlowPlayer doesn't know anything about the `<video>` element. It won't magically transform a `<video>` tag into a Flash object. But HTML5 is well designed to handle this, because you can nest an `<object>` element within a `<video>` element. Browsers that don't support HTML5 video will ignore the `<video>` element and simply render the nested `<object>` instead, which will invoke the Flash plug-in and play the movie through FlowPlayer. Browsers that support HTML5 video will find a video source they can play and play it, *and ignore the nested `<object>` element altogether.*

That last bit is the key to the whole puzzle: HTML5 specifies that all elements (other than `<source>` elements) that are children of a `<video>` element must be ignored altogether. That allows you to use HTML5 video in newer browsers and fall back to Flash gracefully in older browsers, without requiring any fancy JavaScript hacks. You can read more about this technique at the Video for Everybody! site (*http://camendesign .com/code/video_for_everybody*).

A Complete Example

Let's look at an example that uses these techniques. I've extended the Video for Everybody! code to include a WebM-formatted video. Using these commands, I encoded the same source video into three formats:

```
## Theora/Vorbis/Ogg
you@localhost$ ffmpeg2theora --videobitrate 200 --max_size 320x240 --output pr6.ogv
                pr6.dv

## H.264/AAC/MP4
you@localhost$ HandBrakeCLI --preset "iPhone & iPod Touch" --vb 200 --width 320
                --two-pass --turbo --optimize --input pr6.dv --output pr6.mp4
```

```
## VP8/Vorbis/WebM
you@localhost$ ffmpeg -pass 1 -passlogfile pr6.dv -threads 16 -token_partitions 4
                -altref 1 -lag 16 -keyint_min 0 -g 250 -mb_static_threshold 0
                -skip_threshold 0 -qmin 1 -qmax 51 -i pr6.dv -vcodec libvpx_vp8
                -an -f rawvideo -y NULffmpeg --videobitrate 200
you@localhost$ ffmpeg -pass 2 -passlogfile pr6.dv -threads 16 -token_partitions 4
                -altref 1 -lag 16 -keyint_min 0 -g 250 -mb_static_threshold 0
                -skip_threshold 0 -qmin 1 -qmax 51 -i pr6.dv -vcodec libvpx_vp8
                -b 204800 -s 320x240 -aspect 4:3 -acodec vorbis -ac 2 -y pr6.mkv
you@localhost$ mkclean --doctype 4 pr6.mkv pr6.webm
```

The final markup uses a `<video>` element for HTML5 video, with a nested `<object>` element for Flash fallback:

```
<video id="movie" width="320" height="240" preload controls>
  <source src="pr6.mp4" type='video/mp4; codecs="avc1.42E01E, mp4a.40.2"' />
  <source src="pr6.webm" type='video/webm; codecs="vp8, vorbis"' />
  <source src="pr6.ogv" type='video/ogg; codecs="theora, vorbis"' />
  <object width="320" height="240" type="application/x-shockwave-flash"
    data="flowplayer-3.2.1.swf">
    <param name="movie" value="flowplayer-3.2.1.swf" />
    <param name="allowfullscreen" value="true" />
    <param name="flashvars" value='config={
     "clip": {"url": "http://wearehugh.com/dih5/good/bbb_480p.mp4",
     "autoPlay":false, "autoBuffering":true}}' />
    <p>Download video as <a href="pr6.mp4">MP4</a>,
     <a href="pr6.webm">WebM</a>, or
     <a href="pr6.ogv">Ogg</a>.</p>
  </object>
</video>
```

With the combination of HTML5 and Flash, you should be able to watch this video in almost any browser and device.

Further Reading

- "The `<video>` element" in the HTML5 specification (*http://bit.ly/a3kpiq*)
- Video for Everybody! (*http://camendesign.com/code/video_for_everybody*)
- "A gentle introduction to video encoding" (*http://diveintomark.org/tag/give*)
- "Theora 1.1 is released—what you need to know" (*http://hacks.mozilla.org/2009/ 09/theora-1-1-released/*), by Christopher Blizzard
- "Configuring servers for Ogg media" (*https://developer.mozilla.org/en/Configuring _servers_for_Ogg_media*)
- "Encoding with the x264 codec" (*http://www.mplayerhq.hu/DOCS/HTML/en/menc -feat-x264.html*)
- "Video type parameters" (*http://wiki.whatwg.org/wiki/Video_type_parameters*)
- Zencoder Video JS (*http://videojs.com*), custom controls for HTML5 video

- "Everything you need to know about HTML5 audio and video" (*http://dev.opera .com/articles/view/everything-you-need-to-know-about-html5-video-and-audio/*), by Simon Pieters

## CHAPTER 6

You Are Here (And So Is Everybody Else)

Diving In

Geolocation is the art of figuring out where you are in the world and (optionally) sharing that information with people you trust. There are many ways to figure out where you are—your IP address, your wireless network connection, which cell tower your phone is talking to, or dedicated GPS hardware that receives latitude and longitude information from satellites in the sky.

Ask Professor Markup

Q: Geolocation sounds scary. Can I turn it off?

A: Privacy is an obvious concern when you're talking about sharing your physical location with a remote web server. The geolocation API explicitly states (*http://www.w3 .org/TR/geolocation-API/#security*): "User Agents must not send location information to websites without the express permission of the user." In other words, if you don't want to share your location, you don't have to.

The Geolocation API

The geolocation API lets you share your location with trusted websites. The latitude and longitude are available to JavaScript on the page, which in turn can send that information back to the remote web server and do fancy location-aware things like finding local businesses or showing your location on a map.

As you can see from Table 6-1, the geolocation API is supported in several major browsers on desktops and mobile devices. Additionally, some older browsers and devices can be supported by wrapper libraries, as we'll see later in this chapter.

Table 6-1. Geolocation API support

IE	Firefox	Safari	Chrome	Opera	iPhone	Android
·	3.5+	5.0+	5.0+	·	3.0+	2.0+

Along with support for the standard geolocation API, there are a plethora of device-specific APIs on other mobile platforms. I'll cover all that later in this chapter.

Show Me the Code

The geolocation API centers around a new property on the global `navigator` object: `navigator.geolocation`.

The simplest use of the geolocation API looks like this:

```
function get_location() {
  navigator.geolocation.getCurrentPosition(show_map);
}
```

There's no detection, no error handling, and no options. Your web application should probably include at least the first two of those. To detect support for the geolocation API (see "Geolocation" on page 24), you can use Modernizr:

```
function get_location() {
  if (Modernizr.geolocation) {
    navigator.geolocation.getCurrentPosition(show_map);
  } else {
    // no native support; maybe try Gears?
  }
}
```

What you do without geolocation support is up to you. I'll explain the Gears fallback option in a minute, but first I want to talk about what happens *during* that call to `getCurrentPosition()`. As I mentioned at the start of this chapter, geolocation support is *opt-in*. That means your browser will never force you to reveal your current physical location to a remote server. The user experience differs from browser to browser. In Mozilla Firefox, calling the `getCurrentPosition()` function of the geolocation API will cause the browser to pop up an "infobar" at the top of the browser window. The infobar looks like Figure 6-1.

Figure 6-1. Geolocation infobar

There's a lot going on here. As the end user, you:

- Are told that a website wants to know your location
- Are told *which* website wants to know your location
- Can click through to Mozilla's "Location-Aware Browsing" help page, which explains what the heck is going on
- Can choose to share your location
- Can choose *not* to share your location
- Can tell your browser to remember your choice (share or don't share) so you never see this infobar again on this website

Furthermore, this infobar is:

- Nonmodal, so it won't prevent you from switching to another browser window or tab
- Tab-specific, so it will disappear if you switch to another browser window or tab and reappear when you switch back to the original tab
- Unconditional, so there is no way for a website to bypass it
- Blocking, so there is no chance that the website can determine your location while it's waiting for your answer

You just saw the JavaScript code that causes this infobar to appear. It's a single function call that takes a callback function (which I called `show_map()`). The call to `getCurrentPosition()` will return immediately, but that doesn't mean that you have access to the user's location. The first time you are guaranteed to have location information is in the callback function. The callback function looks like this:

```javascript
function show_map(position) {
  var latitude = position.coords.latitude;
  var longitude = position.coords.longitude;
  // let's show a map or do something interesting!
}
```

The callback function will be called with a single parameter, an object with two properties: `coords` and `timestamp`. The timestamp is just that, the date and time when the location was calculated. (Since this is all happening asynchronously, you can't really know when that will happen in advance. It might take some time for the user to read the infobar and agree to share her location, devices with dedicated GPS hardware may take some more time to connect to a GPS satellite, and so on.) The `coords` object has properties like `latitude` and `longitude` that represent exactly what they sound like: the user's physical location in the world. The `position` object's properties are listed in Table 6-2.

Table 6-2. Properties of the position object

Property	Type	Notes
coords.latitude	double	Decimal degrees
coords.longitude	double	Decimal degrees
coords.altitude	double or null	Meters above the reference ellipsoid
coords.accuracy	double	Meters
coords.altitudeAccuracy	double or null	Meters
coords.heading	double or null	Degrees clockwise from true north
coords.speed	double or null	Meters/second
timestamp	DOMTimeStamp	Like a Date() object

Only three of the properties are guaranteed to be there (`coords.latitude`, `coords.longitude`, and `coords.accuracy`). The rest might come back as `null`, depending on the capabilities of your device and the backend positioning server with which it communicates. The `heading` and `speed` properties are calculated based on the user's previous position, if possible.

Handling Errors

Geolocation is complicated. So many things can go wrong. I've mentioned the "user consent" angle already. If your web application wants the user's location but the user doesn't want to give it to you, you're screwed. The user always wins. But what does that look like in code? It looks like the second argument to the `getCurrentPosition()` function—an error handling callback function:

```
navigator.geolocation.getCurrentPosition(
    show_map, handle_error)
```

If anything goes wrong, your error callback function will be called with a `PositionError` object. It has the properties listed in Table 6-3.

Table 6-3. Properties of the PositionError object

Property	Type	Notes
code	short	An enumerated value
message	DOMString	Not intended for end users

The `code` property will be one of the following:

- `PERMISSION_DENIED` (1) if the user clicks the "Don't Share" button or otherwise denies you access to his location.
- `POSITION_UNAVAILABLE` (2) if the network is down or the positioning satellites can't be contacted.

- TIMEOUT (3) if the network is up but it takes too long to calculate the user's position. How long is "too long"? I'll show you how to define that in the next section.

- UNKNOWN_ERROR (0) if anything else goes wrong.

For example:

```
function handle_error(err) {
  if (err.code == 1) {
    // user said no!
  }
}
```

Ask Professor Markup

Q: *Does the geolocation API work on the International Space Station, on the moon, or on other planets?*

A: The geolocation specification (*http://www.w3.org/TR/geolocation-API/#coordinates _interface*) states: "The geographic coordinate reference system used by the attributes in this interface is the World Geodetic System (2d) [WGS84]. No other reference system is supported." The International Space Station is orbiting Earth, so astronauts on the station (*http://twitter.com/Astro_TJ*) can describe their location by latitude, longitude, and altitude. However, the World Geodetic System is Earth-centric, so it can't be used to describe locations on the moon or on other planets.

Choices! I Demand Choices!

Some popular mobile devices—like the iPhone and Android phones—support *two* methods of figuring out where you are. The first method triangulates your position based on your relative proximity to different cellular towers operated by your phone carrier. This method is fast and doesn't require any dedicated GPS hardware, but it only gives you a rough idea of where you are. Depending on how many cell towers are in your area, this "rough idea" could be accurate to as little as one city block or as much as a kilometer in every direction.

The second method actually uses dedicated GPS hardware on your device to talk to dedicated GPS positioning satellites that are orbiting the Earth. GPS can usually pinpoint your location to within a few meters. The downside is that the dedicated GPS chip on your device draws a lot of power, so phones and other general-purpose mobile devices usually turn off the chip until it's needed. That means there will be a startup delay while the chip initializes its connection with the GPS satellites in the sky. If you've ever used Google Maps on an iPhone or other smartphone, you've seen both methods in action. First you see a large circle that approximates your position (finding the nearest cell tower), then a smaller circle (triangulating with other cell towers), then a single dot with an exaction position (given by GPS satellites).

The reason I mention this is that, depending on your web application, you may not need high accuracy. For example, if you're looking for nearby movie listings, a "low-accuracy" location is probably good enough. There aren't *that* many movie theaters around, even in dense cities, and you'll probably be listing several of them anyway. On the other hand, if you're giving turn-by-turn directions in real time, you really *do* need to know exactly where the user is so you can say "turn right in 20 meters" or whatever.

The getCurrentPosition() function takes an optional third argument, a PositionOptions object. There are three properties you can set in a PositionOptions object (see Table 6-4). All the properties are optional; you can set any, all, or none of them.

Table 6-4. PositionOptions object properties

Property	Type	Default	Notes
enableHighAccuracy	boolean	false	true might be slower
timeout	long	(no default)	In milliseconds
maximumAge	long	0	In milliseconds

The enableHighAccuracy property is exactly what it sounds like. If it's set to true, and the device can support it, and the user consents to sharing her exact location, the device will try to provide it. Both iPhones and Android phones have separate permissions for low- and high-accuracy positioning, so it is possible that calling getCurrentPosition() with enableHighAccuracy:true will fail, but calling it with enableHighAccuracy:false will succeed.

The timeout property specifies the number of milliseconds your web application is willing to wait for a position. This timer doesn't start counting down until *after* the user gives permission to even try to calculate her position. You're not timing the user; you're timing the network.

The maximumAge property allows the device to answer immediately with a cached position. For example, let's say you call getCurrentPosition() for the very first time, the user consents, and your success callback function is called with a position that was calculated at exactly 10:00 AM. Then suppose that exactly one minute later, at 10:01 AM, you call getCurrentPosition() again with a maximumAge property of 75000:

```
navigator.geolocation.getCurrentPosition(
  success_callback, error_callback, {maximumAge: 75000});
```

What you're saying is that you don't necessarily need the user's *current* location. You would be satisfied with knowing where he was 75 seconds (75000 milliseconds) ago. In this case, the device knows where the user was 60 seconds (60000 milliseconds) ago, because it calculated the location the first time you called getCurrentPosition(). Since this is within the specified window, the device doesn't bother to recalculate the user's current location. It just returns exactly the same information it returned the first time: the same latitude and longitude, accuracy, and timestamp (10:00 AM).

Before you ask for the user's location, you should think about just how much accuracy you need and set `enableHighAccuracy` accordingly. If you will need to find the user's location more than once, you should think about how old the information can be and still be useful, and set `maximumAge` accordingly. If you need to find the user's location *continuously*, `getCurrentPosition()` is not for you. You need to upgrade to `watchPosition()`.

The `watchPosition()` function has the same structure as `getCurrentPosition()`. It takes two callback functions—a required one for success and an optional one for error conditions—and it can also take an optional `PositionOptions` object that has all the same properties you just learned about. The difference is that your callback function will be called *every time the user's location changes*. There is no need to actively poll the position. The device will determine the optimal polling interval, and it will call your callback function whenever it determines that the user's position has changed. You can use this to update a visible marker on a map, provide instructions on where to go next, or whatever you like. It's entirely up to you.

The `watchPosition()` function itself returns a number. You should probably store this number somewhere. If you ever want to stop watching the user's location changes, you can call the `clearWatch()` method and pass it this number, and the device will stop calling your callback function. If you've ever used the `setInterval()` and `clearInterval()` functions in JavaScript, this works the same way.

What About IE?

Internet Explorer does not support the W3C geolocation API that I've just described (see "The Geolocation API" on page 117). But don't despair! Gears (*http://tools.google.com/gears/*) is an open source browser plug-in from Google that works on Windows, Mac, Linux, Windows Mobile, and Android platforms. It provides a number of features for older browsers, including a geolocation API. It's not quite the same as the W3C geolocation API, but it serves the same purpose.

While we're on the subject of legacy platforms, I should point out that there are a number of device-specific geolocation APIs on mobile phone platforms. BlackBerry, Nokia, Palm, and OMTP BONDI all provide their own geolocation APIs. Of course, they all work differently from Gears, which in turn works differently from the W3C geolocation API. Wheeeeee!

geo.js to the Rescue

geo.js (*http://code.google.com/p/geo-location-javascript/*) is an open source, MIT-licensed JavaScript library that smooths over the differences between the W3C geolocation API, the Gears API, and the various APIs provided by mobile platforms. To use it, you'll need to add two `<script>` elements at the bottom of your page. (Technically, you could put them anywhere, but putting scripts in your `<head>` will make your page load more slowly. So don't do that!)

The first script is *gears_init.js* (*http://code.google.com/apis/gears/gears_init.js*), which initializes Gears if it's installed. The second script is *geo.js* (*http://geo-location-javascript .googlecode.com/svn/trunk/js/geo.js*). You can include them in your page using code like this:

```
<!DOCTYPE html>
<html>
<head>
  <meta charset="utf-8">
  <title>Dive Into HTML 5</title>
</head>
<body>
  ...
  <script src="gears_init.js"></script>
  <script src="geo.js"></script>
</body>
</html>
```

Now you're ready to use whichever geolocation API is installed:

```
if (geo_position_js.init()) {
  geo_position_js.getCurrentPosition(geo_success, geo_error);
}
```

Let's take that one step at a time. First, you need to explicitly call an `init()` function. The `init()` function returns `true` if a supported geolocation API is available:

```
if (geo_position_js.init()) {
```

Calling the `init()` function does not actually find the user's location; it just verifies that finding the location is possible. To actually find the user's location, you need to call the `getCurrentPosition()` function:

```
geo_position_js.getCurrentPosition(geo_success, geo_error);
```

The `getCurrentPosition()` function will trigger the browser to ask for permission to find and share the user's location. If geolocation is being provided by Gears, this will pop up a dialog asking if the user trusts the website to use Gears. If the browser natively supports the geolocation API, the dialog will look different. For example, Firefox 3.5 will display an infobar at the top of the page asking whether the user wants to share her location with your website.

The `getCurrentPosition()` function takes two callback functions as arguments. If the `getCurrentPosition()` function was successful in finding the location—that is, if the user gave permission and the geolocation API actually worked its magic—it will call the function passed in as the first argument. In this example, the success callback function is called `geo_success`:

```
geo_position_js.getCurrentPosition(geo_success, geo_error);
```

The success callback function takes a single argument, which contains the position information:

```
function geo_success(p) {
  alert("Found you at latitude " + p.coords.latitude +
      ", longitude " + p.coords.longitude);
}
```

If the getCurrentPosition() function could not find the user's location—either because he declined to give permission or because the geolocation API failed for some reason—it will call the function passed in as the second argument. In this example, the failure callback function is called geo_error:

```
geo_position_js.getCurrentPosition(geo_success, geo_error);
```

The failure callback function takes no arguments:

```
function geo_error() {
  alert("Could not find you!");
}
```

geo.js does not currently support the watchPosition() function. If you need continuous location information, you'll need to actively poll getCurrentPosition() yourself.

A Complete Example

Let's work through an example of using *geo.js* to attempt to get the user's location and display a map of the immediate surroundings.

When the page loads, it will need to call geo_position_js.init() to determine whether geolocation is available through any of the interfaces that *geo.js* supports. If so, you can set up a link the user can click to look up her location. Clicking that link calls the lookup_location() function, shown here:

```
function lookup_location() {
  geo_position_js.getCurrentPosition(show_map, show_map_error);
}
```

If the user gives consent to track her location, *and* the backend service was actually able to determine that location, *geo.js* calls the first callback function, show_map(), with a single argument, loc. The loc object has a coords property that contains latitude, longitude, and accuracy information. (This example doesn't use the accuracy information.) The rest of the show_map() function uses the Google Maps API to set up an embedded map:

```
function show_map(loc) {
  $("#geo-wrapper").css({'width':'320px','height':'350px'});
  var map = new GMap2(document.getElementById("geo-wrapper"));
  var center = new GLatLng(loc.coords.latitude, loc.coords.longitude);
  map.setCenter(center, 14);
  map.addControl(new GSmallMapControl());
  map.addControl(new GMapTypeControl());
  map.addOverlay(new GMarker(center, {draggable: false, title: "You are here (more or
```

```
    less)"}));
  }
```

If *geo.js* is unable to determine the location, it calls the second callback function, `show_map_error()`:

```
function show_map_error() {
  $("#live-geolocation").html('Unable to determine your location.');
}
```

Further Reading

- W3C geolocation API (*http://www.w3.org/TR/geolocation-API/*)
- Gears (*http://tools.google.com/gears/*)
- BlackBerry geolocation API (*http://www.tonybunce.com/2008/05/08/Blackberry -Browser-Amp-GPS.aspx*)
- Nokia geolocation API (*http://www.forum.nokia.com/infocenter/index.jsp?topic=/ Web_Developers_Library/GUID-4DDE31C7-EC0D-4EEC-BC3A -A0B0351154F8.html*)
- Palm geolocation API (*http://developer.palm.com/index.php?option=com_content &view=article&id=1673#GPS-getCurrentPosition*)
- OMTP BONDI geolocation API (*http://bondi.omtp.org/1.0/apis/geolocation.html*)
- *geo.js* (*http://code.google.com/p/geo-location-javascript/*), the geolocation API wrapper script

## CHAPTER 7

The Past, Present, and Future of Local Storage for Web Applications

Diving In

Persistent local storage is one of the areas where native client applications have traditionally held an advantage over web applications. For native applications, the operating system typically provides an abstraction layer for storing and retrieving application-specific data like preferences or runtime state. These values may be stored in the registry, INI files, XML files, or some other place, according to platform convention. If your native client application needs local storage beyond key/value pairs, you can embed your own database, invent your own file format, or implement any number of other solutions.

Historically, web applications have had none of these luxuries. Cookies were invented early in the Web's history, and indeed they can be used for persistent local storage of small amounts of data. But they have several potentially dealbreaking downsides:

- Cookies are included with every HTTP request, thereby slowing down your web application by needlessly transmitting the same data over and over.
- Cookies are included with every HTTP request, thereby sending data unencrypted over the Internet (unless your entire web application is served over SSL).
- Cookies are limited to about 4 KB of data—enough to slow down your application (see above), but not enough to be terribly useful.

What we really want is:

- A lot of storage space...
- on the client...
- that persists beyond a page refresh...
- and isn't transmitted to the server.

There have been a number of attempts to achieve this, all ultimately unsatisfactory in different ways.

A Brief History of Local Storage Hacks Before HTML5

In the beginning, there was only Internet Explorer. Or at least, that's what Microsoft wanted the world to think. To that end, during the first of the Great Browser Wars, Microsoft invented a great many things and included them in its browser-to-end-all-browser-wars, Internet Explorer. One of these things was called DHTML Behaviors, and one of these behaviors was called userData.

userData allows web pages to store up to 64 KB of data per domain, in a hierarchical XML-based structure. (Trusted domains, such as intranet sites, can store 10 times that amount. And hey, 640 KB ought to be enough for anybody!) IE does not present any form of permissions dialog, and there is no allowance for increasing the amount of storage available.

In 2002, Adobe introduced a feature in Flash 6 that gained the unfortunate and misleading name of "Flash cookies." Within the Flash environment, the feature is properly known as Local Shared Objects, or LSOs. Briefly, it allows Flash objects to store up to 100 KB of data per domain. In 2005 Brad Neuberg developed an early prototype of a Flash-to-JavaScript bridge called the AJAX Massive Storage System, or AMASS, but it was limited by some of Flash's design quirks. By 2006, with the advent of ExternalInterface in Flash 8, accessing LSOs from JavaScript became an order of magnitude easier and faster. Brad rewrote AMASS and integrated it into the popular Dojo Toolkit under the moniker dojox.storage. With this solution, each domain is given the usual 100 KB of storage "for free." Beyond that, it prompts the user for each order of magnitude increase in data storage (1 MB, 10 MB, and so on).

Then, in 2007, Google launched Gears, an open source browser plug-in aimed at providing additional capabilities in browsers. (We've previously discussed Gears in the context of providing a geolocation API in Internet Explorer (see "What About IE?" on page 123). Gears provides an API to an embedded SQL database based on SQLite. After obtaining permission from the user once, Gears can store unlimited amounts of data per domain in SQL database tables.

In the meantime, Brad Neuberg and others continued to hack away on dojox.storage to provide a unified interface to all these different plug-ins and APIs. By 2009, dojox.storage could autodetect (and provide a unified interface on top of) Adobe Flash, Gears, Adobe AIR, and an early prototype of HTML5 Storage that was only implemented in older versions of Firefox.

As you survey these solutions, a pattern emerges: all of them are either specific to a single browser, or reliant on a third-party plug-in. Despite heroic efforts to paper over the differences (in dojox.storage), they all expose radically different interfaces, have different storage limitations, and present different user experiences. So this is the problem that HTML5 set out to solve: to provide a standardized API, implemented natively and consistently in multiple browsers, without having to rely on third-party plug-ins.

Introducing HTML5 Storage

What I refer to as "HTML5 Storage" is actually a specification named Web Storage. This was at one time part of the HTML5 specification proper, but was split out into its own specification for uninteresting political reasons. Certain browser vendors also refer to it as "Local Storage" or "DOM Storage." The naming situation is made even more complicated by some related, similarly named, emerging standards that I'll discuss later in this chapter.

So what is HTML5 Storage? Simply put, it's a way for web pages to store named key/value pairs locally, within the client web browser. Like the data stored in cookies, this data persists even after you navigate away from the website, close your browser tab, exit your browser, or what have you. But unlike with cookies, this data is never transmitted to the remote web server (unless you go out of your way to send it manually). And unlike all previous attempts at providing persistent local storage (described in the preceding section), it is implemented natively in web browsers, so it is available even when third-party browser plug-ins are not.

Which browsers? As Table 7-1 shows, HTML5 is supported by the latest versions of pretty much all browsers...even Internet Explorer!

Table 7-1. HTML5 Storage support

IE	Firefox	Safari	Chrome	Opera	iPhone	Android
8.0+	3.5+	4.0+	4.0+	10.5+	2.0+	2.0+

From your JavaScript code, you'll access HTML5 Storage through the `localStorage` object on the global `window` object. Before you can use it, you should detect whether the browser supports it (see "Local Storage" on page 21):

```
function supports_html5_storage() {
  return ('localStorage' in window) && window['localStorage'] !== null;
}
```

Or, instead of writing this function yourself, you can use Modernizr (see "Modernizr: An HTML5 Detection Library" on page 16) to detect support for HTML5 Storage:

```
if (Modernizr.localstorage) {
  // window.localStorage is available!
} else {
  // no native support for HTML5 Storage :(
  // maybe try dojox.storage or a third-party solution
}
```

Using HTML5 Storage

HTML5 Storage is based on named key/value pairs. You store data based on a named key, and then you can retrieve that data with the same key:

```
interface Storage {
  getter any getItem(in DOMString key);
  setter creator void setItem(in DOMString key, in any data);
};
```

The named key is a string. The data can be any type supported by JavaScript, including strings, Booleans, integers, or floats. However, the data is actually stored as a string. If you are storing and retrieving anything other than strings, you will need to use functions like parseInt() or parseFloat() to coerce your retrieved data into the expected Java-Script datatype.

Calling setItem() with a named key that already exists will silently overwrite the previous value. Calling getItem() with a nonexistent key will return null rather than throwing an exception.

Like other JavaScript objects, you can treat the localStorage object as an associative array. Instead of using the getItem() and setItem() methods, you can simply use square brackets. For example, this snippet of code:

```
var foo = localStorage.getItem("bar");
// ...
localStorage.setItem("bar", foo);
```

could be rewritten to use square-bracket syntax instead:

```
var foo = localStorage["bar"];
// ...
localStorage["bar"] = foo;
```

There are also methods for removing the value for a given named key and clearing the entire storage area (that is, deleting all the keys and values at once):

```
interface Storage {
  deleter void removeItem(in DOMString key);
  void clear();
};
```

Calling removeItem() with a nonexistent key will do nothing.

Finally, there is a property to get the total number of values in the storage area, and to iterate through all of the keys by index (to get the name of each key):

```
interface Storage {
  readonly attribute unsigned long length;
  getter DOMString key(in unsigned long index);
};
```

If you call key() with an index that is not between 0 and (length–1), the function will return null.

Tracking Changes to the HTML5 Storage Area

If you want to keep track programmatically of when the storage area changes, you can trap the storage event. The storage event is fired on the window object whenever setItem(), removeItem(), or clear() is called *and actually changes something.* For example, if you set an item to its existing value or call clear() when there are no named keys, the storage event will not fire because nothing actually changed in the storage area.

The storage event is supported everywhere the localStorage object is supported, which includes Internet Explorer 8. IE 8 does not support the W3C standard addEventListener (although that will finally be added in IE 9). Therefore, to hook the storage event, you'll need to check which event mechanism the browser supports. (If you've done this before with other events, you can skip to the end of this section. Trapping the storage event works the same way as trapping any other event. If you prefer to use jQuery or some other JavaScript library to register your event handlers, you can do that with the storage event, too.) Here's how:

```
if (window.addEventListener) {
  window.addEventListener("storage", handle_storage, false);
} else {
  window.attachEvent("onstorage", handle_storage);
};
```

The handle_storage() callback function will be called with a StorageEvent object, except in Internet Explorer, where the event object is stored in window.event:

```
function handle_storage(e) {
  if (!e) { e = window.event; }
}
```

At this point, the variable e will be a StorageEvent object, which has the useful properties listed in Table 7-2.

Table 7-2. StorageEvent object properties

Property	Type	Description
key	String	The named key that was added, removed, or modified
oldValue	Any	The previous value (now overwritten), or null if a new item was added
newValue	Any	The new value, or null if an item was removed
url[a]	String	The page that called the method that triggered this change

[a] The url property was originally called uri. Some browsers shipped with that property before the specification changed. For maximum compatibility, you should check whether the url property exists and, if not, check for the uri property instead.

The storage event is not cancelable. From within the handle_storage() callback function, there is no way to stop the change from occurring. It's simply a way for the browser to tell you, "Hey, this just happened. There's nothing you can do about it now; I just wanted to let you know."

Limitations in Current Browsers

In talking about the history of local storage hacks using third-party plug-ins (see "A Brief History of Local Storage Hacks Before HTML5" on page 128), I made a point of mentioning the limitations of each technique, such as storage limits. However, I haven't mentioned anything about the limitations of the now-standardized HTML5 Storage.

By default, each origin gets 5 MB of storage space. This is surprisingly consistent across browsers, although it is phrased as no more than a suggestion in the HTML5 Storage specification. One thing to keep in mind is that you're storing strings, not data in its original format. If you're storing a lot of integers or floats, the difference in representation can really add up: each digit in that float is being stored as a character, not in the usual representation of a floating-point number.

If you exceed your storage quota, a `QUOTA_EXCEEDED_ERR` exception will be thrown. "No" is the answer to the next obvious question, "Can I ask the user for more storage space?" At the time of writing, no browser supports any mechanism for web developers to request more storage space. Some browsers, such as Opera, allow the user to control each site's storage quota, but it is purely a user-initiated action, not something that you as a web developer can build into your web application.

HTML5 Storage in Action

Let's look at an example of HTML5 Storage in action. Think back to the Halma game we constructed in Chapter 4 (see "A Complete Example" on page 75). There's a small problem with the game: if you close the browser window mid-game, you'll lose your progress. But with HTML5 Storage, we can save the progress locally, within the browser itself. You can see a live demonstration at *http://diveintohtml5.org/examples/localstorage-halma.html*. Make a few moves, close the browser tab, and then reopen it. If your browser supports HTML5 Storage, the demonstration page should magically remember your exact position within the game, including the number of moves you've made, the positions of each of the pieces on the board, and even whether a particular piece is selected.

How does it work? Every time a change occurs within the game, we call this function:

```
function saveGameState() {
    if (!supportsLocalStorage()) { return false; }
    localStorage["halma.game.in.progress"] = gGameInProgress;
    for (var i = 0; i < kNumPieces; i++) {
      localStorage["halma.piece." + i + ".row"] = gPieces[i].row;
      localStorage["halma.piece." + i + ".column"] = gPieces[i].column;
    }
    localStorage["halma.selectedpiece"] = gSelectedPieceIndex;
    localStorage["halma.selectedpiecehasmoved"] gSelectedPieceHasMoved;
    localStorage["halma.movecount"] = gMoveCount;
    return true;
}
```

As you can see, it uses the `localStorage` object to save whether there is a game in progress (`gGameInProgress`, a Boolean). If so, it iterates through the pieces (`gPieces`, a JavaScript `Array`) and saves the row and column number of each piece. Then it saves some additional game state, including which piece is selected (`gSelectedPieceIndex`, an integer), whether the piece is in the middle of a potentially long series of hops (`gSelectedPieceHasMoved`, a Boolean), and the total number of moves made so far (`gMoveCount`, an integer).

On page load, instead of automatically calling a `newGame()` function that would reset these variables to hardcoded values, we call a `resumeGame()` function. Using HTML5 Storage, the `resumeGame()` function checks whether any state about a game in progress is stored locally. If so, it restores those values using the `localStorage` object:

```
function resumeGame() {
    if (!supportsLocalStorage()) { return false; }
    gGameInProgress = (localStorage["halma.game.in.progress"] == "true");
    if (!gGameInProgress) { return false; }
    gPieces = new Array(kNumPieces);
    for (var i = 0; i < kNumPieces; i++) {
      var row = parseInt(localStorage["halma.piece." + i + ".row"]);
      var column = parseInt(localStorage["halma.piece." + i + ".column"]);
      gPieces[i] = new Cell(row, column);
    }
    gNumPieces = kNumPieces;
    gSelectedPieceIndex = parseInt(localStorage["halma.selectedpiece"]);
    gSelectedPieceHasMoved = localStorage["halma.selectedpiecehasmoved"] == "true";
    gMoveCount = parseInt(localStorage["halma.movecount"]);
    drawBoard();
    return true;
}
```

The most important part of this function is the caveat that I mentioned earlier in this chapter, which I'll repeat here: *Data is stored as strings. If you are storing something other than a string, you'll need to coerce it yourself when you retrieve it.* For example, the flag for whether there is a game in progress (`gGameInProgress`) is a Boolean. In the `saveGameState()` function, we just stored it and didn't worry about the datatype:

```
localStorage["halma.game.in.progress"] = gGameInProgress;
```

But in the `resumeGame()` function, we need to treat the value we got from the local storage area as a string and manually construct the proper Boolean value ourselves:

```
gGameInProgress = (localStorage["halma.game.in.progress"] == "true");
```

Similarly, the number of moves is stored in `gMoveCount` as an integer. In the `saveGameState()` function, we just stored it:

```
localStorage["halma.movecount"] = gMoveCount;
```

But in the `resumeGame()` function, we need to coerce the value to an integer, using the `parseInt()` function built into JavaScript:

```
gMoveCount = parseInt(localStorage["halma.movecount"]);
```

Beyond Named Key/Value Pairs: Competing Visions

While the past is littered with hacks and workarounds (see "A Brief History of Local Storage Hacks Before HTML5" on page 128), the present condition of HTML5 Storage is surprisingly rosy. A new API has been standardized and implemented across all major browsers, platforms, and devices. As a web developer, that's just not something you see every day, is it? But there is more to life than 5 MB of named key/value pairs, and the future of persistent local storage is…how shall I put it? Well, there are a number of competing visions.

One vision is an acronym that you probably know already: SQL. In 2007, Google launched Gears, an open source cross-browser plug-in that included an embedded database based on SQLite. This early prototype later influenced the creation of the Web SQL Database specification. Web SQL Database (formerly known as "WebDB") provides a thin wrapper around a SQL database, allowing you to do things like this from JavaScript:

```
openDatabase('documents', '1.0', 'Local document storage', 5*1024*1024,
function (db) {
  db.changeVersion('', '1.0', function (t) {
    t.executeSql('CREATE TABLE docids (id, name)');
  }, error);
});
```

As you can see, most of the action resides in the string you pass to the `executeSql()` method. This string can be any supported SQL statement, including `SELECT`, `UPDATE`, `INSERT`, and `DELETE`. It's just like backend database programming, except you're doing it from JavaScript! Oh joy!

Table 7-3 shows which browsers have implemented the Web SQL Database specification.

Table 7-3. Web SQL Database support

IE	Firefox	Safari	Chrome	Opera	iPhone	Android
·	·	4.0+	4.0+	10.5+	3.0+	·

Of course, if you've used more than one database product in your life, you are aware that "SQL" is more of a marketing term than a hard-and-fast standard. (Some would say the same of "HTML5," but never mind that.) Sure, there is an actual SQL specification—it's called SQL-92—but there is no database server in the world that conforms to that and only that specification. There's Oracle's SQL, Microsoft's SQL, MySQL's SQL, PostgreSQL's SQL, and SQLite's SQL. And each of these products adds new SQL features over time, so even saying "SQLite's SQL" is not sufficient to pin down exactly what you're talking about—you need to say "the version of SQL that shipped with SQLite Version X.Y.Z."

All of which brings us to the following disclaimer, currently residing at the top of the Web SQL Database specification:

> This specification has reached an impasse: all interested implementors have used the same SQL backend (Sqlite), but we need multiple independent implementations to proceed along a standardisation path. Until another implementor is interested in implementing this spec, the description of the SQL dialect has been left as simply a reference to Sqlite, which isn't acceptable for a standard.

It is against this backdrop that I will introduce you to another competing vision for advanced, persistent, local storage for web applications: the Indexed Database API, formerly known as "WebSimpleDB," now affectionately known as "IndexedDB."

The Indexed Database API exposes what's called an *object store*. An object store shares many concepts with a SQL database. There are "databases" with "records," and each record has a set number of "fields." Each field has a specific datatype, which is defined when the database is created. You can select a subset of records, then enumerate them with a "cursor." Changes to the object store are handled within "transactions."

If you've done any SQL database programming, these terms probably sound familiar. The primary difference is that the object store has no structured query language. You don't construct a statement like `SELECT * from USERS where ACTIVE = 'Y'`. Instead, you use methods provided by the object store to open a cursor on the database named `USERS`, enumerate through the records, filter out records for inactive users, and use accessor methods to get the values of each field in the remaining records. The early walk-through of IndexedDB (*http://hacks.mozilla.org/2010/06/comparing-indexeddb-and-webdatabase/*) is a good tutorial on how IndexedDB works, giving side-by-side comparisons of IndexedDB and Web SQL Database.

At the time of writing, IndexedDB hasn't been implemented in any major browser. In early June 2010, Mozilla said that it would "have some test builds in the next few weeks", but there is no word yet on whether it will even ship in Firefox 4. (By contrast, Mozilla has stated that it will never implement Web SQL Database.) Google has stated that it is considering IndexedDB support, and even Microsoft has said that IndexedDB "is a great solution for the Web".

So what can you, as a web developer, do with IndexedDB? At the moment, absolutely nothing. A year from now? Maybe something. Check the "Further Reading" section for links to some good tutorials to get you started.

Further Reading

HTML5 Storage:

- HTML5 Storage specification (*http://dev.w3.org/html5/webstorage/*)
- "Introduction to DOM Storage" (*http://msdn.microsoft.com/en-us/library/cc197062(VS.85).aspx*) on MSDN

- "Web Storage: easier, more powerful client-side data storage" (*http://dev.opera*
.com/articles/view/web-storage/), by Shwetank Dixit
- "Introduction to DOM Storage" (*https://developer.mozilla.org/en/dom/storage*) on
the Mozilla Developer Center. (Note: most of this page is devoted to Firefox's
prototype implementation of a `globalStorage` object, a nonstandard precursor to
`localStorage`. Mozilla added support for the standard `localStorage` interface in
Firefox 3.5.)
- "Unlock local storage for mobile Web applications with HTML 5" (*http://www*
.ibm.com/developerworks/xml/library/x-html5mobile2/), a tutorial on IBM
DeveloperWorks

Early work by Brad Neuberg et al. (pre-HTML5):

- "Internet Explorer Has Native Support for Persistence?!?!" (*http://codinginparadise*
.org/weblog/2005/08/ajax-internet-explorer-has-native.html), about the `userData`
object in IE
- Dojo Storage (*http://docs.google.com/View?docid=dhkhksk4_8gdp9gr#dojo_stor*
age), part of a larger tutorial about the (now-defunct) Dojo Offline library
- `dojox.storage.manager` API reference (*http://api.dojotoolkit.org/jsdoc/HEAD/dojox*
.storage.manager)
- `dojox.storage` Subversion repository (*http://svn.dojotoolkit.org/src/dojox/trunk/*
storage/)

Web SQL Database:

- Web SQL Database specification (*http://dev.w3.org/html5/webdatabase/*)
- "Introducing Web SQL Databases" (*http://html5doctor.com/introducing-web-sql*
-databases/), by Remy Sharp
- Web Database demonstration (*http://html5demos.com/database*)
- *persistence.js* (*http://zef.me/2774/persistence-js-an-asynchronous-javascript-orm*
-for-html5gears), an "asynchronous JavaScript ORM" built on top of Web SQL
Database and Gears

IndexedDB:

- Indexed Database API specification (*http://dev.w3.org/2006/webapi/IndexedDB/*)
- "Beyond HTML5: Database APIs and the Road to IndexedDB" (*http://hacks.mo*
zilla.org/2010/06/beyond-html5-database-apis-and-the-road-to-indexeddb/), by
Arun Ranganathan and Shawn Wilsher
- "Firefox 4: An early walk-through of IndexedDB" (*http://hacks.mozilla.org/2010/*
06/comparing-indexeddb-and-webdatabase/), by Arun Ranganathan

## CHAPTER 8

Let's Take This Offline

Diving In

What is an offline web application? At first glance, it sounds like a contradiction in terms. Web pages are things you download and render. Downloading implies a network connection. How can you download when you're offline? Of course, you can't. But you *can* download when you're online. And that's how HTML5 offline applications work.

At its simplest, an offline web application is just a list of URLs pointing to HTML, CSS, or JavaScript files, images, or any other kinds of resources that may be present. The home page of the offline web application points to this list, called a *manifest file*, which is just a text file located elsewhere on the web server. A web browser that implements HTML5 offline applications will read the list of URLs from the manifest file, download the resources, cache them locally, and automatically keep the local copies up to date as they change. When you try to access the web application without a network connection, your web browser will automatically switch over to the local copies instead.

From there, most of the work is up to you, as the web developer. There's a flag in the DOM that will tell you whether you're online or offline, and there are events that fire when your status changes (one minute you're offline and the next minute you're online, or vice versa). But that's pretty much it. If your application creates data or saves state, it's up to you to store that data locally (see Chapter 7) while you're offline and synchronize it with the remote server once you're back online. In other words, HTML5 can take your web application offline, but what you do once you're there is up to you. Table 8-1 shows which browsers support offline web applications.

Table 8-1. Offline support

IE	Firefox	Safari	Chrome	Opera	iPhone	Android
·	✓	✓	✓	·	✓	✓

The Cache Manifest

An offline web application revolves around a cache manifest file. As I've already mentioned, the manifest file is a list of all of the resources that your web application might need to access while it's disconnected from the network. In order to bootstrap the process of downloading and caching these resources, you need to point to the manifest file, using the `manifest` attribute on your `<html>` element:

```
<!DOCTYPE HTML>
<html manifest="/cache.manifest">
<body>
...
</body>
</html>
```

Your cache manifest file can be located anywhere on your web server, but it must be served with the content type `text/cache-manifest`. If you are running an Apache-based web server, you can probably just put an `AddType` directive in the *.htaccess* file at the root of your web directory:

```
AddType text/cache-manifest .manifest
```

Then make sure that the name of your cache manifest file ends with *.manifest*. If you use a different web server or a different configuration of Apache, consult your server's documentation on controlling the `Content-Type` header.

Ask Professor Markup

Q: *My web application spans several pages. Do I need a* `manifest` *attribute in each page, or can I just put it in the home page?*

A: Every page of your web application needs a `manifest` attribute that points to the cache manifest for the entire application.

OK, so every one of your HTML pages points to your cache manifest file, and your cache manifest file is being served with the proper `Content-Type` header. But what goes *in* the manifest file? This is where things get interesting.

The first line of every cache manifest file is this:

```
CACHE MANIFEST
```

After that, all manifest files are divided into three parts: the "explicit" section, the "fallback" section, and the "online whitelist" section. Each section has a header, on its own line. If the manifest file doesn't have any section headers, all the listed resources are implicitly in the "explicit" section. Try not to dwell on the terminology, lest your head explode.

Here is a valid manifest file. It lists three resources—a CSS file, a JavaScript file, and a JPEG image:

```
CACHE MANIFEST
/clock.css
/clock.js
/clock-face.jpg
```

This cache manifest file has no section headers, so all the listed resources are in the "explicit" section by default. Resources in the "explicit" section will get downloaded and cached locally and will be used in place of their online counterparts whenever you are disconnected from the network. Thus, upon loading this cache manifest file, your browser will download *clock.css*, *clock.js*, and *clock-face.jpg* from the root directory of your web server. You can then unplug your network cable and refresh the page, and all of those resources will be available offline.

Ask Professor Markup

Q: *Do I need to list my HTML pages in my cache manifest?*

A: Yes and no. If your entire web application is contained in a single page, just make sure that page points to the cache manifest using the `manifest` attribute. When you navigate to an HTML page with a `manifest` attribute, the page itself is assumed to be part of the web application, so you don't need to list it in the manifest file itself. However, if your web application spans multiple pages, you should list all of the HTML pages in the manifest file; otherwise, the browser will not know that there are other HTML pages that need to be downloaded and cached.

Network Sections

Here is a slightly more complicated example. Suppose you want your clock application to track visitors, using a *tracking.cgi* script that is loaded dynamically from an <img src> attribute. Caching this resource would defeat the purpose of tracking, so this resource should never be cached and never be available offline. Here is how you do that:

```
CACHE MANIFEST
NETWORK:
/tracking.cgi
CACHE:
/clock.css
/clock.js
/clock-face.jpg
```

This cache manifest file includes *section headers*. The line marked `NETWORK:` is the beginning of the "online whitelist" section. Resources in this section are never cached and are not available offline. (Attempting to load them while offline will result in an error.) The line marked `CACHE:` is the beginning of the "explicit" section. The rest of the cache manifest file is the same as the previous example. Each of the three resources listed will be cached and available offline.

Fallback Sections

There is one more type of section in a cache manifest file: a *fallback section*. In a fallback section, you can define substitutions for online resources that, for whatever reason, can't be cached or weren't cached successfully. The HTML5 specification offers this clever example of using a fallback section:

```
CACHE MANIFEST
FALLBACK:
/ /offline.html
NETWORK:
*
```

What does this do? First, consider a site that contains millions of pages, like Wikipe dia. You couldn't possibly download the entire site, nor would you want to. But suppose you could make *part* of it available offline. How would you decide which pages to cache? How about this: every page you ever looked at on a hypothetical offline-enabled Wikipedia would be downloaded and cached. That would include every encyclopedia entry that you ever visited, every talk page (where you can have makeshift discussions about a particular encyclopedia entry), and every edit page (where you can actually make changes to that particular entry).

That's what this cache manifest does. Suppose every HTML page on Wikipedia (entry, talk page, edit page, history page) pointed to this cache manifest file. When you visit any page that points to a cache manifest, your browser says, "Hey, this page is part of an offline web application, is it one I know about?" If your browser hasn't ever downloaded this particular cache manifest file, it will set up a new offline "appcache" (short for "application cache"), download all the resources listed in the cache manifest, and then add the current page to the appcache. If your browser does know about this cache manifest, it will simply add the current page to the existing appcache. Either way, the page you just visited ends up in the appcache. This is important. It means that you can have an offline web application that "lazily" adds pages as you visit them. You don't need to list every single one of your HTML pages in your cache manifest.

Now look at the fallback section. The fallback section in this cache manifest contains only one line. The first part of the line (before the space) is not a URL. It's really a URL *pattern*. The single character (/) will match any page on your site, not just the home page. When you try to visit a page while you're offline, your browser will look for it in the appcache. If your browser finds the page in the appcache (because you visited it while online, and the page was implicitly added to the appcache at that time), it will display the cached copy of the page. If your browser doesn't find the page in the appcache, instead of displaying an error message, it will display the page */offline.html*, as specified in the second half of the line in the fallback section.

Finally, let's examine the network section. The network section in this cache manifest also has just a single line, which contains just a single character (*). This character has special meaning in a network section. It's called the "online whitelist wildcard flag." That's a fancy way of saying that anything that isn't in the appcache can still be downloaded from the original web address, as long as you have an Internet connection. This is important for an "open-ended" offline web application. Continuing with our example, it means that while you're browsing this hypothetical offline-enabled Wikipedia *online*, your browser will fetch images and videos and other embedded resources normally, even if they are in a different domain. (This is very common in large websites, even if they aren't part of an offline web application: HTML pages are generated and served locally, while images and videos are served from a CDN on another domain.) Without this wildcard flag, our hypothetical offline-enabled Wikipedia would behave strangely when you were online—specifically, it wouldn't load any externally hosted images or videos!

Is this example complete? No. Wikipedia is more than just HTML files; it uses common CSS, JavaScript, and images on each page. Each of these resources would need to be listed explicitly in the `CACHE:` section of the manifest file in order for pages to display and behave properly offline. But the point of the fallback section is that you can have an "open-ended" offline web application that extends beyond the resources you've listed explicitly in the manifest file.

The Flow of Events

So far, I've talked about offline web applications, the cache manifest, and the offline application cache ("appcache") in vague, semimagical terms. Things are downloaded, browsers make decisions, and everything "Just Works." You know better than that, right? I mean, this is web development we're talking about. Nothing ever "Just Works."

First, let's talk about the flow of events, specifically DOM events. When your browser visits a page that points to a cache manifest, it fires off a series of events on the `window.applicationCache` object, as I describe below. I know this looks complicated, but trust me, this is the simplest version I could come up with that didn't leave out important information. Here's the process:

1. As soon as it notices a `manifest` attribute on the `<html>` element, your browser fires a `checking` event. (All the events listed here are fired on the `window.applicationC ache` object.) The `checking` event is always fired, regardless of whether you have previously visited this page or any other page that points to the same cache manifest.

2. If your browser has never seen this cache manifest before:
   - It will fire a *downloading* event, then start to download the resources listed in the cache manifest.
   - While it's downloading, your browser will periodically fire `progress` events, which contain information on how many files have been downloaded already and how many files are still queued to be downloaded.
   - After all resources listed in the cache manifest have been downloaded successfully, the browser fires one final event, `cached`. This is your signal that the offline

web application is fully cached and ready to be used offline. That's it; you're done.

3. On the other hand, if you have previously visited this page or any other page that points to the same cache manifest, your browser already knows about this cache manifest and may already have some resources in the appcache. In fact, it may have the entire working offline web application in the appcache. So now the question is, has the cache manifest changed since the last time your browser checked it?

   - If the answer is no, the cache manifest has not changed. In this case, your browser will immediately fire a noupdate event. That's it; you're done.

   - If the answer is yes, the cache manifest *has* changed. In this case, your browser will fire a downloading event and start redownloading every single resource listed in the cache manifest.

   While it's downloading, your browser will periodically fire progress events, which contain information on how many files have been downloaded already and how many files are still queued to be downloaded.

   After all resources listed in the cache manifest have been redownloaded successfully, the browser will fire one final event, updateready. This is your signal that the new version of your offline web application is fully cached and ready to be used offline. *The new version is not yet in use.* To "hot-swap" to the new version without forcing the user to reload the page, you can manually call the window.applicationC ache.swapCache() function.

If, at any point in this process, something goes horribly wrong, your browser will fire an error event and stop. Here is a hopelessly abbreviated list of things that could go wrong:

- The cache manifest returned an HTTP 404 (Page Not Found) or 410 (Permanently Gone) error.

- The cache manifest was found and hadn't changed, but the HTML page that pointed to the manifest failed to download properly.

- The cache manifest was found and had changed, but the browser failed to download one of the resources listed in the cache manifest.

The Fine Art of Debugging, a.k.a. "Kill Me! Kill Me Now!"

I want to call out two important points here. The first is something you just read, but probably didn't really sink in, so here it is again: *if even a single resource listed in your cache manifest file fails to download properly, the entire process of caching your offline web application will fail.* Your browser will fire the error event, but there will be no indication of what the actual problem was. This can make debugging offline web applications extremely frustrating.

The second important point is something that is not, technically speaking, an error, but it will look like a serious browser bug until you realize what's going on. It has to do with exactly how your browser checks whether a cache manifest file has changed. This is a three-phase process. This is boring but important, so pay attention. Here's the procedure:

1. Via normal HTTP semantics, your browser will check whether the cache manifest has expired. Just like with any other file being served over HTTP, your web server will typically include metainformation about the file in the HTTP response headers. Some of these HTTP headers (`Expires` and `Cache-Control`) tell your browser how it is allowed to cache the file without ever asking the server whether it has changed. This kind of caching has nothing to do with offline web applications. It happens for pretty much every HTML page, stylesheet, script, image, or other resource on the Web.

2. If the cache manifest has expired (according to its HTTP headers), your browser will ask the server whether there is a new version and, if so, will download it. To do this, your browser issues an HTTP request that includes the last-modified date of the cache manifest file, which your web server included in the HTTP response headers the last time your browser downloaded the file. If the web server determines that the manifest file hasn't changed since that date, it will simply return a 304 (Not Modified) status code. Again, none of this is specific to offline web applications. It happens for virtually all resources on the Web.

3. If the web server thinks the manifest file has changed since that date, it will return an HTTP 200 (OK) status code, followed by the contents of the new file along with new `Cache-Control` headers and a new last-modified date. This ensures that steps 1 and 2 will work properly the next time. (HTTP is cool; web servers are always planning for the future. If your web server absolutely must send you a file, it does everything it can to ensure that it doesn't need to send it twice for no reason.) Once it's downloaded the new cache manifest file, your browser will check the contents against the copy it downloaded last time. If the contents of the cache manifest file are the same as they were last time, your browser won't redownload any of the resources listed in the manifest.

Any one of these steps can trip you up while you're developing and testing your offline web application. For example, say you deploy one version of your cache manifest file, then 10 minutes later, you realize you need to add another resource to it. No problem, right? Just add another line and redeploy. Bzzt. Here's what will happen: you reload the page, your browser notices the `manifest` attribute, it fires the `checking` event, and then...nothing. Your browser stubbornly insists that the cache manifest file has not changed. Why? Because, by default, your web server is probably configured to tell browsers to cache static files for a few hours (via HTTP semantics, using `Cache-Control` headers). That means your browser will never get past step 1 of that three-phase process. Sure, the web server knows that the file has changed, but your browser never even gets around to asking the web server. Why? Because the last time your browser downloaded the cache manifest, the web server told it to cache the resource for a few hours (via HTTP semantics, using `Cache-Control` headers). And now, 10 minutes later, that's exactly what your browser is doing.

To be clear, this is not a bug, it's a feature. Everything is working exactly the way it's supposed to. If web servers didn't have a way to tell browsers (and intermediate proxies) to cache things, the Web would collapse overnight. But that's no comfort after you've spent a few hours trying to figure out why your browser won't notice your updated cache manifest. (And even better, if you wait long enough, it will mysteriously start working again! Because the HTTP cache expired! Just like it's supposed to! Kill me! Kill me now!)

So here's one thing you should absolutely do: reconfigure your web server so that your cache manifest file is not cacheable by HTTP semantics. If you're running an Apache-based web server, these two lines in your *.htaccess* file will do the trick:

```
ExpiresActive On
ExpiresDefault "access"
```

This will actually disable caching for every file in that directory and all subdirectories. That's probably not what you want in production, so you should either qualify this with a `<Files>` directive so it affects only your cache manifest file, or create a subdirectory that contains nothing but this *.htaccess* file and your cache manifest file. As usual, configuration details vary by web server, so consult your server's documentation for how to control HTTP caching headers.

Disabling HTTP caching on the cache manifest file itself won't solve all your problems, though. You'll still have times when you've changed one of the resources in the appcache, but it's still at the same URL on your web server. Here, step 2 of the three-phase process will screw you. If your cache manifest file hasn't changed, the browser will never notice that one of the previously cached resources has changed. Consider the following example:

```
CACHE MANIFEST
# rev 42
clock.js
clock.css
```

If you change *clock.css* and redeploy it, you won't see the changes, because the cache manifest file itself hasn't changed. Every time you make a change to one of the resources in your offline web application, you'll need to change the cache manifest file itself. This can be as simple as changing a single character. The easiest way I've found to accomplish this is to include a comment line with a revision number in the manifest file. Any time you change one of the resources, change the revision number in the comment. The web server will return the newly changed cache manifest file, your browser will notice that the contents of the file have changed, and it will kick off the process to redownload all the resources listed in the manifest:

```
CACHE MANIFEST
# rev 43
```

```
clock.js
clock.css
```

Let's Build One!

Remember the Halma game that we introduced in Chapter 4 (see "A Complete Example" on page 75) and later improved by saving state with persistent local storage (see "HTML5 Storage in Action" on page 132)? Let's take our Halma game offline.

To do that, we need a manifest that lists all the resources the game needs. Well, there's the main HTML page, a single JavaScript file that contains all the game code, and...that's it. There are no images, because all the drawing is done programmatically via the canvas API (see Chapter 4), and all the necessary CSS styles are in a `<style>` element at the top of the HTML page. So, this is our cache manifest:

```
CACHE MANIFEST
halma.html
../halma-localstorage.js
```

A word about paths. I've created an *offline/* subdirectory in the *examples/* directory, and this cache manifest file lives inside the subdirectory. Because the HTML page will need one minor addition to work offline (more on that in a minute), I've created a separate copy of the HTML file, which also lives in the *offline/* subdirectory. But because there are no changes to the JavaScript code itself since we added local storage support (see "HTML5 Storage in Action" on page 132), I'm literally reusing the same *.js* file, which lives in the parent directory (*examples/*). Altogether, the files look like this:

```
/examples/localstorage-halma.html
/examples/halma-localstorage.js
/examples/offline/halma.manifest
/examples/offline/halma.html
```

In the cache manifest file (*/examples/offline/halma.manifest*), we want to reference two files. First is the offline version of the HTML file (*/examples/offline/halma.html*), which is listed in the manifest file without any path prefix because the two files are in the same directory. Second is the JavaScript file, which lives in the parent directory (*/examples/halma-localstorage.js*) and is listed in the manifest file using relative URL notation: *../halma-localstorage.js*. This is just like how you might use a relative URL in an `<img src>` attribute. As you'll see in the next example, you can also use absolute paths (that start at the root of the current domain) or even absolute URLs (that point to resources in other domains).

Now, in the HTML file, we need to add the `manifest` attribute that points to the cache manifest file:

```
<!DOCTYPE html>
<html lang="en" manifest="halma.manifest">
```

And that's it! When an offline-capable browser first loads the offline-enabled HTML page, it will download the linked cache manifest file and start downloading all the referenced resources and storing them in the offline application cache. From then on, the offline application algorithm will take over whenever you revisit the page. You can play the game offline, and since it remembers its state locally, you can leave and come back as often as you like.

Further Reading

Standards:

- Offline web applications in the HTML5 specification (*http://bit.ly/cCkWZa*)

Browser vendor documentation:

- "Offline resources in Firefox" (*https://developer.mozilla.org/En/Offline_resources _in_Firefox*) on the Mozilla Developer Center
- "HTML5 Offline Application Cache" (*http://developer.apple.com/safari/library/ documentation/iPhone/Conceptual/SafariJSDatabaseGuide/OfflineApplicationC ache/OfflineApplicationCache.html*), part of the "Safari Client-Side Storage and Offline Applications Programming Guide" (*http://developer.apple.com/safari/li brary/documentation/iPhone/Conceptual/SafariJSDatabaseGuide/Introduction/In troduction.html*)

Tutorials and demos:

- "Gmail for Mobile HTML5 Series: Using Appcache to Launch Offline - part 1" (*http://googlecode.blogspot.com/2009/04/gmail-for-mobile-html5-series-using .html*), by Andrew Grieve
- "Gmail for Mobile HTML5 Series: Using Appcache to Launch Offline - part 2" (*http://googlecode.blogspot.com/2009/05/gmail-for-mobile-html5-series-part-2 .html*), by Andrew Grieve
- "Gmail for Mobile HTML5 Series: Using Appcache to Launch Offline - part 3" (*http://googlecode.blogspot.com/2009/05/gmail-for-mobile-html5-series-part-3 .html*), by Andrew Grieve
- "Debugging HTML 5 Offline Application Cache" (*http://jonathanstark.com/blog/ 2009/09/27/debugging-html-5-offline-application-cache/*), by Jonathan Stark
- "An HTML5 offline image editor and uploader application" (*http://hacks.mozilla .org/2010/02/an-html5-offline-image-editor-and-uploader-application/*), by Paul Rouget

## CHAPTER 9

A Form of Madness

Diving In

Everybody knows about web forms, right? Make a `<form>`, add a few `<input type="text">` elements and maybe an `<input type="password">`, finish it off with an `<input type="submit">` button, and you're done.

You don't know the half of it. HTML5 defines over a dozen new input types that you can use in your forms. And when I say "use," I mean you can use them right now—without any shims, hacks, or workarounds. Now don't get too excited; I don't mean to say that all of these exciting new features are actually supported in every browser. Oh goodness no, I don't mean that at all. In modern browsers, yes, your forms will kick all kinds of ass. In legacy browsers, your forms will still work, but with less ass kicking. Which is to say, all of these features degrade gracefully in every browser. Even IE 6.

Placeholder Text

The first improvement HTML5 brings to web forms is the ability to set placeholder text in an input field. Placeholder text is displayed inside the input field as long as the field is empty and not focused. As soon as you click on (or tab to) the input field, the placeholder text disappears.

You've probably seen placeholder text before. For example, Mozilla Firefox 3.5 now includes placeholder text in the location bar that reads "Search Bookmarks and History", as shown in Figure 9-1.

Figure 9-1. Placeholder text in Firefox's search box

When you click on (or tab to) the location bar, the placeholder text disappears (Figure 9-2).

Figure 9-2. Placeholder text disappears on focus

Ironically, Firefox 3.5 does not support adding placeholder text to your own web forms. C'est la vie. Browser support for placeholders is shown in Table 9-1.

Table 9-1. Placeholder support

IE	Firefox	Safari	Chrome	Opera	iPhone	Android
•	3.7+	4.0+	4.0+	•	•	•

Here's how you can include placeholder text in your own web forms:

```
<form>
  <input name="q" placeholder="Search Bookmarks and History">
  <input type="submit" value="Search">
</form>
```

Browsers that don't support the `placeholder` attribute will simply ignore it. No harm, no foul.

Ask Professor Markup

Q: Can I use HTML markup in the `placeholder` attribute? I want to insert an image, or maybe change the colors.

A: The `placeholder` attribute can only contain text, not HTML markup. However, there are some vendor-specific CSS extensions (*http://trac.webkit.org/export/37527/trunk/ LayoutTests/fast/forms/placeholder-pseudo-style.html*) that allow you to style the placeholder text in some browsers.

Autofocus Fields

Many websites use JavaScript to focus the first input field of a web form automatically. For example, the home page of Google.com will autofocus the input box so you can type your search keywords without having to position the cursor in the search box. While this is convenient for most people, it can be annoying for power users or people with special needs. If you press the space bar expecting to scroll the page, the page will not scroll because the focus is already in a form input field. Instead, you'll type a space in the field. If you focus a different input field while the page is still loading, the site's autofocus script may "helpfully" move the focus back to the original input field upon completion, disrupting your flow and causing you to type in the wrong place.

Because the autofocusing is done with JavaScript, it can be tricky to handle all of these edge cases, and there is little recourse for people who don't want a web page to "steal" the focus.

To solve this problem, HTML5 introduces an autofocus attribute on all web form controls. The autofocus attribute does exactly what it says on the tin: as soon as the page loads, it moves the input focus to a particular input field. But because it's just markup instead of script, the behavior will be consistent across all websites. Also, browser vendors (or extension authors) can offer users a way to disable the autofocusing behavior. Table 9-2 shows which browsers support autofocus.

Table 9-2. Autofocus support

IE	Firefox	Safari	Chrome	Opera	iPhone	Android
·	·	4.0+	3.0+	10.0+	✓	✓

Here's how you can set a form field to autofocus:

```
<form>
  <input name="q" autofocus>
  <input type="submit" value="Search">
</form>
```

Browsers that don't support the autofocus attribute will simply ignore it.

What's that? You say you want your autofocus fields to work in all browsers, not just these fancy-pants HTML5 browsers? You can keep your current autofocus script. Just make two small changes:

1. Add the autofocus attribute to your HTML markup.
2. Detect whether the browser supports the autofocus attribute (see "Form Autofocus" on page 27), and run your own autofocus script only if the browser doesn't support autofocus natively:

```
<form name="f">
  <input id="q" autofocus>
  <script>
    if (!("autofocus" in document.createElement("input"))) {
      document.getElementById("q").focus();
    }
  </script>
  <input type="submit" value="Go">
</form>
...
```

Go to *http://diveintohtml5.org/examples/input-autofocus-with-fallback.html* to see an example of autofocus with fallback.

Email Addresses

For over a decade, web forms comprised just a few kinds of fields—the most common are listed in Table 9-3.

Table 9-3. Input types in HTML 4

Field type	HTML code	Notes
Checkbox	`<input type="checkbox">`	Can be toggled on or off
Radio button	`<input type="radio">`	Can be grouped with other inputs
Password field	`<input type="password">`	Echoes dots instead of characters as the user types
Drop-down list	`<select><option>...`	
File picker	`<input type="file">`	Pops up an "open file" dialog
Submit button	`<input type="submit">`	
Plain text	`<input type="text">`	The type attribute can be omitted

All of these input types still work in HTML5. If you're "upgrading to HTML5" (perhaps by changing your doctype; see "The Doctype" on page 31), you don't need to make a single change to your web forms. Hooray for backward compatibility!

However, HTML5 defines several new field types, and for reasons that will become clear in a moment, there is no reason *not* to start using them.

The first of these new input types is for email addresses. It looks like this:

```
<form>
  <input type="email">
  <input type="submit" value="Go">
</form>
```

I was about to write a sentence that started with "In browsers that don't support `type="email"`...," but I stopped myself. Why? Because I'm not sure what it would mean to say that a browser doesn't support `type="email"`. All browsers "support" `type="email"`. They may not do anything special with it (you'll see a few examples of special treatment in a moment), but browsers that don't recognize `type="email"` will treat it as `type="text"` and render it as a plain text field.

I cannot emphasize enough how important this is. The Web has millions of forms that ask you to enter an email address, and all of them use `<input type="text">`. You see a text box, you type your email address in the text box, and that's that. Then along comes HTML5, which defines `type="email"`. Do browsers freak out? No. Every single browser on Earth treats an unknown `type` attribute as `type="text"`—even IE 6. So you can "upgrade" your web forms to use `type="email"` right now.

What would it mean to say that a browser *does* support `type="email"`? Well, it can mean any number of things. The HTML5 specification doesn't mandate any particular user interface for the new input types. Opera styles the form field with a small email icon. Other HTML5 browsers, like Safari and Chrome, simply render it as a text box— exactly like `type="text"`—so your users will never know the difference (unless they view the page source).

And then there's the iPhone.

The iPhone does not have a physical keyboard. All "typing" is done by tapping on an onscreen keyboard that pops up at appropriate times, like when you focus a form field in a web page. Apple did something very clever in the iPhone's web browser: it recognizes several of the new HTML5 input types, and *dynamically changes the onscreen keyboard* to optimize for that kind of input.

For example, email addresses are text, right? Sure, but they're a special kind of text. That is, virtually all email addresses contain the @ sign and at least one period (`.`), but they're unlikely to contain any spaces. So when an iPhone user focuses on an `<input type="email">` element, she gets an onscreen keyboard that contains a smaller-than-usual space bar, plus dedicated keys for the @ and `.` characters, as shown in Figure 9-3.

To sum up: there's no downside to converting all your email address form fields to `type="email"` immediately. Virtually no one will even notice, except iPhone users, who probably won't notice either. But the ones who do notice will smile quietly and thank you for making their web experience just a little easier.

Web Addresses

Web addresses—known to many as URLs, and to a few pedants as URIs—are another type of specialized text. The syntax of a web address is constrained by the relevant Internet standards. If someone asks you to enter a web address into a form, he'll be expecting something like `http://www.google.com`, not "125 Farwood Road." Forward slashes and periods are common, but spaces are forbidden. And every web address has a domain suffix like ".com" or ".org".

Behold...(drum roll please)...`<input type="url">`. On the iPhone, it looks like Figure 9-4.

Figure 9-3. Keyboard optimized for entering an email address

Figure 9-4. Keyboard optimized for entering a URL

Just as it does for email address fields, the iPhone provides a special virtual keyboard that's optimized for web addresses. The space bar has been completely replaced with three virtual keys: a period, a forward slash, and a ".com" button. You can long-press the ".com" button to choose other common suffixes, like ".org" or ".net".

Browsers that don't support HTML5 will treat `type="url"` exactly like `type="text"`, so there's no downside to using it for all your web address–inputting needs.

Numbers As Spinboxes

Next up: numbers. Asking for a number is, in many ways, trickier than asking for an email or web address. First of all, numbers are more complicated than you might think. Quick: pick a number. −1? No, I meant a number between 1 and 10. 7½? No, no, not a fraction, silly. π? Now you're just being irrational.

My point is, you don't often ask for "just a number." It's more likely that you'll ask for a number in a particular range, and you may only want certain kinds of numbers within that range—maybe whole numbers but not fractions or decimals, or something more esoteric like numbers divisible by 10. HTML5 has you covered. Let's look at an example:

```
<input type="number"
       min="0"
       max="10"
       step="2"
       value="6">
```

Let's take that one attribute at a time (you can follow along with a live example if you like):

- `type="number"` means that this is a number field.
- `min="0"` specifies the minimum acceptable value for this field.
- `max="10"` is the maximum acceptable value.
- `step="2"`, combined with the `min` value, defines the acceptable numbers in the range: 0, 2, 4, and so on, up to the `max` value.
- `value="6"` is the default value. This should look familiar. It's the same attribute name you've always used to specify values for form fields. (I mention it here to drive home the point that HTML5 builds on previous versions of HTML. You don't need to relearn how to do stuff you're already doing.)

That's the markup side of a number field. Keep in mind that all of those attributes are optional. If you have a minimum but no maximum, you can specify a `min` attribute but no `max` attribute. The default step value is 1, and you can omit the `step` attribute unless you need a different step value. If there's no default value, the `value` attribute can be an empty string or even omitted altogether.

But HTML5 doesn't stop there. For the same low, low price of free, you get these handy JavaScript methods as well:

`input.stepUp(n)`
    Increases the field's value by *n*

`input.stepDown(n)`
    Decreases the field's value by *n*

`input.valueAsNumber`
    Returns the current value as a floating-point number (the `input.value` property is always a string)

Having trouble visualizing it? Well, the exact interface of a number control is up to your browser, and different browser vendors have implemented support in different ways. On the iPhone, where input is difficult to begin with, the browser once again optimizes the virtual keyboard for numeric input as shown in Figure 9-5.

Figure 9-5. Keyboard optimized for entering a number

In the desktop version of Opera, the same `type="number"` field is rendered as a "spinbox" control, with little up and down arrows that you can click to change the value (Figure 9-6).

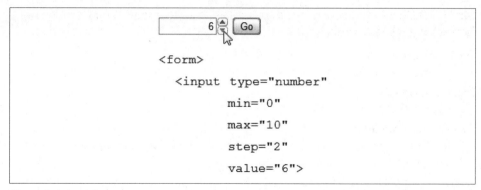

Figure 9-6. A spinbox

Opera respects the `min`, `max`, and `step` attributes, so you'll always end up with an acceptable numeric value. If you bump up the value to the maximum, the up arrow in the spinbox is grayed out (Figure 9-7).

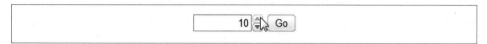

Figure 9-7. A spinbox at its maximum value

As with all the other input types I've discussed in this chapter, browsers that don't support `type="number"` will treat it as `type="text"`. The default value will show up in the field (since it's stored in the `value` attribute), but the other attributes, like `min` and `max`, will be ignored. You're free to implement them yourself, or you can reuse one of the many JavaScript frameworks that have already implemented spinbox controls. Just check for the native HTML5 support (see "Input Types" on page 25) first, like this:

```
if (!Modernizr.inputtypes.number) {
  // no native support for type="number" fields
  // maybe try Dojo or some other JavaScript framework
}
```

Numbers As Sliders

Spinboxes, discussed in the preceding section, are not the only way to represent numeric input. You've probably also seen "slider" controls that look like Figure 9-8.

Figure 9-8. A slider

You can now have slider controls in your web forms, too. The markup looks eerily similar to that for spinbox controls:

```
<input type="range"
       min="0"
       max="10"
       step="2"
       value="6">
```

The available attributes are the same as those for `type="number"`—`min`, `max`, `step`, `value`—and they mean the same thing. The only difference is the user interface. Instead of a field for typing, browsers are expected to render `type="range"` as a slider control. At the time of writing, the latest versions of Safari, Chrome, and Opera all do this. (Sadly, the iPhone renders it as a simple text box. It doesn't even optimize its onscreen keyboard for numeric input.) All other browsers simply treat the field as `type="text"`, so there's no reason you can't start using `type="range"` immediately.

Date Pickers

HTML 4 did not include a date picker control. Various JavaScript frameworks have picked up the slack—for example, Dojo, jQuery UI, YUI, and Closure Library—but of course each of these solutions requires "buying into" the framework on which the date picker is built.

HTML5 finally defines a way to include a native date picker control without having to script it yourself. In fact, it defines six: date, month, week, time, date + time, and date + time − timezone.

So far, as Table 9-4 illustrates, support is…sparse.

Table 9-4. Date picker support

Input type	Opera	Every other browser
`type="date"`	9.0+	•
`type="month"`	9.0+	•
`type="week"`	9.0+	•
`type="time"`	9.0+	•
`type="datetime"`	9.0+	•
`type="datetime-local"`	9.0+	•

Figure 9-9 shows how Opera renders an `<input type="date">`.

If you need a time to go with that date, Opera also supports `<input type="date time">`, as shown in Figure 9-10.

If you only need a month and year (perhaps a credit card expiration date), Opera can render an `<input type="month">`, as shown in Figure 9-11.

Figure 9-9. A date picker

Figure 9-10. A date/time picker

Figure 9-11. A month picker

Less common, but also available, is the ability to pick a specific week of a year with `<input type="week">`; see Figure 9-12.

Last but not least, you can pick a time with `<input type="time">`, as shown in Figure 9-13.

Figure 9-12. A week picker

Figure 9-13. A time picker

It's likely that other browsers will eventually support these input types. In the meantime, just like type="email" (see "Email Addresses" on page 150) and the other input types, these form fields will be rendered as plain text boxes in browsers that don't recognize type="date" and the other variants. If you like, you can simply use <input type="date"> and friends, make Opera users happy, and wait for other browsers to catch up. Alternatively, you can use <input type="date">, detect whether the browser has native support for date pickers (see "Input Types" on page 25), and fall back to a scripted solution of your choice:

```
<form>
  <input type="date">
</form>
...
<script>
  var i = document.createElement("input");
  i.setAttribute("type", "date");
  if (i.type == "text") {
    // No native date picker support :(
    // Use Dojo/jQueryUI/YUI/Closure/some other solution to create one,
    // then dynamically replace that <input> element.
  }
</script>
```

Search Boxes

OK, this one is subtle. Well, the idea is simple enough, but the implementations may require some explanation. Here goes....

Search. Not just Google Search or Yahoo! Search. (Well, those too.) Think of any search box, on any page, on any site. Amazon has a search box. Newegg has a search box. Most blogs have a search box. How are they marked up? `<input type="text">`, just like every other text box on the Web. With HTML5, we can fix that:

```
<form>
  <input name="q" type="search">
  <input type="submit" value="Find">
</form>
```

In some browsers, you won't notice any difference from a regular text box. But if you're using Safari on Mac OS X, it will look like Figure 9-14.

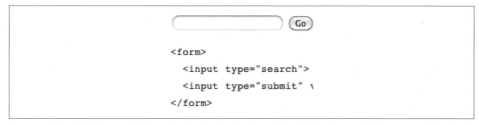

Figure 9-14. A search box

Can you spot the difference? The input box has rounded corners! I know, I know, you can hardly contain your excitement. But wait, there's more! When you actually start typing in the `type="search"` box, Safari inserts a small "x" button on the right side of the box. Clicking the "x" clears the contents of the field. (Google Chrome, which shares much technology with Safari under the hood, also exhibits this behavior.) Both of these small tweaks are done to match the look and feel of native search boxes in iTunes and other Mac OS X client applications (Figure 9-15).

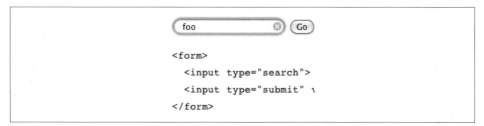

Figure 9-15. A focused search box

The Apple website uses `<input type="search">` for its site-search box, to help give the site a "Mac-like" feel. But there's nothing Mac-specific about it. It's just markup, so each browser on each platform can choose to render the search box according to platform-specific conventions. As with all the other new input types, browsers that don't recognize `type="search"` will treat it like `type="text"`, so there is absolutely no reason not to start using `type="search"` for all your search boxes today.

Color Pickers

HTML5 also defines `<input type="color">`, which lets you pick a color and returns that color's hexadecimal representation. No browser supports it yet, which is a shame, because I've always loved the Mac OS color picker. Maybe someday.

And One More Thing...

In this chapter, I've talked about new input types and new features like autofocus form fields, but I haven't mentioned what is perhaps the most exciting part of HTML5 forms: automatic input validation. Consider the common problem of entering an email address into a web form. You probably have some client-side validation in JavaScript, followed by server-side validation in PHP or Python or some other server-side scripting language. There are two big problems with validating email addresses in JavaScript:

- A surprising number of your visitors (probably around 10 percent) won't have JavaScript enabled.
- You'll get it wrong.

Seriously, you'll get it wrong. Determining whether a random string of characters is a valid email address is unbelievably complicated (*http://www.regular-expressions.info/email.html*). The harder you look, the more complicated it gets (*http://www.ex-parrot.com/pdw/Mail-RFC822-Address.html*). Did I mention it's really, really complicated (*http://haacked.com/archive/2007/08/21/i-knew-how-to-validate-an-email-address-until-i.aspx*)? Wouldn't it be easier to offload the entire headache to your browser?

The screenshot in Figure 9-16 is from Opera 10, although the functionality has been present since Opera 9. The only markup involved is setting the `type` attribute to `"email"` (see "Email Addresses" on page 150). When an Opera user tries to submit a form with an `<input type="email">` field, Opera automatically offers RFC-compliant email validation, even if scripting is disabled.

Opera also offers validation of web addresses entered into `<input type="url">` fields and numbers in `<input type="number">` fields. The validation of numbers even takes into account the `min` and `max` attributes, so Opera will not let users submit the form if they enter a number that is too large (Figure 9-17).

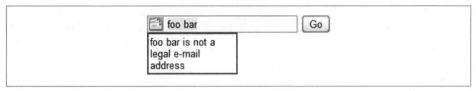

Figure 9-16. Opera validates type="email"

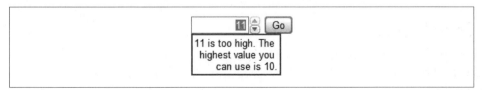

Figure 9-17. Opera validates type="number"

Unfortunately, no other browser supports automatic HTML5 form validation yet, so you're going to be stuck with script-based fallbacks for a little while.

Further Reading

Specifications and standards:

- `<input>` types (*http://bit.ly/akweH4*)
- The `<input placeholder>` attribute (*http://bit.ly/caGl8N*)
- The `<input autofocus>` attribute (*http://bit.ly/db1Fj4*)

JavaScript libraries:

- Modernizr (*http://www.modernizr.com*), an HTML5 detection library

## CHAPTER 10

"Distributed," "Extensibility," and Other Fancy Words

Diving In

There are over 100 elements (*http://simon.html5.org/html5-elements*) in HTML5. Some are purely semantic (see Chapter 3), and others are just containers for scripted APIs (see Chapter 4). Throughout the history of HTML (see Chapter 1), standards wonks have argued about which elements should be included in the language. Should HTML include a `<figure>` element? A `<person>` element? How about a `<rant>` element? Decisions are made, specs are written, authors author, implementors implement, and the Web lurches ever forward.

Of course, HTML can't please everyone. No standard can. Some ideas don't make the cut. For example, there is no `<person>` element in HTML5. (There's no `<rant>` element either, damn it!) There's nothing stopping you from including a `<person>` element in a web page, but it won't validate, it won't work consistently across browsers (see "A Long Digression into How Browsers Handle Unknown Elements" on page 42), and it might conflict with future HTML specs if it's added later.

So if making up your own elements isn't the answer, what's a semantically inclined web author to do? There have been attempts to extend previous versions of HTML. The most popular method is with microformats (*http://microformats.org*), which use the `class` and `rel` attributes in HTML 4. Another option is RDFa (*http://www.w3.org/TR/rdfa-syntax/*), which was originally designed to be used in XHTML (see "Postscript" on page 14) but is now being ported to HTML as well.

Both microformats and RDFa have their strengths and weaknesses. They take radically different approaches toward the same goal: extending web pages with additional semantics that are not part of the core HTML language. I don't intend to turn this chapter into a format flamewar. (That would definitely require a `<rant>` element!) Instead, I want to focus on a third option that is part of, and tightly integrated into, HTML5 itself: microdata.

What Is Microdata?

Each word in the following sentence is important, so pay attention.

Professor Markup Says

Microdata annotates the DOM with scoped name/value pairs from custom vocabularies.

Now what does that mean? Let's start from the end and work backward. Microdata centers around *custom vocabularies*. Think of "the set of all HTML5 elements" as one vocabulary. This vocabulary includes elements to represent a section or an article (see "New Semantic Elements in HTML5" on page 41), but it doesn't include elements to represent a person or an event. If you want to represent a person on a web page, you'll need to define your own vocabulary. Microdata lets you do this. Anyone can define a microdata vocabulary and start embedding custom properties in his own web pages.

The next thing to know about microdata is that it works with *name/value pairs*. Every microdata vocabulary defines a set of named properties. For example, a Person vocabulary could define properties like `name` and `photo`. To include a specific microdata property on your web page, you provide the property name in a specific place. Depending on where you declare the property name, microdata has rules about how to extract the property value. (More on this in the next section.)

Along with named properties, microdata relies heavily on the concept of "scoping." The simplest way to think of microdata scoping is to think about the natural parent-child relationship of elements in the DOM. The `<html>` element (see "The Root Element" on page 33) usually contains two children, `<head>` (see "The `<head>` Element" on page 34) and `<body>`. The `<body>` element usually contains multiple children, each of which may have child elements of its own. For example, your page might include an `<h1>` element within an `<hgroup>` element within a `<header>` element (see "Headers" on page 45) within the `<body>` element. Similarly, a data table might contain `<td>` elements within `<tr>` elements within a `<table>` element (within the `<body>`). Microdata reuses the hierarchical structure of the DOM itself to provide a way to say "all the properties within *this* element are taken from *this* vocabulary." This allows you to use several microdata vocabularies on the same page. You can even nest microdata vocabularies within other vocabularies, all by reusing the natural structure of the DOM. (I'll show multiple examples of nested vocabularies throughout this chapter.)

I've already touched on the DOM, but let me elaborate on that. Microdata is about applying additional semantics to *data that's already visible on your web page*. Microdata is not designed to be a standalone data format. It's a complement to HTML. As you'll see in the next section, microdata works best when you're already using HTML correctly, but the HTML vocabulary isn't quite expressive enough. Microdata is great for fine-tuning the semantics of data that's already in the DOM. If the data you're

---

semantifying isn't in the DOM, you should step back and reevaluate whether microdata is the right solution.

Does Professor Markup's statement make more sense now? I hope so. Let's see how this works in action.

The Microdata Data Model

Defining your own microdata vocabulary is easy. First you need a namespace, which is just a URL. The namespace URL can point to a working web page, although that's not strictly required. Let's say I want to create a microdata vocabulary that describes a person. If I own the *data-vocabulary.org* domain, I'll use the URL *http://data-vocabulary.org/Person* as the namespace for my microdata vocabulary. That's an easy way to create a globally unique identifier: pick a URL on a domain that you control.

In this vocabulary, I need to define some named properties. Let's start with three basic properties:

- `name` (the user's full name)
- `photo` (a link to a picture of the user)
- `url` (a link to a site associated with the user, like a blog or a Google profile)

Two of these properties are URLs, and the other is plain text. Each of them lends itself to a natural form of markup, even before you start thinking about microdata or vocabularies. Imagine that you have a profile page or an "about" page. Your name is probably marked up as a heading, like an `<h1>` element. Your photo is probably an `<img>` element, since you want people to see it. And any URLs associated with your profile are probably already marked up as hyperlinks, because you want people to be able to click them. For the sake of discussion, let's say your entire profile is also wrapped in a `<section>` element to separate it from the rest of the page content. Thus:

```
<section>
  <h1>Mark Pilgrim</h1>
  <p><img src="http://www.example.com/photo.jpg" alt="[me smiling]"></p>
  <p><a href="http://diveintomark.org/">weblog</a></p>
</section>
```

Microdata's data model is name/value pairs. A microdata property name (like `name` or `photo` or `url` in this example) is always declared on an HTML element. The corresponding property value is then taken from the element's DOM. For most HTML elements, the property value is simply the text content of the element. However, there are a handful of exceptions, as Table 10-1 illustrates.

Table 10-1. Where do microdata property values come from?

Element	Value
`<meta>`	content attribute
`<audio>`	src attribute
`<embed>`	
`<iframe>`	
`<img>`	
`<source>`	
`<video>`	
`<a>`	href attribute
`<area>`	
`<link>`	
`<object>`	data attribute
`<time>`	datetime attribute
All other elements	Text content

"Adding microdata" to your page is a matter of adding a few attributes to the HTML elements you already have. The first thing you always do is declare which microdata vocabulary you're using, by adding an `itemtype` attribute. The second thing you always do is declare the scope of the vocabulary, using an `itemscope` attribute. In this example, all the data we want to semantify is in a `<section>` element, so we'll declare the `itemtype` and `itemscope` attributes on the `<section>` element:

```
<section itemscope itemtype="http://data-vocabulary.org/Person">
```

Your name is the first bit of data within the `<section>` element. It's wrapped in an `<h1>` element. The `<h1>` element doesn't require any special processing, so it falls under the "all other elements" rule in Table 10-1, where the microdata property value is simply the text content of an element (this would work equally well if your name was wrapped in a `<p>`, `<div>`, or `<span>` element):

```
<h1 itemprop="name">Mark Pilgrim</h1>
```

In English, this says: "Here is the `name` property of the http://data-vocabulary.org/Person vocabulary. The value of the property is `Mark Pilgrim`."

Next up is the `photo` property. This is supposed to be a URL. According to Table 10-1, the "value" of an `<img>` element is its `src` attribute. Hey look, the URL of your profile photo is already in an `<img src>` attribute! All you need to do is declare that the `<img>` element is the `photo` property:

```
<p><img itemprop="photo"
        src="http://www.example.com/photo.jpg"
        alt="[me smiling]"></p>
```

In English, this says: "Here is the photo property of the http://data-vocabulary.org/ Person vocabulary. The value of the property is http://www.example.com/photo.jpg."

Finally, the url property is also a URL. According to Table 10-1, the "value" of an <a> element is its href attribute. And once again, this fits perfectly with your existing markup. All you need to do is say that your existing <a> element is the url property:

```
<a itemprop="url" href="http://diveintomark.org/">dive into mark</a>
```

In English, this says: "Here is the url property of the http://data-vocabulary.org/ Person vocabulary. The value of the property is http://diveintomark.org/."

Of course, if your markup looks a little different, that's not a problem. You can add microdata properties and values to any HTML markup, even really gnarly 20th century era, tables-for-layout, oh-God-why-did-I-agree-to-maintain-this markup. While I don't recommend this kind of markup, it is still very common, and you can still add microdata to it:

```
<TABLE>
  <TR><TD>Name<TD>Mark Pilgrim
  <TR><TD>Link<TD>
    <A href=# onclick=goExternalLink()>http://diveintomark.org/</A>
</TABLE>
```

To mark up the name property, just add an itemprop attribute on the table cell that contains the name. Table cells have no special rules in the microdata property value table, so they get the default value, where the microdata property is the text content:

```
<TR><TD>Name<TD itemprop="name">Mark Pilgrim
```

Adding the url property looks trickier. This markup doesn't use the <a> element properly. Instead of putting the link target in the href attribute, it has nothing useful in the href attribute and it uses JavaScript in the onclick attribute to call a function (not shown) that extracts the URL and navigates to it. For extra "oh crap, please stop doing that" bonus points, let's pretend that the function also opens the link in a tiny pop-up window with no scroll bars. Wasn't the Internet fun last century?

Anyway, you can still convert this into a microdata property; you just need to be a little creative. Using the <a> element directly is out of the question. The link target isn't in the href attribute, and there's no way to override the rule that says "in an <a> element, look for the microdata property value in the href attribute." But you *can* add a wrapper element around the entire mess, and use that to add the url microdata property:

```
<TABLE itemscope itemtype="http://data-vocabulary.org/Person">
  <TR><TD>Name<TD>Mark Pilgrim
  <TR><TD>Link<TD>
    <span itemprop="url">
      <A href=# onclick=goExternalLink()>http://diveintomark.org/</A>
    </span>
</TABLE>
```

Because the `<span>` element has no special processing, it uses the default rule, "the microdata property is the text content." "Text content" doesn't mean "all the markup inside this element" (like you would get with, say, the `innerHTML` DOM property). It means "just the text, ma'am." In this case, `http://diveintomark.org/` is the text content of the `<a>` element inside the `<span>` element.

To sum up: you can add microdata properties to any markup. You'll find it easier to add microdata if you're using HTML correctly than if your HTML markup sucks, but it can always be done.

Marking Up People

The starter examples in the previous section weren't completely made up. There really is a microdata vocabulary for marking up information about people, and it really is that easy. Let's take a closer look.

The easiest way to integrate microdata into a personal website is on your "about" page. You *do* have an "about" page, don't you? If not, you can follow along as I extend this sample "about" page (*http://diveintohtml5.org/examples/person.html*) with additional semantics. The final result is here: *http://diveintohtml5.org/examples/person-plus-micro data.html*.

Let's look at the raw markup first, before any microdata properties have been added:

```
<section>
  <img width="204" height="250"
      src="http://diveintohtml5.org/examples/2000_05_mark.jpg"
      alt="[Mark Pilgrim, circa 2000]">

  <h1>Contact Information</h1>
  <dl>
    <dt>Name</dt>
    <dd>Mark Pilgrim</dd>

    <dt>Position</dt>
    <dd>Developer advocate for Google, Inc.</dd>

    <dt>Mailing address</dt>
    <dd>
      100 Main Street<br>
      Anytown, PA 19999<br>
      USA
    </dd>
  </dl>
  <h1>My Digital Footprints</h1>
```

```
<ul>
  <li><a href="http://diveintomark.org/">weblog</a></li>
  <li><a href="http://www.google.com/profiles/pilgrim">Google profile</a></li>
  <li><a href="http://www.reddit.com/user/MarkPilgrim">Reddit.com profile</a></li>
  <li><a href="http://www.twitter.com/diveintomark">Twitter</a></li>
</ul>
</section>
```

The first thing you always need to do is declare the vocabulary you're using and the scope of the properties you want to add. You do this by adding the `itemtype` and `itemscope` attributes on the outermost element that contains the other elements that contain the actual data. In this case, that's a `<section>` element:

```
<section itemscope itemtype="http://data-vocabulary.org/Person">
```

 You can follow along online with the changes made throughout this section. Before: *http://diveintohtml5.org/examples/person.html*; after: *http://diveintohtml5.org/examples/person-plus-microdata.html*.

Now you can start defining microdata properties from the `http://data-vocabulary.org/Person` vocabulary. But what are those properties? As it happens, you can see the list of properties by navigating to *http://data-vocabulary.org/Person*. The microdata specification does not require this, but I'd say it's certainly a "best practice." After all, if you want developers to actually *use* your microdata vocabulary, you need to document it. And where better to put your documentation than the vocabulary URL itself? Table 10-2 lists the properties of the Person vocabulary.

Table 10-2. Person vocabulary

Property	Description
name	Name
nickname	Nickname
photo	An image link
title	The person's title (for example, "Financial Manager")
role	The person's role (for example, "Accountant")
url	Link to a web page, such as the person's home page
affiliation	The name of an organization with which the person is associated (for example, an employer)
friend	Identifies a social relationship between the person described and another person
contact	Identifies a social relationship between the person described and another person
acquaintance	Identifies a social relationship between the person described and another person
address	The location of the person (can have the subproperties `street-address`, `locality`, `region`, `postal-code`, and `country-name`)

The first thing in this sample "about" page is a picture of me. Naturally, it's marked up with an `<img>` element. To declare that this `<img>` element is my profile picture, all we need to do is add `itemprop="photo"` to it:

```
<img itemprop="photo" width="204" height="250"
    src="http://diveintohtml5.org/examples/2000_05_mark.jpg"
    alt="[Mark Pilgrim, circa 2000]">
```

Where's the microdata property value? It's already there, in the `src` attribute. If you recall from Table 10-1, the "value" of an `<img>` element is its `src` attribute. Every `<img>` element has a `src` attribute—otherwise it would just be a broken image—and the `src` is always a URL. See? If you're using HTML correctly, microdata is easy.

Furthermore, this `<img>` element isn't alone on the page. It's a child element of the `<section>` element, the one we just declared with the `itemscope` attribute. Microdata reuses the parent-child relationships of elements on the page to define the scoping of microdata properties. In plain English, we're saying: "This `<section>` element represents a person. Any microdata properties you might find on the children of the `<section>` element are properties of that person." If it helps, you can think of the `<section>` element as the subject of a sentence. The `itemprop` attribute represents the verb of the sentence—something like "is pictured at"—and the microdata property value represents the object of the sentence:

This person [explicit, from `<section itemscope itemtype="...">`]

is pictured at [explicit, from `<img itemprop="photo">`]

`http://diveintohtml5.org/examples/2000_05_mark.jpg` [implicit, from `<img src>` attribute]

The subject only needs to be defined once, by putting `itemscope` and `itemtype` attributes on the outermost `<section>` element. The verb is defined by putting the `itemprop="photo"` attribute on the `<img>` element. The object of the sentence doesn't need any special markup at all, because Table 10-1 says that the property value of an `<img>` element is its `src` attribute.

Moving on to the next bit of markup, we see an `<h1>` header and the beginnings of a `<dl>` list. Neither the `<h1>` nor the `<dl>` needs to be marked up with microdata. Not every piece of HTML needs to be a microdata property. Microdata is about the properties themselves, not the markup or headers surrounding the properties. This `<h1>` isn't a property; it's just a header. Similarly, the `<dt>` that says "Name" is just a label, not a property:

```
<h1>Contact Information</h1>
  <dl>
    <dt>Name</dt>
    <dd>Mark Pilgrim</dd>
```

So where is the real information? It's in the `<dd>` element, so that's where we need to put the `itemprop` attribute. Which property is it? It's the `name` property. Where is the property value? It's the text within the `<dd>` element. Does that need to be marked up?

Table 10-1 says no, `<dd>` elements have no special processing, so the property value is just the text within the element:

```
<dd itemprop="name">Mark Pilgrim</dd>
```

What did we just say, in English? "This person's name is Mark Pilgrim." Well OK then. Onward.

The next two properties are a little tricky. This is the markup, pre-microdata:

```
<dt>Position</dt>
<dd>Developer advocate for Google, Inc.</dd>
```

If you look at the definition of the Person vocabulary, the text "Developer advocate for Google, Inc." actually encompasses *two* properties: `title` ("Developer advocate") and `affiliation` ("Google, Inc."). How can you express that in microdata? The short answer is, you can't. Microdata doesn't have a way to break up runs of text into separate properties. You can't say "the first 18 characters of this text are one microdata property, and the last 12 characters of this text are another microdata property."

But all is not lost. Imagine that you wanted to style the text "Developer advocate" in a different font from the text "Google, Inc." CSS can't do that either. So what would you do? You would first need to wrap the different bits of text in dummy elements, like `<span>`, then apply different CSS rules to each `<span>` element.

This technique is also useful for microdata. There are two distinct pieces of information here: a `title` and an `affiliation`. If you wrap each piece in a dummy `<span>` element, you can declare that each `<span>` is a separate microdata property:

```
<dt>Position</dt>
<dd><span itemprop="title">Developer advocate</span> for
    <span itemprop="affiliation">Google, Inc.<span></dd>
```

Ta-da! In English, this says: "This person's title is 'Developer advocate.' This person is employed by Google, Inc." Two sentences, two microdata properties. A little more markup, but a worthwhile tradeoff.

The same technique is useful for marking up street addresses. The Person vocabulary defines an `address` property, which itself is a microdata item. That means the address has its own vocabulary (*http://data-vocabulary.org/Address*) and defines its own properties: `street-address`, `locality`, `region`, `postal-code`, and `country-name`.

If you're a programmer, you are probably familiar with dot notation to define objects and their properties. Think of the relationship like this:

- `Person`
- `Person.address`
- `Person.address.street-address`
- `Person.address.locality`
- `Person.address.region`

- `Person.address.postal-code`
- `Person.address.country-name`

In this example, the entire street address is contained in a single `<dd>` element. (Once again, the `<dt>` element is just a label, so it plays no role in adding semantics with microdata.) Notating the `address` property is easy. Just add an `itemprop` attribute on the `<dd>` element:

```
<dt>Mailing address</dt>
<dd itemprop="address">
```

But remember, the `address` property is itself a microdata item. That means we need to add the `itemscope` and `itemtype` attributes too:

```
<dt>Mailing address</dt>
<dd itemprop="address" itemscope
    itemtype="http://data-vocabulary.org/Address">
```

We've seen all of this before, but only for top-level items. A `<section>` element defines `itemtype` and `itemscope`, and all the elements within the `<section>` element that define microdata properties are "scoped" within that specific vocabulary. But this is the first time we've seen *nested* scopes—defining a new `itemtype` and `itemscope` (on the `<dd>` element) within an existing one (on the `<section>` element). This nested scope works exactly like the HTML DOM. The `<dd>` element has a certain number of child elements, all of which are scoped to the vocabulary defined on the `<dd>` element. Once the `<dd>` element is closed with a corresponding `</dd>` tag, the scope reverts to the vocabulary defined by the parent element (`<section>`, in this case).

The properties of the Address vocabulary suffer the same problem we encountered with the `title` and `affiliation` properties. There's just one long run of text, but we want to break it up into several separate microdata properties. The solution is the same. We wrap each distinct piece of information in a dummy `<span>` element, then declare microdata properties on each `<span>` element:

```
<dd itemprop="address" itemscope
    itemtype="http://data-vocabulary.org/Address">
  <span itemprop="street-address">100 Main Street</span><br>
  <span itemprop="locality">Anytown</span>,
  <span itemprop="region">PA</span>
  <span itemprop="postal-code">19999</span>
  <span itemprop="country-name">USA</span>
</dd>
</dl>
```

In English: "This person has a mailing address. The street address part of the mailing address is '100 Main Street.' The locality part is 'Anytown.' The region is 'PA.' The postal code is '19999.' The country name is 'USA.'" Easy peasy.

Ask Professor Markup

Q: Is this mailing address format U.S.-specific?

A: No. The properties of the Address vocabulary are generic enough that they can describe most mailing addresses in the world. Not all addresses will have values for every property, but that's OK. Some addresses might require fitting more than one "line" into a single property, but that's OK too. For example, if your mailing address has a street address and a suite number, they would both go into the `street-address` subproperty:

```
<p itemprop="address" itemscope
    itemtype="http://data-vocabulary.org/Address">
  <span itemprop="street-address">
    100 Main Street
    Suite 415
  </span>
  ...
</p>
```

There's one more thing on this sample "about" page: a list of URLs. The Person vocabulary has a property for this, called `url`. A `url` property can be anything, really. (Well, it has to be a URL, but you probably guessed that.) What I mean is that the definition of the `url` property is very loose. The property can be any sort of URL that you want to associate with a Person: a blog, a photo gallery, or a profile on another site like Facebook or Twitter.

The other important thing to note here is that a single Person can have multiple `url` properties. Technically, any property can appear more than once, but until now, we haven't taken advantage of that. For example, you could have two `photo` properties, each pointing to a different image URL. Here, I want to list four different URLs: my weblog, my Google profile page, my user profile on Reddit, and my Twitter account. In HTML, that's a list of links: four `<a>` elements, each in its own `<li>` element. In microdata, each `<a>` element gets an `itemprop="url"` attribute:

```
<h1>My Digital Footprints</h1>
<ul>
  <li><a href="http://diveintomark.org/"
        itemprop="url">weblog</a></li>
  <li><a href="http://www.google.com/profiles/pilgrim"
        itemprop="url">Google profile</a></li>
  <li><a href="http://www.reddit.com/user/MarkPilgrim"
        itemprop="url">Reddit.com profile</a></li>
  <li><a href="http://www.twitter.com/diveintomark"
        itemprop="url">Twitter</a></li>
</ul>
```

According to Table 10-1, <a> elements have special processing. The microdata property value is the href attribute, not the child text content. The text of each link is actually ignored by a microdata processor. Thus, in English, this says: "This person has a URL at *http://diveintomark.org/*. This person has another URL at *http://www.google.com/profiles/pilgrim*. This person has another URL at *http://www.reddit.com/user/MarkPilgrim*. This person has another URL at *http://www.twitter.com/diveintomark*."

Introducing Google Rich Snippets

I want to step back for just a moment and ask, "Why are we doing this?" Are we adding semantics just for the sake of adding semantics? Don't get me wrong; I enjoy fiddling with angle brackets as much as the next webhead. But why microdata? Why bother?

There are two major classes of applications that consume HTML and, by extension, HTML5 microdata:

- Web browsers
- Search engines

For browsers, HTML5 defines a set of DOM APIs for extracting microdata items, properties, and property values from a web page. As I write this, no browser supports this API. Not a single one. So that's...kind of a dead end, at least until browsers catch up and implement the client-side APIs.

The other major consumer of HTML is search engines. What could a search engine do with microdata properties about a person? Imagine this: instead of simply displaying the page title and an excerpt of text, the search engine could integrate some of that structured information and display it. Full name, job title, employer, address, maybe even a little thumbnail of a profile photo. Would that catch your attention? It would catch mine.

Google supports microdata as part of its Rich Snippets program (*http://www.google.com/support/webmasters/bin/answer.py?hl=en&answer=99170*). When Google's web crawler parses your page and finds microdata properties that conform to the http://data-vocabulary.org/Person vocabulary, it parses out those properties and stores them alongside the rest of the page data. Google even provides a handy tool that shows how Google "sees" your microdata properties. Testing it against our sample microdata-enabled "about" page (*http://diveintohtml5.org/examples/person-plus-microdata.html*) yields this output:

```
Item
  Type: http://data-vocabulary.org/person
  photo = http://diveintohtml5.org/examples/2000_05_mark.jpg
  name = Mark Pilgrim
  title = Developer advocate
  affiliation = Google, Inc.
  address = Item( 1 )
  url = http://diveintomark.org/
```

```
url = http://www.google.com/profiles/pilgrim
url = http://www.reddit.com/user/MarkPilgrim
url = http://www.twitter.com/diveintomark

Item 1
  Type: http://data-vocabulary.org/address
  street-address = 100 Main Street
  locality = Anytown
  region = PA
  postal-code = 19999
  country-name = USA
```

It's all there: the `photo` property from the `<img src>` attribute, all four URLs from the list of `<a href>` attributes, and even the address object (listed as "Item 1") and all five of its subproperties.

And how does Google use all of this information? That depends. There are no hard-and-fast rules about how microdata properties should be displayed, which ones should be displayed, or whether they should be displayed at all. If someone searches for "Mark Pilgrim," *and* Google determines that this "about" page should rank in the results, *and* Google decides that the microdata properties it originally found on that page are worth displaying, the search result listing might look something like Figure 10-1.

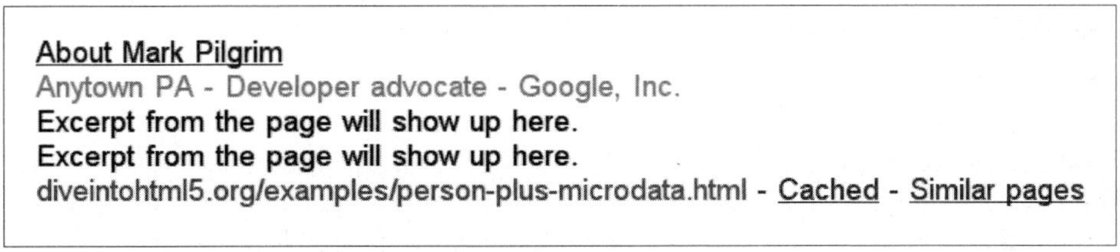

About Mark Pilgrim
Anytown PA - Developer advocate - Google, Inc.
Excerpt from the page will show up here.
Excerpt from the page will show up here.
diveintohtml5.org/examples/person-plus-microdata.html - <u>Cached</u> - <u>Similar pages</u>

Figure 10-1. Sample search result for a microdata-enhanced Person listing

The first line, "About Mark Pilgrim," is actually the title of the page, given in the `<title>` element. That's not terribly exciting; Google does that for every page. But the second line is full of information taken directly from the microdata annotations we added to the page. "Anytown PA" was part of the mailing address, marked up with the `http://data-vocabulary.org/Address` vocabulary. "Developer advocate" and "Google, Inc." were two properties from the `http://data-vocabulary.org/Person` vocabulary (`title` and `affiliation`, respectively).

This is really quite amazing. You don't need to be a large corporation making special deals with search engine vendors to customize your search result listings. Just take 10 minutes and add a couple of HTML attributes to annotate the data you were already publishing anyway.

Marking Up Organizations

Microdata isn't limited to a single vocabulary. "About" pages are nice, but you probably only have one of them. Still hungry for more? Let's learn how to mark up organizations and businesses.

I've created a sample page of business listings (*http://diveintohtml5.org/examples/organ ization.html*). Let's look at the original HTML markup, without microdata:

```
<article>
  <h1>Google, Inc.</h1>
  <p>
    1600 Amphitheatre Parkway<br>
    Mountain View, CA 94043<br>
    USA
  </p>
  <p>650-253-0000</p>
  <p><a href="http://www.google.com/">Google.com</a></p>
</article>
```

 You can follow along online with the changes made throughout this section. Before: *http://diveintohtml5.org/examples/organization.html*; after: *http://diveintohtml5.org/examples/organization-plus-microdata .html*.

Short and sweet. All the information about the organization is contained within the `<article>` element, so let's start there:

```
<article itemscope itemtype="http://data-vocabulary.org/Organization">
```

As with marking up people, you need to set the `itemscope` and `itemtype` attributes on the outermost element. In this case, the outermost element is an `<article>` element. The `itemtype` attribute declares the microdata vocabulary you're using (in this case, *http://data-vocabulary.org/Organization*), and the `itemscope` attribute declares that all of the properties you set on child elements relate to this vocabulary.

So what's in the Organization vocabulary? It's very simple and straightforward. In fact, some of it should already look familiar. Table 10-3 lists the relevant properties.

Table 10-3. Organization vocabulary

Property	Description
name	The name of the organization (for example, "Initech").
url	A link to the organization's home page.
address	The location of the organization. Can contain the subproperties `street-address`, `locality`, `region`, `postal-code`, and `country-name`.
tel	The telephone number of the organization.
geo	The geographical coordinates of the location. Always contains two subproperties, `latitude` and `longitude`.

The first bit of markup within the outermost `<article>` element is an `<h1>`. This `<h1>` element contains the name of a business, so we'll put an `itemprop="name"` attribute directly on it:

```
<h1 itemprop="name">Google, Inc.</h1>
```

According to Table 10-1, `<h1>` elements don't need any special processing. The microdata property value is simply the text content of the `<h1>` element. In English, we just said: "The name of the Organization is 'Google, Inc.'"

Next up is a street address. Marking up the address of an Organization works exactly the same way as marking up the address of a Person. First, add an `itemprop="address"` attribute to the outermost element of the street address (in this case, a `<p>` element). That states that this is the **address** property of the Organization. But what about the properties of the address itself? We also need to define the **item type** and **itemscope** attributes to say that this is an Address item that has its own properties:

```
<p itemprop="address" itemscope
   itemtype="http://data-vocabulary.org/Address">
```

Finally, we need to wrap each distinct piece of information in a dummy `<span>` element so we can add the appropriate microdata property name (`street-address`, `locality`, `region`, `postal-code`, and `country-name`) on each `<span>` element:

```
<p itemprop="address" itemscope
   itemtype="http://data-vocabulary.org/Address">
  <span itemprop="street-address">1600 Amphitheatre Parkway</span><br>
  <span itemprop="locality">Mountain View</span>,
  <span itemprop="region">CA</span>
  <span itemprop="postal-code">94043</span><br>
  <span itemprop="country-name">USA</span>
</p>
```

In English, we just said: "This Organization has an address. The street address part is '1600 Amphitheatre Parkway'. The locality is 'Mountain View'. The region part is 'CA'. The postal code is '94043'. The name of the country is 'USA'."

Next up: a telephone number for the Organization. Telephone numbers are notoriously tricky, and the exact syntax is country-specific. (And if you want to call another country, it's even worse.) In this example, we have a United States telephone number, in a format suitable for calling from elsewhere in the United States:

```
<p itemprop="tel">650-253-0000</p>
```

(Hey, in case you didn't notice, the Address vocabulary went out of scope when its `<p>` element was closed. Now we're back to defining properties in the Organization vocabulary.)

If you want to list several telephone numbers—maybe one for United States customers and one for international customers—you can do that. Any microdata property can be repeated. Just make sure each telephone number is in its own HTML element, separate from any label you may give it:

```
<p>
   US customers: <span itemprop="tel">650-253-0000</span><br>
   UK customers: <span itemprop="tel">00 + 1* + 6502530000</span>
</p>
```

According to Table 10-1, neither the `<p>` element nor the `<span>` element has special processing. The value of the microdata `tel` property is simply the text content. The Organization microdata vocabulary makes no attempt to subdivide the different parts of a telephone number. The entire `tel` property is just freeform text. If you want to put the area code in parentheses, or use spaces instead of dashes to separate the numbers, you can do that. If a microdata-consuming client wants to parse the telephone number, that's entirely up to it.

Next, we have another familiar property: `url`. Just like associating a URL with a Person as described in the preceding section, you can associate a URL with an Organization. This could be the company's home page, a contact page, a product page, or anything else. If it's a URL about, from, or belonging to the Organization, mark it up with an `itemprop="url"` attribute:

```
<p><a itemprop="url" href="http://www.google.com/">Google.com</a></p>
```

According to Table 10-1, the `<a>` element has special processing. The microdata property value is the value of the `href` attribute, not the link text. In English, this says: "This organization is associated with the URL *http://www.google.com/*." It doesn't say anything more specific about the association, and it doesn't include the link text, "Google.com."

Finally, I want to talk about geolocation. No, not the W3C geolocation API (see Chapter 6). I'm talking about how to mark up the physical location for an Organization using microdata.

To date, all of our examples have focused on marking up *visible* data. That is, you have an `<h1>` with a company name, so you add an `itemprop` attribute to the `<h1>` element to declare that the (visible) header text is, in fact, the name of an Organization. Or you have an `<img>` element that points to a photo, so you add an `itemprop` attribute to the `<img>` element to declare that the (visible) image is a photo of a Person.

In this example, geolocation information isn't like that. There is no visible text that gives the exact latitude and longitude (to four decimal places!) of the Organization. In fact, the sample Organization page without microdata has no geolocation information at all. It has a link to Google Maps, but even the URL of that link does not contain latitude and longitude coordinates. (It contains similar information in a Google-specific format.) Even if we had a link to a hypothetical online mapping service that did take latitude and longitude coordinates as URL parameters, microdata has no way of separating out the different parts of a URL. You can't declare that the first URL query parameter is the latitude, the second URL query parameter is the longitude, and the rest of the query parameters are irrelevant.

To handle edge cases like this, HTML5 provides a way to annotate *invisible* data. This technique should only be used as a last resort. If there is a way to display or render the data you care about, you should do so. Invisible data that only machines can read tends to "go stale" very quickly. That is, it's likely that someone will come along later and update the visible text but forget to update the invisible data. This happens more often than you think, and it *will* happen to you too.

Still, there are cases where invisible data is unavoidable. Perhaps your boss *really* wants machine-readable geolocation information but doesn't want to clutter up the interface with pairs of incomprehensible six-digit numbers. Invisible data is the only option. The only saving grace here is that you can put the invisible data immediately after the visible text that it describes, which may help remind the person who comes along later and updates the visible text that she needs to update the invisible data right after it.

In this example, we can create a dummy `<span>` element within the same `<article>` element as all the other Organization properties, then put the invisible geolocation data inside the `<span>` element:

```
<span itemprop="geo" itemscope
  itemtype="http://data-vocabulary.org/Geo">
  <meta itemprop="latitude" content="37.4149" />
  <meta itemprop="longitude" content="-122.078" />
</span>
</article>
```

Geolocation information is defined in its own vocabulary, like the address of a Person or Organization. Therefore, this `<span>` element needs three attributes:

`itemprop="geo"`
  Says that this element represents the `geo` property of the surrounding Organization.

```
itemtype="http://data-vocabulary.org/Geo"
```
Says which microdata vocabulary this element's properties conform to.

```
itemscope
```
Says that this element is the enclosing element for a microdata item with its own vocabulary (given in the `itemtype` attribute). All the properties within this element are properties of the Geo vocabulary (`http://data-vocabulary.org/Geo`), not the surrounding Organization vocabulary (`http://data-vocabulary.org/Organiza tion`).

The next big question that this example answers is, "How do you annotate invisible data?" You do this with the `<meta>` element. In previous versions of HTML, you could only use the `<meta>` element within the `<head>` of your page (see "The <head> Element" on page 34). In HTML5, you can use the `<meta>` element anywhere. And that's exactly what we're doing here:

```
<meta itemprop="latitude" content="37.4149" />
```

According to Table 10-1, the `<meta>` element has special processing. The microdata property value is the `content` attribute. Since this attribute is never visibly displayed, we have the perfect setup for unlimited quantities of invisible data. With great power comes great responsibility. In this case, the responsibility is on you to ensure that this invisible data stays in sync with the visible text around it.

There is no direct support for the Organization vocabulary in Google Rich Snippets, so I don't have any pretty sample search result listings to show you. But organizations feature heavily in the next two case studies, events and reviews, and those *are* supported by Google Rich Snippets.

Marking Up Events

Stuff happens. Some stuff happens at predetermined times. Wouldn't it be nice if you could tell search engines exactly when stuff was about to happen? There's an angle bracket for that.

Let's start by looking at a sample schedule of my speaking engagements (*http://divein tohtml5.org/examples/event.html*):

```
<article>
  <h1>Google Developer Day 2009</h1>
  <img width="300" height="200"
      src="http://diveintohtml5.org/examples/gdd-2009-prague-pilgrim.jpg"
      alt="[Mark Pilgrim at podium]">
  <p>
    Google Developer Days are a chance to learn about Google
    developer products from the engineers who built them. This
    one-day conference includes seminars and "office hours"
    on web technologies like Google Maps, OpenSocial, Android,
    AJAX APIs, Chrome, and Google Web Toolkit.
  </p>
```

```
<p>
  <time datetime="2009-11-06T08:30+01:00">2009 November 6, 8:30</time>
    &ndash;
  <time datetime="2009-11-06T20:30+01:00">20:30</time>
</p>
<p>
  Congress Center<br>
  5th května 65<br>
  140 21 Praha 4<br>
  Czech Republic
</p>
<p><a href="http://code.google.com/intl/cs/events/developerday/2009/home.html">
    GDD/Prague home page</a></p>
</article>
```

 You can follow along online with the changes made throughout this section. Before: *http://diveintohtml5.org/examples/event.html*; after: *http://diveintohtml5.org/examples/event-plus-microdata.html*.

All the information about the event is contained within the `<article>` element, so that's where we need to put the `itemtype` and `itemscope` attributes:

```
<article itemscope itemtype="http://data-vocabulary.org/Event">
```

The URL for the Event vocabulary is *http://data-vocabulary.org/Event*, which also happens to contain a nice little chart describing the vocabulary's properties. And what are those properties? Table 10-4 lists them.

Table 10-4. Event vocabulary

Property	Description
summary	The name of the event.
url	A link to the event details page.
location	The location or venue of the event. Can optionally be represented by a nested Organization (see "Marking Up Organizations" on page 176) or Address (see "Marking Up People" on page 171).
description	A description of the event.
startDate	The starting date and time of the event in ISO date format.
endDate	The ending date and time of the event in ISO date format.
duration	The duration of the event in ISO duration format.
eventType	The category of the event (for example, "Concert" or "Lecture"). This is a freeform string, not an enumerated attribute.
geo	The geographical coordinates of the location. Always contains two subproperties, latitude and longitude.
photo	A link to a photo or image related to the event.

The Event's name is in an `<h1>` element. According to Table 10-1, `<h1>` elements have no special processing. The microdata property value is simply the text content of the `<h1>` element. So, all we need to do is add the `itemprop` attribute to declare that this `<h1>` element contains the name of the Event:

```
<h1 itemprop="summary">Google Developer Day 2009</h1>
```

In English, this says: "The name of this Event is 'Google Developer Day 2009.'"

This event listing has a photo, which can be marked up with the `photo` property. As you would expect, the photo is already marked up with an `<img>` element. Like the `photo` property in the Person vocabulary (see "The Microdata Data Model" on page 166), the `Event` photo property is a URL. Since Table 10-1 says that the property value of an `<img>` element is its `src` attribute, the only thing we need to do is add the `itemprop` attribute to the `<img>` element:

```
<img itemprop="photo" width="300" height="200"
     src="http://diveintohtml5.org/examples/gdd-2009-prague-pilgrim.jpg"
     alt="[Mark Pilgrim at podium]">
```

In English, this says: "The photo for this Event is at *http://diveintohtml5.org/examples/gdd-2009-prague-pilgrim.jpg.*"

Next up is a longer description of the Event, which is just a paragraph of freeform text:

```
<p itemprop="description">Google Developer Days are a chance to
learn about Google developer products from the engineers who built
them. This one-day conference includes seminars and "office
hours" on web technologies like Google Maps, OpenSocial,
Android, AJAX APIs, Chrome, and Google Web Toolkit.</p>
```

The next bit is something new. Events generally occur on specific dates and start and end at specific times. In HTML5, dates and times should be marked up with the `<time>` element (see "Dates and Times" on page 49), and we are already doing that here. So the question becomes, how do we add microdata properties to these `<time>` elements? Looking back at Table 10-1, we see that the `<time>` element has special processing. The value of a microdata property on a `<time>` element is the value of the `datetime` attribute. And hey, the `startDate` and `endDate` properties of the Event vocabulary take an ISO-style date, just like the `datetime` property of a `<time>` element. Once again, the semantics of the core HTML vocabulary dovetail nicely with the semantics of our custom microdata vocabulary. Marking up start and end dates with microdata is as simple as:

1. Using HTML correctly in the first place (using `<time>` elements to mark up dates and times)
2. Adding a single `itemprop` attribute:

```
<p>
  <time itemprop="startDate" datetime="2009-11-06T08:30+01:00">2009 November 6, 8:30</time>
  &ndash;
  <time itemprop="endDate" datetime="2009-11-06T20:30+01:00">20:30</time>
</p>
```

In English, this says: "This Event starts on November 6, 2009, at 8:30 in the morning, and goes until November 6, 2009, at 20:30 (times local to Prague, GMT+1)."

Next up is the `location` property. The definition of the Event vocabulary says that this can be either an Organization or an Address. In this case, the Event is being held at a venue that specializes in conferences, the Congress Center in Prague. Marking it up as an Organization allows us to include the name of the venue as well as its address.

First, let's declare that the `<p>` element that contains the address is the `location` property of the Event, and that this element is also its own microdata item that conforms to the `http://data-vocabulary.org/Organization` vocabulary:

```
<p itemprop="location" itemscope
    itemtype="http://data-vocabulary.org/Organization">
```

Next, mark up the name of the Organization by wrapping the name in a dummy `<span>` element and adding an `itemprop` attribute to the `<span>` element:

```
<span itemprop="name">Congress Center</span><br>
```

`"name"` is defining a property in the Organization vocabulary, not the Event vocabulary. The `<p>` element defined the beginning of the scope of the Organization properties, and that `<p>` element hasn't yet been closed with a `</p>` tag. Any microdata properties we define here are properties of the most recently scoped vocabulary. Nested vocabularies are like a stack. We haven't yet popped the stack, so we're still talking about properties of the Organization.

In fact, we're going to add a third vocabulary onto the stack—an Address for the Organization for the Event:

```
<span itemprop="address" itemscope
    itemtype="http://data-vocabulary.org/Address">
```

Once again, we want to mark up every piece of the address as a separate microdata property, so we need a slew of dummy `<span>` elements to hang our `itemprop` attributes onto (if I'm going too fast for you here, go back and read about marking up the address of a Person (see "Marking Up People" on page 171) and marking up the address of an Organization (see "Marking Up Organizations" on page 177)):

```
<span itemprop="street-address">5th května 65</span><br>
<span itemprop="postal-code">140 21</span>
<span itemprop="locality">Praha 4</span><br>
<span itemprop="country-name">Czech Republic</span>
```

There are no more properties of the Address, so we close the `<span>` element that started the Address scope and pop the stack:

```
</span>
```

There are also no more properties of the Organization, so we close the `<p>` element that started the Organization scope and pop the stack again:

```
</p>
```

Now we're back to defining properties on the Event. The next property is geo, to represent the physical location of the Event. This uses the same Geo vocabulary that we used to mark up the physical location of an Organization in the previous section. We need a `<span>` element to act as the container; it gets the `itemtype` and `itemscope` attributes. Within that `<span>` element, we need two `<meta>` elements, one for the `latitude` property and one for the `longitude` property:

```
<span itemprop="geo" itemscope itemtype="http://data-vocabulary.org/Geo">
  <meta itemprop="latitude" content="50.047893" />
  <meta itemprop="longitude" content="14.4491" />
</span>
```

Because we've closed the `<span>` that contained the Geo properties, we're back to defining properties on the Event. The last property is the `url` property, which should look familiar. Associating a URL with an Event works the same way as associating a URL with a Person (see "Marking Up People" on page 173) and associating a URL with an Organization (see "Marking Up Organizations" on page 178). If you're using HTML correctly (marking up hyperlinks with `<a href>`), declaring that the hyperlink is a microdata `url` property is simply a matter of adding the `itemprop` attribute:

```
<p>
  <a itemprop="url"
     href="http://code.google.com/intl/cs/events/developerday/2009/home.html">
     GDD/Prague home page
  </a>
</p>
</article>
```

The sample event page (*http://diveintohtml5.org/examples/event.html*) also lists a second event, my speaking engagement at the ConFoo conference in Montreal. For brevity, I'm not going to go through that markup line by line. It's essentially the same as the event in Prague: an Event item with nested Geo and Address items. I just mention it in passing to reiterate that a single page can have multiple events, each marked up with microdata.

The Return of Google Rich Snippets

According to Google's Rich Snippets Testing Tool, this is the information that Google's crawlers will glean from our sample event listing page (*http://diveintohtml5.org/exam ples/event-plus-microdata.html*):

```
Item
    Type: http://data-vocabulary.org/Event
    summary = Google Developer Day 2009
    eventType = conference
    photo = http://diveintohtml5.org/examples/gdd-2009-prague-pilgrim.jpg
    description = Google Developer Days are a chance to learn about Google developer
                  products from the engineers who built them. This one-day
                  conference includes seminars and office hours on web technologies
                  like Goo...
    startDate = 2009-11-06T08:30+01:00
```

```
endDate = 2009-11-06T20:30+01:00
location = Item(__1)
geo = Item(__3)
url = http://code.google.com/intl/cs/events/developerday/2009/home.html

Item
    Id: __1
    Type: http://data-vocabulary.org/Organization
    name = Congress Center
    address = Item(__2)

Item
    Id: __2
    Type: http://data-vocabulary.org/Address
    street-address = 5th května 65
    postal-code = 140 21
    locality = Praha 4
    country-name = Czech Republic

Item
    Id: __3
    Type: http://data-vocabulary.org/Geo
    latitude = 50.047893
    longitude = 14.4491
```

As you can see, all the information we added in microdata is there. Properties that are separate microdata items are given internal IDs (`Item(__1)`, `Item(__2)`, and so on), but this is not part of the microdata specification. It's just a convention that Google's testing tool uses to linearize the sample output and show you the grouping of nested items and their properties.

So how might Google choose to represent this sample page in its search results? (Again, I have to preface this with the disclaimer that this is just an example; Google may change the format of its search results at any time, and there is no guarantee that Google will even pay attention to your microdata markup.) It might look like Figure 10-2.

<u>Mark Pilgrim's event calendar</u>
Excerpt from the page will show up here.
Excerpt from the page will show up here.
<u>Google Developer Day 2009</u>   Fri, Nov 6   Congress Center, Praha 4, Czech Republic
<u>ConFoo.ca 2010</u>   Wed, Mar 10   Hilton Montreal Bonaventure, Montréal, Québec, Canada
diveintohtml5.org/examples/event-plus-microdata.html - <u>Cached</u> - <u>Similar pages</u>

Figure 10-2. Sample search result for a microdata-enhanced Event listing

After the page title and autogenerated excerpt text, Google starts using the microdata markup we added to the page to display a little table of events. Note the date format: "Fri, Nov 6." That is not a string that appeared anywhere in our HTML or microdata markup. We used two fully qualified ISO-formatted strings, `2009-11-06T08:30+01:00` and `2009-11-06T20:30+01:00`. Google took those two dates, figured out that they were on the same day, and decided to display a single date in a more friendly format.

Now look at the physical addresses. Google chose to display just the venue name + locality + country, not the exact street address. This is made possible by the fact that we split up the address into five subproperties—`name`, `street-address`, `region`, `locality`, and `country-name`—and marked up each part of the address as a different microdata property. Google takes advantage of that to show an abbreviated address. Other consumers of the same microdata markup might make different choices about what to display or how to display it. There's no right or wrong choice here. It's up to you to provide as much data as possible, as accurately as possible. It's up to the rest of the world to interpret it.

Marking Up Reviews

Here's another example of making the Web (and possibly search result listings) better through markup: business and product reviews.

This is a short review I wrote of my favorite pizza place near my house. (This is a real restaurant, by the way. If you're ever in Apex, NC, I highly recommend it.) Let's look at the original markup (*http://diveintohtml5.org/examples/review.html*):

```
<article>
  <h1>Anna's Pizzeria</h1>
  <p>★★★★☆ (4 stars out of 5)</p>
  <p>New York-style pizza right in historic downtown Apex</p>
  <p>
    Food is top-notch. Atmosphere is just right for a "neighborhood
    pizza joint." The restaurant itself is a bit cramped; if you're
    overweight, you may have difficulty getting in and out of your
    seat and navigating between other tables. Used to give free
    garlic knots when you sat down; now they give you plain bread
    and you have to pay for the good stuff. Overall, it's a winner.
  </p>
  <p>
    100 North Salem Street<br>
    Apex, NC 27502<br>
    USA
  </p>
  <p>- reviewed by Mark Pilgrim, last updated March 31, 2010</p>
</article>
```

 You can follow along online with the changes made throughout this section. Before: *http://diveintohtml5.org/examples/review.html*; after: *http://diveintohtml5.org/examples/review-plus-microdata.html*.

This review is contained in an `<article>` element, so that's where we'll put the `itemtype` and `itemscope` attributes. Here's the namespace URL for this vocabulary:

```
<article itemscope itemtype="http://data-vocabulary.org/Review">
```

What are the available properties in the Review vocabulary? I'm glad you asked. They're listed in Table 10-5.

Table 10-5. Review vocabulary

Property	Description
itemreviewed	The name of the item being reviewed. Can be a product, service, business, etc.
rating	A numerical quality rating for the item, on a scale from 1 to 5. Can also be a nested Rating using the http://data-vocabulary.org/Rating vocabulary to use a nonstandard scale.
reviewer	The name of the author who wrote the review.
dtreviewed	The date that the item was reviewed in ISO date format.
summary	A short summary of the review.
description	The body of the review.

The first property is simple: itemreviewed is just text, and here it's contained in an <h1> element, so that's where we should put the itemprop attribute:

```
<h1 itemprop="itemreviewed">Anna's Pizzeria</h1>
```

I'm going to skip over the actual rating and come back to that at the end.

The next two properties are also straightforward. The summary property is a short description of what you're reviewing, and the description property is the body of the review:

```
<p itemprop="summary">New York-style pizza right in historic downtown Apex</p>
<p itemprop="description">
  Food is top-notch. Atmosphere is just right for a "neighborhood
  pizza joint." The restaurant itself is a bit cramped; if you're
  overweight, you may have difficulty getting in and out of your
  seat and navigating between other tables. Used to give free
  garlic knots when you sat down; now they give you plain bread
  and you have to pay for the good stuff. Overall, it's a winner.
</p>
```

The location and geo properties aren't anything we haven't tackled before (refer back to the previous sections on marking up the address of a Person, marking up the address of an Organization, and marking up geolocation information):

```
<p itemprop="location" itemscope
   itemtype="http://data-vocabulary.org/Address">
  <span itemprop="street-address">100 North Salem Street</span><br>
  <span itemprop="locality">Apex</span>,
  <span itemprop="region">NC</span>
  <span itemprop="postal-code">27502</span><br>
  <span itemprop="country-name">USA</span>
</p>
<span itemprop="geo" itemscope
      itemtype="http://data-vocabulary.org/Geo">
  <meta itemprop="latitude" content="35.730796" />
```

```
<meta itemprop="longitude" content="-78.851426" />
</span>
```

The final line presents a familiar problem: it contains two bits of information in one element. The name of the reviewer is `Mark Pilgrim`, and the review date is `March 31, 2010`. How do we mark up these two distinct properties? As usual, we can wrap them in their own elements (see "Marking Up People" on page 171) and put an `itemprop` attribute on each element. In fact, the date in this example should have been marked up with a `<time>` element in the first place, so that provides a natural hook on which to hang our `itemprop` attribute. The reviewer name can just be wrapped in a dummy `<span>` element:

```
<p>
  <span itemprop="reviewer">Mark Pilgrim</span>, last updated
  <time itemprop="dtreviewed" datetime="2010-03-31">
    March 31, 2010
  </time>
</p>
</article>
```

OK, let's talk ratings. The trickiest part of marking up a review is the rating. By default, ratings in the Review vocabulary are on a scale of 1–5, with 1 being "terrible" and 5 being "awesome." If you want to use a different scale, you can definitely do that. But let's talk about the default scale first:

```
<p>★★★★☆ (<span itemprop="rating">4</span> stars out of 5)</p>
```

If you're using the default 1–5 scale, the only property you need to mark up is the rating itself (4, in this case). But what if you want to use a different scale? You can do that; you just need to declare the limits of the scale you're using. For example, if you wanted to use a scale of 0–10, you would still declare the `itemprop="rating"` property, but instead of giving the rating value directly, you would use a nested Rating with the vocabulary of `http://data-vocabulary.org/Rating` to declare the worst and best values in your custom scale and the actual rating value within that scale:

```
<p itemprop="rating" itemscope
   itemtype="http://data-vocabulary.org/Rating">
  ★★★★★★★★★☆
  (<span itemprop="value">9</span> on a scale of
  <span itemprop="worst">0</span> to
  <span itemprop="best">10</span>)
</p>
```

In English, this says: "The product I'm reviewing has a rating value of 9 on a scale of 0–10."

Did I mention that review microdata could affect search result listings? Oh yes, it can. Here is the "raw data" that the Google Rich Snippets tool extracted from my microdata-enhanced review (*http://www.google.com/webmasters/tools/richsnippets?url=//divein tohtml5.org/examples/review-plus-microdata.html*):

```
Item
  Type: http://data-vocabulary.org/Review
  itemreviewed = Anna's Pizzeria
  rating = 4
  summary = New York-style pizza right in historic downtown Apex
  description = Food is top-notch. Atmosphere is just right ...
  address = Item(__1)
  geo = Item(__2)
  reviewer = Mark Pilgrim
  dtreviewed = 2010-03-31

Item
  Id: __1
  Type: http://data-vocabulary.org/Organization
  street-address = 100 North Salem Street
  locality = Apex
  region = NC
  postal-code = 27502
  country-name = USA

Item
  Id: __2
  Type: http://data-vocabulary.org/Geo
  latitude = 35.730796
  longitude = -78.851426
```

Figure 10-3 (modulo the whims of Google, the phase of the moon, and so on and so forth) shows what my review might look like in a search result listing.

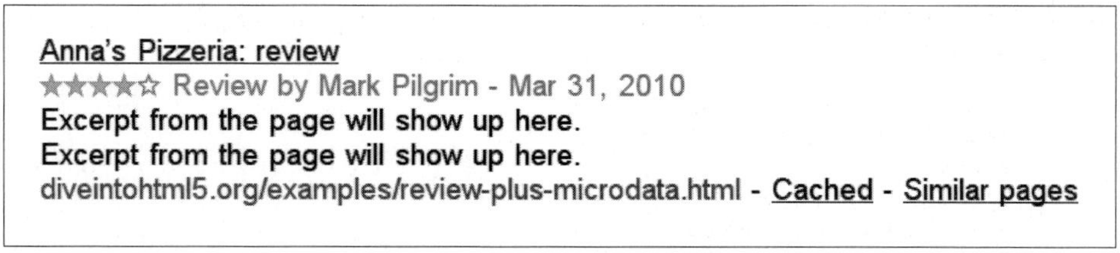

Figure 10-3. Sample search result for a microdata-enhanced Review listing

Angle brackets don't impress me much, but I have to admit, that's pretty cool.

Further Reading

Microdata resources:

- Live microdata playground (*http://foolip.org/microdatajs/live/*)
- HTML5 microdata specification (*http://bit.ly/ckt9Rj*)

Google Rich Snippets resources:

- "About rich snippets and structured data" (*http://www.google.com/support/web masters/bin/answer.py?hl=en&answer=99170*)
- "People" (*http://www.google.com/support/webmasters/bin/answer.py?hl=en&an swer=146646*)
- "Businesses and organizations" (*http://www.google.com/support/webmasters/bin/ answer.py?hl=en&answer=146861*)
- "Events" (*http://www.google.com/support/webmasters/bin/answer.py?hl=en&an swer=164506*)
- "Reviews" (*http://www.google.com/support/webmasters/bin/answer.py?hl=en&an swer=146645*)
- "Review ratings" (*http://www.google.com/support/webmasters/bin/answer.py?hl= en&answer=172705*)
- Google Rich Snippets Testing Tool (*http://www.google.com/webmasters/tools/richs nippets*)
- Google Rich Snippets Tips and Tricks (*http://knol.google.com/k/google-rich-snip pets-tips-and-tricks*)

The All-in-One Almost-Alphabetical Guide to Detecting Everything

Confused? Read Chapter 2 for a conceptual introduction. Want an all-in-one library instead? Try Modernizr (*http://www.modernizr.com*).

List of Elements

<audio>

http://bit.ly/cZxl7K

```
return !!document.createElement('audio').canPlayType;
```

<audio> in MP3 format

http://en.wikipedia.org/wiki/MP3

```
var a = document.createElement('audio');
return !!(a.canPlayType && a.canPlayType('audio/mpeg;').replace(/no/, ''));
```

<audio> in Vorbis format

http://en.wikipedia.org/wiki/Vorbis

```
var a = document.createElement('audio');
return !!(a.canPlayType && a.canPlayType('audio/ogg;
        codecs="vorbis"').replace(/no/, ''));
```

<audio> in WAV format

http://en.wikipedia.org/wiki/WAV

```
var a = document.createElement('audio');
return !!(a.canPlayType && a.canPlayType('audio/wav;
        codecs="1"').replace(/no/, ''));
```

<audio> in AAC format

http://en.wikipedia.org/wiki/Advanced_Audio_Coding

```
var a = document.createElement('audio');
return !!(a.canPlayType && a.canPlayType('audio/mp4;
        codecs="mp4a.40.2"').replace(/no/, ''));
```

<canvas>

See Chapter 4

```
return !!document.createElement('canvas').getContext;
```

<canvas> text API

See "Text" on page 63

```
var c = document.createElement('canvas');
return c.getContext && typeof c.getContext('2d').fillText == 'function';
```

<command>

http://bit.ly/aQt2Fn

```
return 'type' in document.createElement('command');
```

<datalist>

http://bit.ly/9WVz5p

```
return 'options' in document.createElement('datalist');
```

<details>

http://bit.ly/cO8mQy

```
return 'open' in document.createElement('details');
```

<device>

http://bit.ly/aaBeUy

```
return 'type' in document.createElement('device');
```

\<form> constraint validation

http://bit.ly/cb9Wmj

```
return 'noValidate' in document.createElement('form');
```

\<iframe sandbox>

http://blog.whatwg.org/whats-next-in-html-episode-2-sandbox

```
return 'sandbox' in document.createElement('iframe');
```

\<iframe srcdoc>

http://blog.whatwg.org/whats-next-in-html-episode-2-sandbox

```
return 'srcdoc' in document.createElement('iframe');
```

\<input autofocus>

See "Autofocus Fields" on page 148

```
return 'autofocus' in document.createElement('input');
```

\<input placeholder>

See "Placeholder Text" on page 147

```
return 'placeholder' in document.createElement('input');
```

\<input type="color">

http://bit.ly/9HkeNn

```
var i = document.createElement('input');
i.setAttribute('type', 'color');
return i.type !== 'text';
```

\<input type="email">

See "Email Addresses" on page 150

```
var i = document.createElement('input');
i.setAttribute('type', 'email');
return i.type !== 'text';
```

\<input type="number">

See "Numbers As Spinboxes" on page 153

```
var i = document.createElement('input');
i.setAttribute('type', 'number');
return i.type !== 'text';
```

<input type="range">

See "Numbers As Sliders" on page 155

```
var i = document.createElement('input');
i.setAttribute('type', 'range');
return i.type !== 'text';
```

<input type="search">

See "Search Boxes" on page 158

```
var i = document.createElement('input');
i.setAttribute('type', 'search');
return i.type !== 'text';
```

<input type="tel">

http://bit.ly/bZm0Q5

```
var i = document.createElement('input');
i.setAttribute('type', 'tel');
return i.type !== 'text';
```

<input type="url">

See "Web Addresses" on page 151

```
var i = document.createElement('input');
i.setAttribute('type', 'url');
return i.type !== 'text';
```

<input type="date">

See "Date Pickers" on page 156

```
var i = document.createElement('input');
i.setAttribute('type', 'date');
return i.type !== 'text';
```

<input type="time">

See "Date Pickers" on page 156

```
var i = document.createElement('input');
i.setAttribute('type', 'time');
return i.type !== 'text';
```

<input type="datetime">

See "Date Pickers" on page 156

```
var i = document.createElement('input');
i.setAttribute('type', 'datetime');
return i.type !== 'text';
```

<input type="datetime-local">

See "Date Pickers" on page 156

```
var i = document.createElement('input');
i.setAttribute('type', 'datetime-local);
return i.type !== 'text';
```

<input type="month">

See "Date Pickers" on page 156

```
var i = document.createElement('input');
i.setAttribute('type', 'month');
return i.type !== 'text';
```

<input type="week">

See "Date Pickers" on page 156

```
var i = document.createElement('input');
i.setAttribute('type', 'week');
return i.type !== 'text';
```

<meter>

http://bit.ly/c0pX0I

```
return 'value' in document.createElement('meter');
```

<output>

http://bit.ly/asJaqH

```
return 'value' in document.createElement('output');
```

<progress>

http://bit.ly/bjDMy6

```
return 'value' in document.createElement('progress');
```

<time>

http://bit.ly/bl62jp

```
return 'valueAsDate' in document.createElement('time');
```

<video>

See Chapter 5

```
return !!document.createElement('video').canPlayType;
```

<video> captions

http://bit.ly/9mLiRr

```
return 'track' in document.createElement('track');
```

<video poster>

http://bit.ly/b6RhzT

```
return 'poster' in document.createElement('video');
```

<video> in WebM format

http://www.webmproject.org

```
var v = document.createElement('video');
return !!(v.canPlayType && v.canPlayType('video/webm; codecs="vp8,
        vorbis"').replace(/no/, ''));
```

<video> in H.264 format

See "H.264" on page 84

```
var v = document.createElement('video');
return !!(v.canPlayType && v.canPlayType('video/mp4; codecs="avc1.42E01E,
        mp4a.40.2"').replace(/no/, ''));
```

<video> in Theora format

See "Theora" on page 84

```
var v = document.createElement('video');
return !!(v.canPlayType && v.canPlayType('video/ogg; codecs="theora,
        vorbis"').replace(/no/, ''));
```

contentEditable

http://bit.ly/aLivbS

```
return 'isContentEditable' in document.createElement('span');
```

Cross-document messaging

http://bit.ly/cUOqXd

```
return !!window.postMessage;
```

Drag and drop

http://bit.ly/aN0RFQ

```
return 'draggable' in document.createElement('span');
```

File API

http://dev.w3.org/2006/webapi/FileAPI/

```
return typeof FileReader != 'undefined';
```

Geolocation

See Chapter 6

```
return !!navigator.geolocation;
```

History

http://bit.ly/9JGAGB

```
return !!(window.history && window.history.pushState &&
window.history.popState);
```

Local storage

http://dev.w3.org/html5/webstorage/

```
return ('localStorage' in window) && window['localStorage'] !== null;
```

Microdata

http://bit.ly/dBGnqr

```
return !!document.getItems;
```

Offline web applications

See Chapter 8

```
return !!window.applicationCache;
```

Server-sent events

http://dev.w3.org/html5/eventsource/

```
return typeof EventSource !== 'undefined';
```

Session storage

http://dev.w3.org/html5/webstorage/

```
try {
  return ('sessionStorage' in window) && window['sessionStorage'] !== null;
} catch(e) {
  return false;
}
```

SVG

http://www.w3.org/TR/SVG/

```
return !!(document.createElementNS && document.createElementNS
('http://www.w3.org/2000/svg', 'svg').createSVGRect);
```

SVG in text/html

http://hacks.mozilla.org/2010/05/firefox-4-the-html5-parser-inline-svg-speed-and-more/

```
var e = document.createElement('div');
e.innerHTML = '<svg></svg>';
return !!(window.SVGSVGElement && e.firstChild instanceof window.SVGSVGElement);
```

WebSimpleDB

http://dev.w3.org/2006/webapi/WebSimpleDB/

```
return !!window.indexedDB;
```

Web Sockets

http://dev.w3.org/html5/websockets/

```
return !!window.WebSocket;
```

Web SQL Database

http://dev.w3.org/html5/webdatabase/

```
return !!window.openDatabase;
```

Web Workers

http://bit.ly/9jheof

```
return !!window.Worker;
```

Undo

http://bit.ly/bs6JFR

```
return typeof UndoManager !== 'undefined';
```

Further Reading

Specifications and standards:

- HTML5 (*http://bit.ly/bYiOQp*)
- Geolocation (*http://www.w3.org/TR/geolocation-API/*)
- Server-Sent Events (*http://dev.w3.org/html5/eventsource/*)
- WebSimpleDB (*http://dev.w3.org/2006/webapi/WebSimpleDB/*)
- Web Sockets (*http://dev.w3.org/html5/websockets/*)
- Web SQL Database (*http://dev.w3.org/html5/webdatabase/*)
- Web Storage (*http://dev.w3.org/html5/webstorage/*)
- Web Workers (*http://bit.ly/9jheof*)

JavaScript libraries:

- Modernizr (*http://www.modernizr.com*), an HTML5 detection library

Index

A

AAC (Advanced Audio Coding), 87
Almost Standards mode, 32
alternate link relation, 37
APIs
    canvas API, 16–18
    canvas text API, 17
    ExplorerCanvas, 74
    geo.js, 123
    geolocation API, 24, 117–120
    Indexed Database API, 135
    Web Worker, 23
applications
    local storage, 127–136
    offline web applications, 23, 137–146
archives, link relations, 38
article element, 41, 47
aside element, 41
audio codecs
    about, 85–88
    encoding Ogg Vorbis video, 91–99
Audio Video Interleave video container format, 82
authors, link relations, 38
autofocus, web forms, 27, 148
autoplay attribute, 110

B

backward compatibility
    about, 11
    XHTML, 13
batch encoding
    H.264 video codec, 107
    Ogg Vorbis video codec, 98

breadcrumbs, link relations, 39
browsers
    audio video support, 88
    autofocus support, 28, 149
    canvas support, 17
    canvas text support, 18
    doctype and modes, 31
    error handling, 13
    geolocation support, 24
    handling unknown elements, 42–45
    headers, 1
    HTML5 input types, 26
    HTML5 support, 15
    JavaScript, 23
    local storage, 132
    microdata support, 29
    Microsoft Internet Explorer, 73, 114, 123
    Midas, 3
    Mosaic, 3
    offline support, 24
    placeholder support, 27
    placeholder text support, 148
    SQL database support, 134

C

cache manifest, offline web applications, 138–141, 143
canPlayType() function, 20
canvas
    about, 16–18
    coordinates, 60
    drawing text, 63–66
    images, 70–73
    paths, 61–63
canvas element, 57

We'd like to hear your suggestions for improving our indexes. Send email to *index@oreilly.com*.

canvas text API, 17
character encoding, 35
codecs
    about, 20
    audio, 85–88, 91–99
    video, 83, 90, 100–109
color pickers, web forms, 160
conditional comments, 74
containers, video, 81
Content-Type header, 1
cookies, compared to HTML5 Storage, 21
coordinates, canvas, 60
custom vocabularies, microdata, 164

D

date pickers, web forms, 156
dates and times, 49
dd element, 170
debugging offline web applications, 142–144
detecting
    autofocus support, 28
    canvas support, 17
    canvas text support, 18
    geolocation support, 24
    HTML5 input types, 26
    HTML5 support, 15
    microdata support, 29
    offline support, 24
    placeholder support, 27
doctype, 31
DOM (Document Object Model)
    about, 15
    detecting canvas support, 17
    detecting canvas text support, 18
    video, 19, 20
DOM events, 141
drawing, 57–79
    canvas coordinates, 60
    gradients, 67
    Halma game example, 75–79
    images, 70–73
    paths, 61–63
    shapes, 58
    text, 63–66

E

elements
    about, 163

article element, 41, 47
aside element, 41
canvas element, 16, 57
dd element, 170
footer element, 41, 53
handling unknown elements, 42–45
head element, 34–40
header element, 41
hgroup element, 41
img element, 2, 8, 70
link relations, 37
mark element, 41
nav element, 41
root element, 33
section element, 41
source element, 112
time element, 41
video element, 18–21
email addresses
    validating in JavaScript, 160
    web forms, 150
error handling
    about, 11
    browsers, 13
    geolocation, 120
events
    DOM events, 141
    marking up, 180–186
    storage events, 131
examples
    geo.js, 125
    Halma game, 75–79, 132, 145
    Video for Everybody!, 114
ExplorerCanvas, 74
external link relations, 38

F

fallback section, cache manifest, 140
feed autodiscovery, 37
ffmpeg2theora, 98
fields
    autofocus, 148
    email addresses, 150
Firefogg, 91–98
Flash Video video container format, 82
FlowPlayer, 114
font sizes, 65
footer element, 41
footers, 52

formats, video, 19
forms (see web forms)

G

Gears plug-in, 128
geo.js, 123–126
geolocation, 117–126
    about, 24
    API, 117–120
    error handling, 120
    geo.js, 123–126
    methods for calculating location, 121
    using invisible data, 179
    vocabulary, 179
getCurrentPosition() function, 118, 120, 122,
        124
Google
    On2, 85
    Rich Snippets, 174, 184
GPS (Global Positioning System), 121
gradients, drawing, 67

H

H.264 video codec, 84, 90, 100–108
Halma game example, 75–79, 132, 145
HandBrake, H.264 video codec, 100–108
head element, 34–40
header element, 41
headers
    about, 45–47
    Content-Type, 1
hgroup element, 41
history
    HTML, 7–11
    HTML5, ix
    local storage prior to HTML5, 128
    standards development, 2–7
    XHTML, 10
    XML, 10
HTML
    competing visions, 11
    development history, 7–11
    page structure, 33
HTML Working Group, 9
HTML5 Storage, 127–136
    about, 21, 129
    future of, 134
    Halma game example, 132

history prior to HTML5, 128
    using, 130–132

I

IE (Internet Explorer)
    audio video support, 89
    canvas and VML support, 73
    geolocation, 123
    styling unknown elements, 42
    video support, 114
images, displaying, 70–73
img element, 2, 8, 70
Indexed Database API, 135
input types
    about, 25
    web forms, 147
iPhone, web forms, 151

J

JavaScript
    autofocus, 27
    running in background, 23

L

language, 34
libraries, Modernizr, 16
license link relation, 39
licensing, H.264 video codec, 90
link relations, 36–40
local storage (see HTML5 Storage)
LSOs (Local Shared Objects), 128

M

mailing address format, 173
mark element, 41
microdata
    about, 28, 164
    data mode, 165–168
Microsoft Internet Explorer
    audio video support, 89
    canvas and VML support, 73
    geolocation, 123
    styling unknown elements, 42
    video support, 114
Midas browser, 3
MIME types
    about, 1

importance of, 10
video, 113
XHTML, 9, 10
Modernizr, 16
Mosaic browser, 3
MP3 (MPEG-1 Audio Layer 3), 86
MPEG-4 video container format, 82

N

namespaces
    microdata, 165
    need for, 33
nav element, 41
navigation
    about, 51
    breadcrumbs, 39
network section, cache manifest, 139
nofollow link relation, 39
noreferrer link relation, 39
numbers, web forms, 153–156

O

objects, DOM, 15
offline web applications, 137–146
    about, 23
    cache manifest, 138–141
    debugging, 142–144
    flow of events, 141
    Halma game example, 145
Ogg video container format, 82
Ogg Vorbis audio codec, 87, 91–99
organizations, marking up, 176–180

P

paths
    about, 145
    canvas, 61–63
people, marking up, 168–176
pingback link relation, 39
placeholder text
    about, 27
    web forms, 147
prefetch link relation, 40
preload attribute, 110
publication date, 50

Q

Quirks mode, 32

R

relative font sizes, 65
reviews, marking up, 186–189
Rich Snippets, 174, 184
root element, 33

S

scoping, microdata, 164
scripting, 12
search boxes, web forms, 158
search link relation, 40
section element, 41
shapes, drawing, 58
sidebar link relation, 40
sliders, numbers as, 155
source element, 112
spinboxes, numbers as, 153
SQL database support, 134
standards
    HTML history, 7–9
    implementations and specifications, 1
    process of creating, 2–7
Standards mode, 32
storage (see HTML5 Storage)
StorageEvent objects, 131
stylesheet link relation, 37

T

tag link relation, 40
tag-sets, XML, 9
text
    canvas text API, 17
    character encoding, 35
    drawing, 63–66
    placeholder text, 27, 147
Theora video codec, 84
time element, 41
times and dates, 49
tracking changes in HTML5 storage area, 131
translations, linking, 38

U

URLs
    microdata, 166
    Person vocabulary, 173
    web forms, 151

V

validating email addresses in JavaScript, 160
video, 81–116
   about, 18–21
   audio codecs, 85–88, 91–99
   browser support, 88
   containers, 81
   markup, 110–113
   Microsoft Internet Explorer, 114
   video codecs, 83, 90, 100–109
   Video for Everybody! example, 114
Vorbis audio codec, 87, 91–99
VP8 video codec, 85

W

W3C (World Wide Web Consortium)
   HTML Working Group, 9
   WHAT Working Group, 13
   Workshop on Web Applications and
         Compound Documents, 11
watchPosition() function, 123
web addresses, web forms, 151
web applications
   local storage, 127–136
   offline, 23, 137–146
web browsers (see browsers)
web forms, 147–161
   autofocus, 27
   autofocus fields, 148
   color pickers, 160
   date pickers, 156
   email addresses, 150
   history, 9
   input types, 25
   numbers, 153–156
   placeholder text, 27, 147
   search boxes, 158
   web addresses, 151
Web workers, 23
WebM video format, 82, 89, 108
WHAT Working Group, and W3C, 13
working groups
   about, 12
   HTML Working Group, 9
   W3C, 11, 13
   WHAT Working Group, 13
Workshop on Web Applications and
         Compound Documents, 11

World Wide Web Consortium (see W3C)

X

XForms, backward compatibility, 13
XHTML
   about, 10
   backward compatibility, 13
   development history, 9
XML
   development history, 10
   tag-sets, 9

About the Author

Mark Pilgrim is a senior developer advocate at Google, Inc. He specializes in open source and open standards. Mark is the author of several technical books, including *Dive Into Python* (APress) and *Dive Into Accessibility*, a free online tutorial on web accessibility. He lives in North Carolina with his wife, two boys, and a big slobbery dog.

Colophon

The animal on the cover of *HTML5: Up and Running* is an alpine chamois (*Rupicapra rupicapra*), a goat- or antelope-like species that is native to the mountain ranges of Europe, including the Carpathians, the Apennines, the Tatras, the Balkans, the Caucasus, and the Alps. Alpine chamois can also be found in New Zealand, having been introduced there in 1907 by Austrian Emperor Franz Joseph I.

Alpine chamois live at relatively high altitudes, and have adapted to steep, rugged, and rocky terrain. They grow to a size of about 75 centimeters tall and weigh between 20 and 30 kilograms (though individuals in New Zealand often weigh about 20 percent less than their European brethren). Both males and females sport short horns that curve backward near the tip and fur that is dark brown during the summer and light gray in the winter. Many chamois also display a characteristically white face and rump, with black stripes under the eyes and along the back.

Adult male chamois live mostly solitary lives, only congregating once a year to compete for the attention of unmated females. Females, however, live in herds with their young. All variety of chamois are popular game animals; their meat is considered tasty and their leather is known to be exceptionally smooth and absorbent. Also, a tuft of hair taken from the back of the neck of a chamois, called a *gamsbart*, is traditionally worn as a hat decoration throughout the alpine countries. This practice may be slightly more difficult in modern times, however, as some subspecies of chamois have gained protection from the European Union. In contrast, the New Zealand Department of Conservation encourages the hunting of alpine chamois, hoping to limit the animal's impact on native flora.

The cover image is from J. G. Wood's *Animate Creation*. The cover font is Adobe ITC Garamond. The text font is Linotype Birka; the heading font is Adobe Myriad Condensed; and the code font is LucasFont's TheSansMonoCondensed.

Related Titles from O'Reilly

Web Programming

ActionScript 3.0 Cookbook

ActionScript 3.0 Design Patterns

ActionScript for Flash MX: The Definitive Guide, 2nd Edition

Adobe AIR 1.5 Cookbook

Adobe AIR for JavaScript Developer's Pocket Guide

Advanced Rails

Ajax Design Patterns

Ajax Hacks

Ajax on Rails

Ajax: The Definitive Guide

Apache 2 Pocket Reference

Apache Cookbook, 2nd Edition

Building Scalable Web Sites

Designing Web Navigation

Dojo: The Definitive Guide

Dynamic HTML: The Definitive Reference, 3rd Edition

Essential ActionScript 3.0

Essential PHP Security

Ferret

Flash CS4: The Missing Manual

Flash Hacks

Head First HTML with CSS & XHTML

Head First JavaScript

Head First PHP & MySQL

High Performance Web Sites

HTTP: The Definitive Guide

JavaScript & DHTML Cookbook, 2nd Edition

JavaScript Pocket Reference, 2nd Edition

JavaScript: The Definitive Guide, 5th Edition

JavaScript: The Good Parts

JavaScript: The Missing Manual

Learning ActionScript 3.0

Learning PHP and MySQL, 2nd Edition

PHP Cookbook, 2nd Edition

PHP Hacks

PHP in a Nutshell

PHP Pocket Reference, 2nd Edition

Programming ColdFusion MX, 2nd Edition

Programming Flex 2

Programming PHP, 2nd Edition

Programming Amazon Web Services

Rails Cookbook

The ActionScript 3.0 Quick Reference Guide

Twitter API: Up and Running

Universal Design for Web Applications

Upgrading to PHP 5

Web Database Applications with PHP and MySQL, 2nd Edition

Website Optimization

Web Site Cookbook

Webmaster in a Nutshell, 3rd Edition

Our books are available at most retail and online bookstores.

To order direct: 1-800-998-9938 • *order@oreilly.com* • *www.oreilly.com*

Online editions of most O'Reilly titles are available by subscription at *safari.oreilly.com*

Buy this book and get access to the online edition for 45 days—for free!

HTML5: Up and Running

By Mark Pilgrim
August 2010, $29.99
ISBN 9780596806026

With Safari Books Online, you can:

Access the contents of thousands of technology and business books

- Quickly search over 7000 books and certification guides
- Download whole books or chapters in PDF format, at no extra cost, to print or read on the go
- Copy and paste code
- Save up to 35% on O'Reilly print books
- **New!** Access mobile-friendly books directly from cell phones and mobile devices

Stay up-to-date on emerging topics before the books are published

- Get on-demand access to evolving manuscripts.
- Interact directly with authors of upcoming books

Explore thousands of hours of video on technology and design topics

- Learn from expert video tutorials
- Watch and replay recorded conference sessions

To try out Safari and the online edition of this book FREE for 45 days, go to **www.oreilly.com/go/safarienabled** and enter the coupon code BOQTREH. To see the complete Safari Library, visit safari.oreilly.com.

Spreading the knowledge of innovators   safari.oreilly.com